What
White
Looks
Like

What
white
Looks
Like

AFRICAN-AMERICAN PHILOSOPHERS ON
THE WHITENESS QUESTION

GEORGE YANCY, EDITOR

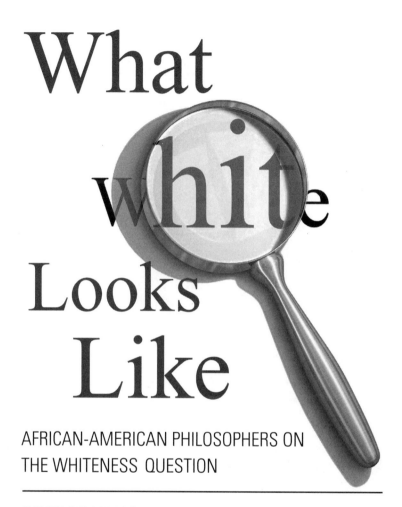

ROUTLEDGE
NEW YORK AND LONDON

Published in 2004 by
Routledge
29 West 35th Street
New York, NY 10001
www.routledge-ny.com

Published in Great Britain by
Routledge
11 New Fetter Lane
London EC4P 4EE
www.routledge.co.uk

Printed in the United States of America on acid-free paper.

10 9 8 7 6 5 4 3 2 1

Library of Congress Cataloging in Publication Data

What white looks like : African-American philosophers on the whiteness question / edited
by George Yancy.
    p. cm.
Includes bibliographical references and index.
    ISBN 0-415-96615-9 (alk. paper) — ISBN 0-415-96616-7 (pbk. : alk. paper)
  1. United States—Race relations—Philosophy.   2. African American philosophy.   3. Race
relations—Philosophy.   4. Ethnicity--Philosophy.   I. Yancy, George.
  E185.615W438 2004
  305.809073—dc22

                                                        2003022741

This Book is Dedicated to the
Eradication of White Supremacy

CONTENTS

ACKNOWLEDGMENTS

Editing books can be somewhat disconcerting. There are personalities with which to deal, time schedules to keep, authors to encourage, author deadlines to maintain, chapters to edit, chapters and introductions of one's own to write, helpful suggestions to make to authors, and so on. With this in mind, I would like to thank the contributors to this volume. Each of them is to be thanked for his/her endurance and dedication to writing philosophically thought-provoking chapters. In the fray of other personal and professional commitments and various obstacles, they came through.

In the spirit of thanking, I would like to acknowledge Damon Zucca, past philosophy editor at Routledge, for his strong show of interest in this project. William Germano, at Routledge, is to be thanked for working with me yet again on another very important philosophical volume. Gilad Foss is to be thanked for his assistance. Mark Henderson, assistant editor at Routledge, is to be especially thanked for his very significant suggestions and for playing such a crucial role in seeing this project to fruition. I would like to thank my production editor Danielle Savin for overseeing the production of the text and keeping me informed about important stages of the text. I would also like to thank Susan Fox, Project Editor, for her patience, diligence, and professionalism. A special thanks goes to Norma McLemore, my copyeditor, for her extraordinarily sharp eye for detail and philosophical insights. Philosophers Bettina Bergo, Linda Alcoff, and Clarence Shole Johnson are to be thanked for their very helpful suggestions regarding various aspects of this volume. Each of them came through when called upon. A special thanks goes to philosopher John McClendon for his responding to the call to write a chapter for this volume with such alacrity. Charles Mills is to be thanked for his critical assessments. I would also like to thank James G. Spady for the many discussions that we have had regarding the structure of whiteness. Those discussions were framed by a very important distinction: It is one thing for whites to theorize whiteness, to talk about deconstructing whiteness, becoming a race traitor; it is another thing for whites to be prepared *to do* something about whiteness, to be prepared to abdicate white cultural and white politicoeconomic power. I would like to thank those white scholars (David R. Roediger, Noel Ignatiev, Peggy MacIntosh, Christine Sleeter, Alice McIntyre, Jessie Daniels, Mike Hill, Greg Moses, Richard Dyer, Jane Lazarre, and others) who have sincerely attempted to deracinate their white-skin privileges, to render benign—assuming that this is even possible—their whiteness and the value that it carries over and above their intentional actions.

I would like to thank my uncle William L. Banks for his encouragement and his principled posture toward his Christian beliefs. Of course, his scholarship and productivity are standards for me to emulate. Uncle William has been there when I most needed him. I would like to thank Ruth Yancy for her enduring show of love. My in-laws, Geoff and Lillian are to be thanked for their support. Lillian is to be especially thanked for her rationale concerning the importance of this text. I would also like to thank Ron Hankison for his honest discussions regarding his own whiteness. In an email discussion, he wrote:

> Even though one may not be "born white," it sure as hell *feels* like one has. There is no self-conscious, ceremonial introduction to the "privileges and power sites" of whiteness. On the contrary, white people are constantly reminding each other of how difficult and perilous life is for them—indeed, for everybody. This is another example of how whiteness does its work—by constantly asserting the opposite of what is "objectively" true, white people constantly reinforce their perception that they are at some kind of terrible risk. And by "feeling" constantly that they are "at risk" (of attack, loss of power, loss of prestige, or, in the most common fear, loss of money) they feel the importance of maintaining a constant, vigilant posture of defense.

I would especially like to thank Adrian, Gabriel, and Elijah. They are three utterly important human beings who make my life rich and meaningful, and, yet, who force me to mourn aspects of human finitude, for they are so incredibly precious to me. *So, I work for them.* For they are the future and must someday seriously confront issues of whiteness, blackness, racism, disrespect, hurtful words, inquisitive gazes, looks that stereotype them as exotica, and so on. Perhaps when burdened with some race-related conundrum, some deeply personal question about racial identity, and the social ontology of racial performance, this work will prove helpful as they turn to Daddy's philosophical voice.

I would also like to give tribute to my wife, Susan J. Hadley. Sometimes acknowledgments lose their significance when stated so many times. Not with this one. Every day I am thankful for her companionship. All our moments together—some trying, others sublime—are testimony to a life lived thankfully, to a committed friendship that requires real work and dedication, to moments of risked vulnerability, and to a strong and loving impulse to continue sharing our lives together despite life's many obstacles and challenges.

CONTRIBUTORS

Robert E. Birt teaches philosophy at Morgan State University in Baltimore, MD. He is editor of *The Quest for Community and Identity: Critical Essays in Africana Social Philosophy* (Rowman & Littlefield, 2002). His research interests include Africana philosophy, existential philosophy, critical theory, and philosophical anthropology. His articles have appeared in *International Philosophical Quarterly, Man and World*, which has since been renamed *The Continental Philosophy Review, Social Science Information, Quest: Journal of African Philosophy*, and *Philosophical Forum*.

Blanche Radford Curry received her Ph.D. in philosophy from Brown University. She teaches philosophy at Fayetteville (N.C.) State University. She has published in *Sage: A Scholarly Journal on Black Women; Educational Foundations;* and the *American Philosophical Association Newsletter on Philosophy and the Black Experience*. She also contributed chapters in *Overcoming Racism and Sexism; Gender and Academe: Feminist Pedagogy and Politics;* and, *Women's Studies in Transition: The Pursuit of Interdisciplinarity*.

Arnold Farr is associate professor of philosophy at Saint Joseph's University in Philadelphia. He is coauthor and coeditor of *Marginal Groups and Mainstream American Culture*. He has published in the *Journal of Social Philosophy* and has published several articles on German idealism, race, and critical theory in volumes edited by others. His areas of research are German idealism, critical theory, race, and liberation philosophy. He recently finished a book titled *Reading Farrakhan/Reading America: An Essay on Racialized Consciousness and the Obstruction of Understanding*.

Lewis R. Gordon is professor of Africana studies and of modern culture and media at Brown University and ongoing visiting professor of philosophy and government at the University of the West Indies at Mona, Jamaica. He also is president of the Caribbean Philosophical Association. He is the author of several books, including *Existentia Africana: Understanding Africana Existential Thought* (Routledge, 2000), and editor of volumes I–V of *Radical Philosophy Review*

Clevis Headley is currently an associate professor of philosophy at Florida Atlantic University. He has published articles in *Man and World*, *Philosophy Today, Semiotica, Teaching Philosophy, Africana Philosophia*, and the *Journal of Social and Political Philosophy*. His published articles focus on Frege, the philosophy of mathematics, critical race theory, and Africana and Afro-Caribbean philosophy. Headley teaches courses in pragmatism, social and political philosophy, existentialism, ethics, and Africana philosophy. His immediate research interest focuses on Africana and Afro-Caribbean philosophy.

Paget Henry is professor of sociology and Africana studies at Brown University. He is the author of *Peripheral Capitalism and Underdevelopment in Antigua*, and *Caliban's Reason: Introducing Afro-Caribbean Philosophy*. Henry is the coeditor (with Paul Buhie) of *CLR James's Caribbean*, and is the current editor of the *CLR James Journal*.

Joy James is professor of Africana studies at Brown University and teaches political and feminist theory. She is the author of *Transcending the Talented Tenth, Resisting State Violence*, and *Shadowboxing: Representations of Black Feminist Politics*. Her current work on incarceration and human rights includes the anthologies *States of Confinement: Policing, Detention and Prisons; Imprisoned Intellectuals: America's Political Prisoners Write on Life, Liberation, and Rebellion;* and the forthcoming *The New Abolitionists*.

Janine Jones teaches philosophy at the University of North Carolina at Greensboro. Her areas of interest include philosophy of mind, metaphysics, philosophy of language, and epistemology. Her current topics of interest are imagining and conceiving. Her published work has appeared in philosophical journals including *Philosophical Studies* and *Philosophia*, and nonphilosophical journals including *Travelers' Tales America, Travelers' Tales Danger*, and *Travelers' Tales Ireland*.

John H. McClendon III is associate professor of African-American studies and American cultural studies at Bates College in Lewiston, Maine. His areas of research are philosophy of African-American studies, philosophy of social science, history of African-American philosophers, African philosophy, philosophy of African-American sports, and Marxist philosophy. He is the editor of the *American Philosophical Association Newsletter on Philosophy and the Black Experience*. He has two forthcoming books, *Marxism in Ebony: A Materialist Philosophical Perspective on African American Studies* and *C.L.R. James's Notes on Dialectics: Left Hegelianism or Marxism-Leninism*. In addition to the study *The State of Black Champaign County* (Urban League of Champaign, Illinois, 1984) and his collaborative contribution to *Afro-American Studies: A Guide for Teachers* with J. Rupert Picott et al. (Associated Publishers, 1977) his publications have appeared in journals and anthologies including Leonard Harris's *Philosophy Born of Struggle* (1983), Jessie Carney Smith's *Notable Black American Women Book II*, the *A.M.E. Church Review*, the *American Philosophical Association Newsletter on Philosophy and the Black Experience*, *Sage Race Relations Abstracts*, the *Review of Ethnic Studies*, *Auslegung*, *Explorations in Ethnic Studies*, *University of Illinois Afro-Scholar Working Papers*, the *Missourian*, the *African Americanist*, and *Freedomways*. McClendon is the former director of the Black Culture Center at the University of Missouri.

Charles W. Mills is professor of philosophy at the University of Illinois at Chicago. He earned his Ph.D. at the University of Toronto and previously taught at the University of Oklahoma. He works in the area of radical political theory and has published numerous articles on Marxism, critical race theory, and Africana philosophy, as well as two books: *The Racial Contract* (1997) and *Blackness Visible: Essays on Philosophy and Race* (1998). A third book, *From Class to Race: Essays in White Marxism and Black Radicalism*, is scheduled to appear by December 2003.

Lucius T. Outlaw, Jr. is presently professor of philosophy, director of the African American studies program, and associate provost for undergraduate education at Vanderbilt University. Foci of his undergraduate and graduate teaching are W.E.B. Du Bois, Ralph Ellison, Alexis de Tocqueville, and matters of race in the founding and development of the United States of America. Recent publications include "On Courage and Democratic Pluralism," in *Courage*, edited by Barbara Darling-Smith (Notre Dame, IN: University of Notre Dame Press, 2002), and "'Afrocentricity': Critical Considerations," in *Companion to African American Philosophy*, edited by Tommy Lott, et al. (Blackwell Publishers, 2003). He is currently working on a book, *In Search of Critical Social Theory in the Interests of Black Folks*, to be published by Rowman & Littlefield.

Paul C. Taylor teaches social philosophy and American ethnic studies at the University of Washington in Seattle. Some of his essays have appeared in the *Journal of Speculative Philosophy*, the *Journal of Aesthetics and Art Criticism*, and the *Michigan Quarterly Review*. He is the author of *Race: A Philosophical Introduction* (Polity Press, 2003).

George Yancy has published in journals including the *Journal of Speculative Philosophy*, the *Review of Metaphysics*, the *Journal of Social Philosophy*, *Philosophy and Social Criticism*, *Radical Philosophy Review*, *Hypatia: A Journal of Feminist Philosophy*, *Encyclopedia of Feminist Theories*, the *Western Journal of Black Studies*, the *AME Church Review*, the *American Philosophical Association Newsletter on Feminism and Philosophy*, the *CLA Journal*, the *Black Arts Quarterly*, *Social Science Quarterly*, *Popular Music and Society*. Yancy's books include *African-American Philosophers: 17 Conversations* (Routledge, 1998), which was named an Outstanding Academic Book by *Choice* for 1999, *Cornel West: A Critical Reader* (Blackwell Publishers, 2001), and *The Philosophical i: Personal Reflections on Life in Philosophy* (Rowman & Littlefield, 2002). He is currently editing a book titled *White on White/Black on Black* (forthcoming from Rowman & Littlefield). He is also editing (with Susan Hadley) a book titled *Narrated Identities: Psychologists Engaged in Self-Construction* (forthcoming from Jessica Kingsley Publishers). Yancy is the recipient of the McAnulty Fellowship (Duquesne University) and the prestigious McCracken Fellowship (New York University). He is book review editor of the *American Philosophical Association Newsletter on Philosophy and the Black Experience*.

Introduction

FRAGMENTS OF A SOCIAL ONTOLOGY OF WHITENESS

George Yancy

I see these souls [the souls of white folk] undressed and from the back and side. I see the working of their entrails. I know their thoughts and they know that I know. This knowledge makes them now embarrassed, now furious! They deny my right to live and be and call me misbirth! My word is to them mere bitterness and my soul, pessimism. And yet as they preach and strut and shout and threaten, crouching as they clutch at rags of facts and fancies to hide their nakedness, they go twisting, flying by my tired eyes and I see them ever stripped—ugly, human.

—W.E.B. Du Bois

WHITES HAVE A WAY OF speaking from a center that they often appear to forget forms the white ideological fulcrum upon which what they say (do not say) or see (do not see) hinges. In short, whites frequently lie to themselves. For example, a respected white philosopher-mentor of mine, upon finding out that I was passionate about pursuing issues in African-American philosophy, advised: "Make sure that you don't get pegged." I quietly thought to myself: "Pegged? I'm doing philosophy!" It immediately occurred to me that the introductory course in philosophy that I had taken with him some years back did not include a single person of color. Yet, he did not see his own philosophical performances—engagements with European and Anglo-American philosophy—as "pegged"; he simply taught philosophy qua philosophy. Such a philosophy only masquerades as universal. Philosophy is always already performed by bodies that are sexed, gendered, and culturally coded in some fashion, and is always already shaped by prior assumptions, interests, concerns, and goals that are historically bounded and pragmatically contextual. His advice carried the normative implication that focusing on African-American philosophy came with a penalty: "If you want to be considered a 'real philosopher,' don't focus on something as marginal as so-called African-American philosophy."

There are many pegged contemporary Kantians and Platonists, but since Plato and Kant are "real" philosophers, concentrating on their systems makes one a "real" philosopher, though pegged. So, it was not an issue about being pegged so much as it was an issue about being pegged as someone doing something as marginal and "insignificant" as African-American philosophy. He apparently failed to see the historical and cultural particularity of his own (white) philosophical preoccupations and normative assumptions, thus rendering my philosophical concerns a mark of disgrace and self-imposed limitation. Like whiteness, his investment in Anglo-American and European philosophers went unmarked. Once thematized, historicized, and analyzed, however, perhaps he would come to understand the hidden normativity of his assumption: "The only real philosophy is done by *white men;* the only real wisdom is *white male wisdom."*

Another example of speaking from this invisible (or unacknowledged) center occurred in a conversation with a friend about the grading system of a philosopher who taught a course in Kantian ethics. As we stood talking one day after class, he revealed his conviction that because he was the only privileged white male in the class, he would receive a low grade from the professor. I found his remark rather disturbing. First, he was presumptuous to think that the professor would do this. Second, he assumed that if he was penalized, it would be because of his status as a white male, not his lack of philosophical acumen. Had I taken the course for credit, which I had not done, written a paper, and received an A, he would apparently have assumed that I received the grade because I was black. At no point would it occur to him that I might have been the better student of philosophy. Given that he received an A- from this same professor in a previous course, this only reinforced his conviction that no matter how hard he tried he would be penalized for being a privileged white male. He did not show an awareness of (or interest in) how this was an insult to me. At a deeper level, perhaps he could not come to terms with his own lack of philosophical acumen and needed an excuse to hide behind. In verbalizing an awareness of his whiteness, he in fact covered over his presumptuous conviction that he could get better grades in philosophy—*precisely because of his whiteness*—than any black were it not for his being penalized for being white. Hence, the normative center of whiteness continued to hold. When I asked him how many other white males were in the previous class in which he received the A-, he replied that there were several others. I think that he also mentioned that there were no blacks in the class. He appeared baffled when I asked:

"So, you're saying that all the white males in that class were penalized because they were white and privileged? What calculus for grading did the professor use given the fact that there was more than one white male?" One could see the disturbing perplexity across his face, perhaps a hint of recognition that he realized the casuistry of his own thinking, but he was still undeterred in his conviction.

A third example occurred in a graduate class in African-American literature. I was one of two blacks in the course and the only black male. All of the other students, with the exception of one woman from the Middle East, were white. One day after discussing Frederick Douglass's *Narrative of the Life of Frederick Douglass, An American Slave, Written by Himself,* and Harriet Jacobs's *Incidents in the Life of a Slave Girl,* I became disappointed with the superficial readings by the other graduate students of these two texts. On this particular day the other black student was absent. So, there I was challenging this sea of whiteness. "After I read these texts, I noticed how angry I became. These texts speak to me as a black male. I feel justifiably angered by the behavior of whites in these texts," I announced. I went on to add: "I would like to know what the rest of you feel about the white racist behavior of the whites in these texts. Do you feel guilty? And how do you feel about the fact that your own whiteness implicates you in a structural white power system from which you are able to gain so many privileges? How do you understand your whiteness vis-à-vis the whites in the texts?"

There was absolute silence. Students were apparently in a contemplative mood, but no one ventured to speak. The professor broke the silence with a very helpful narrative about her having been born in the South. She provided an insightful account of her own social and racial location as a way of negotiating how she too felt angered by the whites in the text, and how she is aware of her own whiteness as a site of power and privilege. One student at least attempted to address my questions, even if only in a groping fashion. One male student said to me as the class ended: "George, I need to get back to you on this. I have not given thought to this before."

My sense is that the students had been reading these very important texts without autocritique. But how does a white person read Douglass without being enraged by the white sadistic behavior of Covey or Mr. Plummer or the hypocrisy of Mr. Auld? How does a white person fail to ask counterfactually: "What if I were Covey or Mr. Plummer?" I certainly posed, "What if I were Douglass?" And surely Mr. Flint's obsessive sexual drive to possess Jacobs should have invited a discussion of contemporary white representations of black women as overly sexed, dark, exotic sexual objects. Sad to say, to my knowledge, there was no such discussion. In this example, the white students understood Mr. Auld, Mr. Flint, Mr. Plummer, Covey, or even Mrs. Hick as "ultraracists." The white students were able to distance themselves from these figures through a process of juxtaposing the "good white" with the "bad white." They saw themselves as "good whites," whites incapable of such acts of racial brutality. Through this process of subterfuge, however, they failed to locate their own center of power, a center that enabled them to make such a distinction without any recognition of their own whiteness as a species of white racism, particularly given the historical accruing value of whiteness and the implications of this accrual upon nonwhite people. Again, the apparently invisible center of whiteness continued to hold.

A key feature of the social ontology of whiteness is that whites attempt to avoid discussing their own social, political, economic, and cultural investments in whiteness. Many whites fail to see their complicity with the systemic workings of white supremacy. By perpetuating the dualism between the "good white" and the "bad white," whites attempt to mute the claim that white racism is not limited to the KKK, neo-Nazi skinheads, White Aryan Resistance, and other white racist groups. In her insightful analysis of what it means to be white, Alice McIntyre uses a participatory action research (PAR) approach to explore how to best get a small group of white female teachers to name their whiteness. Describing an episode in which one of the teachers manages to avoid facing her whiteness through the deployment of the above dualistic way of thinking, McIntyre notes:

> Faith's struggle with whether or not she is a racist becomes embedded in an all too common game that white people play with themselves. We compare the various degrees of racism. On the other hand, the participants conceptualize whites as rednecks, people with a Ku Klux Klan mentality. On the other hand, the participants label some whites as more open-minded and liberal, better educated, and trying to be 'better' people. And then there are the whites who are somewhere in between those two extremes. The participants vacillated about their own locations on this artificially constructed continuum of racism.[1]

In the process of avoiding the implications of her whiteness, Faith attempts to shift attention away from her whiteness by focusing attention on the "extremism" of white supremacy. The interesting point here, though, is that "throughout the history of the U.S., the 'extremism' of the far right has often converged with the cultural and political center."[2] Jessie Daniels, in her qualitative content analysis of white supremacist discourse, also raises the issue of dualistic thinking as a means of shifting the conversation away from the pervasive and systemic nature of whiteness. Discussing how this phenomenon functions within the framework of academia, she writes: "By obfuscating the connections between white supremacist movements and the white supremacist context in which they exist, traditional paradigms 'e-race' the central importance of being 'white.' And, more to the point, these interpretations leave unexamined—indeed, completely irrelevant within such a framework—the privileged position of white academics, or the ways white supremacy (with all the connections to class, gender, and sexuality in place), are inscribed in academic institutions."[3] Tracing the theme of how whites attempt to derail a direct analysis of the centrism of white supremacy, Daniels argues that nationally syndicated shows tend to let many whites off the proverbial hook by portraying white racism to be contained, isolated, and marginal. What she says is worth quoting in full:

> In a different milieu, nationally syndicated shows—such as "Donahue," "Geraldo," "Oprah," and "Sally"—offer an important lens for viewing white supremacists because they provide millions of Americans with their (perhaps only) knowledge of white supremacists. I contend that the format of talk shows frames racism, as it is expressed by white supremacists, so as to make it appear contained, distant, and nonthreatening; and, the shows in which white supremacists appear distance racism by marginalizing their views in a variety of ways. First the producers of these shows marginalize white supremacists by consistently referring to the groups as "hate groups." Shows featuring white supremacists appear with titles such as, "I'm Proud to be a Racist," "Young Hate Mongers," "I'm Raising My Kids to be Racists," and "Hatemonger Moms." Through rhetoric such as "racist," a label that only the most committed white supremacists utilize, as well as, "hate" and "hatemonger," terms even white supremacists do not embrace, the shows signal audiences that the guests are members of a lunatic fringe bearing not the slightest connection to the vast majority of viewers. Talk-show audiences are alerted to tune in to "see what racists are like." Framing the appearance of white supremacists in this way preempts any other interrogation of racism by the audience, the host, or society at large.[4]

My point is that whiteness often does not speak its name, which is a function of both its power and its bad faith. I do realize, for example, that the KKK is far from being shy about its aims, identity, and motivations. This is also true with regard to the unequivocal self-naming and self-consciousness of whites in the American South and whites in South Africa during apartheid. There was nothing invisible about Jim Crow or Afrikaner nationalism. The point here is that many so-called innocent whites have come to deny the racist implications of their whiteness. Such individuals tend to see themselves as (raceless) liberals, atomic individuals whose whiteness is muted by such self-proclamations as: "I'm not a racist!!! I've never used the 'N' word. Indeed, I have many friends who are black. I believe that people have the freedom to be what they want to be. When I see a black person, I don't see race, I see a person. I've never been part of a white lynch mob, and I didn't own any slaves. Blacks have been given so much. They can now eat anywhere they desire. They're no longer restricted to the back of the bus. I thought this is why there was a civil rights movement in the first place. Frankly, I'm not sure what the fuss is all about." This form of discourse is characteristic of whiteness's ontology. It speaks from within the safe space of what McIntyre refers to as white talk: It is "talk that serves to insulate white people from examining their/our individual and collective role(s) in the perpetuation of racism."[5] In this way, whites are able to localize the virulent nature of whiteness, thus attempting to render whiteness/white supremacy an anomaly. Hence, such events as the brutal beating of Rodney King by white police officers (1991), the sodomizing of Abner Louima (1997) with a plunger handle by white New York police officers, the burning alive and beheading of Garnett Paul Johnson (1997) by two white men, the dragging to death of James Byrd Jr. (1998) by three white men, and the shooting and killing of Amadou Diallo (1999), who reached for his wallet and was shot at 41 times and hit with 19 bullets, are seen as rare exceptions to the rule of whiteness's innocence. Such brutal white racist acts provide many whites with ways of effectively dealing with their own white racism: "I'm no racist, because I would never do something so cruel and unconscionable." And while such whites are more than happy to proclaim their moral superiority, divulge their love of black folk, hide behind their power of self-definition, I feel my blackness defined beyond my control, slipping away from me, stigmatized as dangerous from birth. I feel that I have become this indistinguishable, amorphous, black seething mass, a token of danger, a threat, a rapist, a criminal, a burden, a beast, a rapacious animal incapable of delayed gratification, a "coon," a "nigger," a slick, dickgrabbing black male. I am simply an instantiation of universal blackness (read: evil). I am deemed obstreperous, irresponsible and worthy of non-being. In white eyes, I am an ontological cipher. Being black while living in white racist America, *I am* King, Louima, Johnson, Byrd, and Diallo.

As long as whiteness constitutes an ensemble of power relations that places whites in positions of advantage and power (that is, puts them in potential and actual positions of power in virtue of their whiteness) vis-à-vis nonwhites, whiteness will never be innocent. So although many blacks and whites occupy the same socioeconomic status, the latter live their value-laden, color-coded flesh in ways that reinforce (and are reinforced by) the larger, systemic processes of white domination. All whites need not occupy the same class position in order for white supremacy to work. And even if many poor whites suffer under white-controlled American capitalism and have class interests similar to those of blacks, this does not negate the extraordinary value placed on whiteness, even on the whiteness of poor whites. After all, to be a poor white does not mean that one inhabits a space of "post-whiteness." Despite Oprah Winfrey's wealth, she is still black. No amount of money will change this. There are many poor whites who still deem themselves more important, valued, and powerful than she, if only because they are white and she is not. It is here that white people (poor or not) live a kind of alienated selfhood, which means that they cannot be fully themselves (white) without dominating (or feeling better than) the Other (nonwhite). Hence, white "superiority" thrives vis-à-vis black "inferiority." Whiteness is parasitic upon blackness.

Within the eyes of whiteness, Oprah, despite her talent and financial success ($1.1 billion), is still inferior because she is black (read: not white). And despite Colin Powell's wielding of political power, he, too, remains black. As long as he behaves such that his blackness recedes and takes a back seat to so-called racially neutral political policies (whether local or foreign), he plays the role of a man without color. He is simply part of the ("color-blind") administration. Once he speaks in a discourse that opposes the white power structure of the administration, his blackness, which was always there, will take center stage and will become hypervisible. The white historically constructed weight of his blackness will come to haunt him. In the eyes of whiteness, he will return to being just another problem, a burden, and in some white eyes, just a "nigger."

Even though Condoleezza Rice's name is painted on a Chevron oil tanker, in the eyes of whiteness, she is deemed the embodiment of unrestricted promiscuity, a "Jezebel," a black "mammy" who makes sure that white folk are content. It is here that one might ask, "How many blacks in American have truly transcended the Veil?"

The power of whiteness (white supremacy) manifests itself in many forms, but it still remains whiteness (white supremacy). Whether it manifests itself in the form of the dragging to death of James Byrd Jr., Trent Lott's praises of white segregationist Strom Thurmond, President Bush's reference to the Crusades in his war on "terrorism," or the little old white woman who clutches her purse as a black man enters the elevator, whiteness remains a synergistic system of transversal relationships of privileges, norms, rights, modes of self-perception and the perception of others, unquestioned presumptions, deceptions, beliefs, "truths," behaviors, advantages, modes of comportment, and sites of power and hegemony that benefit whites individually and institutionally. Under the system of white hegemony, poor whites also manage to reap aesthetic and psychological rewards as a result of possessing the valued property of whiteness. Hence, whether poor or wealthy, whiteness constitutes an invisible knapsack of unearned assets that they (white people) can rely upon.[6] Let us face it, whiteness is a form of inheritance and like any inheritance one need not accept it. Poor whites benefit from walking in clothing stores without the encumbrance of being followed and subjected to surveillance. Is it fair to say that they are white supremacists because of this? To the extent that they leave this aspect of whiteness's social ontology unmarked and uninterrupted, they do occupy a space of being supreme, for they move and have their being in ways that do not challenge the very white social order that comes to mark the black body as suspicious, as criminal. Indeed, they do not challenge the white power system that continues to mark the white body as preferable, privileged, and supreme. It would be like a white spectator who watches the lynching and burning of a black body and refuses to protest, to fight against this spectacle of white psychopathology. Such a white constitutes a crucial element in the equation of such a site of white supremacy. No longer distinguishable—because of his/her dead silence—from the one who tied the noose or lit the fire, such a white abdicates his/her freedom to speak out in opposition to such madness. He/she has become one with the mob, a white massive force, acting as one white supremacist entity. Self-consciously signing a contract is not requisite for membership in this white supremacist spectacle. It is enough that you are a *white*, silent witness.

The police officers guilty of murdering Amadou Diallo—notwithstanding other variables that may help to explain what went terribly wrong that day—acted from a center of whiteness. This center informed their actions; it is a center that comes replete with "knowledge" about the black body as criminal, as rapacious, as a problem. Why so many shots? The black body has been historically scripted as almost superhuman, possessing animal strength and hyperendurance. Perhaps this is why Rodney King *had* to be beaten so many times. He just would not stay down. "What incredible strength *these* people possess. Just look at Serena Williams." Like the black ontologically criminal nature of Amadou's black body, a construction that no doubt informed the decisions of the police officers, even if unconscious, the black body of a black male walking into an elevator can be seen as criminal. Well dressed, a black man enters an elevator where an old white woman waits to reach her floor. She sees the black body. Over and above how it is clothed, she sees a criminal, a brute, a black surface that triggers the white imaginary: "What does he want, my money, my body, my life?" She clutches her purse, eagerly anticipating the arrival of her floor, "knowing" that this black predator will soon strike. She refuses to make direct eye contact so as not to trigger the anger, the rage, in this black beast. Of course, not only does she ontologically freeze the black male identity, her own identity becomes frozen. For she is unwilling to move beyond just seeing a criminal, which ultimately means that she is unwilling to move beyond her own whiteness. It is her failure to call into question, self-reflexively, her own assumptions and modes of being that is criminal.

In both cases, the social ontology of whiteness has created and sustained a form of interpersonal distance partly informed by mythopoetic constructions about blackness. Of course, it is through the culturally-constructed centrality of whiteness's supremacist ontology that these constructions appear at all. The black body *is* by nature criminal, because the white body *is* by nature innocent, pure, and good. Whiteness sets itself up as the thesis. Blackness, within the dialectical logic of whiteness, *must* be the antithesis. The black body, in both situations, is ontologically mapped; its coordinates lead to that which is always immediately visible: the black surface. There is only the visible, the concrete, the seen, all there, all at once: a single Black *thing*, unindividuated, threatening, ominous, *black*. The white thinks that he/she takes no part in this construction. After all, it is not as if he or she ever said: "Today, I will self-consciously become a white supremacist. I will construct the black as criminal and inferior, while deeming everything white to be of the highest order." This reduces whiteness to a form of voluntarism that could be used to exculpate whites from their racist actions, that is, whites could use this form of reasoning to nullify any responsibility for their racist actions. The fact of the matter is that this form of voluntarism is naïve and lacks complexity in the realm of social action; hence, it does not free whites from the duty of taking responsibility for their acts of white racism. Freedom still remains. One can cease to cooperate with structures of white power; cease to perform white racist acts; and, hence, help to dismantle structures of white power. Whites must come to see how they have become seduced by whiteness, and how they make choices based upon that seduction. The problem is that one's whiteness, a center from which one has always already cut up the social world, makes sense of things, evaluates and judges, remains invisible while the discursive field of white power/knowledge continues to open up a social space of intelligibility in terms of which the black/white body appears. The white(s) in the above two cases are beyond epistemic humility. Or, perhaps they are beyond any means of persuasion (rational, evidential, rhetorical) that would help to disrupt what has become a kind of "world-picture." There is no more to know and nothing more to be done differently. Seeing the blackness is sufficient. Judgment has already been rendered: Guilty! Take the white woman on the elevator. She looks with eyes that are informed by white *mythos* and structured through white historical power. The black body is therefore always already *codified*. She then begins the *ritual* of clutching at her purse. This ritual is not simply an effect of mythos and codification. Rather, the ritual is generative; it reinforces the reality, solidity, and "truth" of the context. Through mythos, codification, and ritualized behavior the black body is then *ontologized*; its being gets frozen into something that should be avoided, a thing rendered suspect a priori. Bryonn Bain, a Harvard Law student, who was a victim of codificational power of the NYPD's equation of blackness with criminality, knows the dangers of something as simple as "walking while black." His blackness was a site of negative ontologization.

One way of challenging whiteness is to interrogate its ontology, its being, as expressed through its imperial and hegemonic gaze. Indeed, such a challenge is designed to critique the representational power of whiteness. For whiteness sees what it wants to see and thus identifies that which it wants to see with that which is. The power and privilege of whiteness obfuscates its own complicity in seeing a "reality" that it constructs as objective. Functioning as the Transcendental Signified, within the specious taxonomy of naturally occurring racial kinds, whiteness is deemed that center from which all other racial *differences* are constituted.

Within Aristotelian metaphysics, whiteness is but a mere accident; it is that which is predicated of something that is not itself an accident. Historically, however, whiteness has come to signify that which is transhistorical, nonaccidental, that which exists in virtue of itself. This process of reification often occludes recognition of the situated, value-laden, constructive force of whiteness, rendering invisible its Procrustean tendencies, myopia, narcissism, solipsism, hegemony, xenophobia, and misanthropy. Perhaps there is something ironically "Kantian" in this. Whiteness fails to call into question its own modes of socioepistemological constructivity, ways that social reality is constituted and regulated. Through this process of "white-world-making," the construction of a world with values, regulations, and policies that provide supportive structures to those identified as "white," a world that whiteness then denies having given birth to, a possible slippage between knowing and being is often difficult to encourage. In short, what whiteness *knows* is what there *is.* As a racist, Kant was no stranger to the reduction of what is "known" about the black to what the black "is." Too bad Kant failed to see (or refused to see) the specifically *cultural* and *racial* "Copernican" implications of what he held to be true about blacks. As space and time are pure forms of intuition, those conditions under which empirical objects appear, counterfactually, Kant could have reasoned: "Race is but a social category through which I construct and constitute others as having a racial status inferior to my own; it is an impure form of intuition through which the nonwhite, in this case the black, appears." As is known, however, Kant's own racial identity (and the racial identities of nonwhites) was constructed through the very metanarrative world-making of whiteness itself.

Whiteness has the power to create an elaborate social subterfuge, leading both whites and nonwhites to believe that the representations in terms of which they live their lives and understand the world and themselves are naturally given, unchangeable ways of being. As argued above, to be known as black, from the constitutive and regulative hegemonic perspective of whiteness, means to be nothing more than black, a mere predictable occurrence in the natural world, a mere *thing,* frozen, signifying an ontology of surfaces; it is to be known as an ontological plenum, a black epidermal surface, whose ways of being are presumed symmetrical with white ways of knowing. The epistemological framework of whiteness (what whites claim *to know* about black people) constructed black people as inferior through regimes of white racist discourse, racist institutions, and oppressive, misanthropic actions. Whiteness, as a value-creating power, creates a distorted Black body/self through the use of theories and practices that define and reinforce certain conceptions of the black body/self. Of course, on this score, whiteness distorts its own status as superior.

Notwithstanding the powerful counter-semiotic systems created, sustained, and reconfigured by black people, blacks internalized white ways of constructing the world and understood themselves as ontologically inferior; whiteness constructed blacks as ugly, and many blacks felt themselves as ugly; whiteness imagined blacks as uncivilized, and many Blacks came to think of themselves as uncivilized. The white imaginary creates such self-serving specious and blatantly false constructions and knowledge claims, an imaginary that conflates being and knowing. Within the white imaginary, blackness became a trope for all things negative, that is, all things not white. However, the white

imaginary would be limited to spinning empty ideational constructions with little or no somatic consequences without powerful infra-
structures, white political institutions, white juridical practices, and so
on, to enforce its white Herrenvolk structure.

It is the hegemony of white ways of knowing, white ways of being,
white ways of emoting, characterizing, silencing, brutalizing, institu-
tionalizing, oppressing, naming, interpreting, seeing, not seeing, terrorizing, policing, mythologizing, distancing, blaming, denying, avoiding,
and inviting that act to occlude other (nonhegemonic) ways of being
and knowing for white folk. To be black, to fall prey to whiteness's
(anti-black) epistemological and ontological modes of structuration, is
to be devoid of ontological depth. From the perspective of whiteness
vis-à-vis black people, Jean-Paul Sartre's existentialist thesis is reversed:
essence precedes existence. The black does not come upon the stage of
human existence unmade, stretching beyond itself toward some task,
project, end. Within the framework of whiteness, the black is already
made, enclosed within him/herself. Whiteness is true transcendence, an
ecstatic mode of being; blackness, however, in its ontological structure,
is true immanence, a thing unable to be other than what it was born to
be, a thing closed upon itself, locked into an ontological realm where
things exist not "for-themselves" but "in-themselves," waiting to be ordered by some external, subjugating, purposive (white) consciousness.

Within the framework of whiteness, the black is not that Other
whose being calls out for recognition, whose being awaits to explode
and disrupt the self-identical sameness of whiteness. For whiteness ad-
mits of no ignorance vis-à-vis the black. Hence, there is no need for
white silence, a moment of quietude that encourages listening to the
black. There is no need for white self-erasure (or at least a form of self-
bracketing) in the presence of blackness. All that is knowable is known
in a single glance, the mere visual registration of blackness is enough.
The black simply *is*. There is no inside. To admit to an inside is already
to admit of the unknown, which already creates space for white inse-
curity, white unknowing. To admit as much would create a slippage between knowing and being, a slippage that could undermine white
security and white self-certainty. To gaze upon the black in a typical social encounter, from the perspective of whiteness, often means seeing
nothing but a body imprinted with culturally and historically embedded
significations—though believed to be fixed, essential significations—
that derive from the power of whiteness to map thoroughly the meaning of what it means to be black (and white).

Within the bounds of a white socio-ontological cartography, then,
whiteness is the hub of economic and political power; it is deemed supe-

rior intellectually, culturally, aesthetically, religiously, and so on. Hence one sees blackness but only through (superior) whiteness. One sees the black (the Other) as an instantiation of white normativity (the same). The black is a white normative sign that carries a surplus of white-constructed significations; the black is neither more nor less than an extension of what whiteness is. In a social ontological encounter with a black person, whiteness does not abandon itself or stray from its familiar white scripts and its familiar acts of scripting; rather, the white body/self performs under the aegis of white normativity. Whiteness fails the crucible of sociality. Out of trepidation and a failure to remit its own power, whiteness refuses to reach across the social ontological divide, a divide that is testimony to the reality that there is more than the One/the same/the white. The appeal of the black tends to go unrecognized. For this requires silence and humility on the part of whiteness. Whiteness, however, is arrogant and solipsistic ("only we, whites, really exist").

Whiteness fails to see itself as alien, as seen, as recognized. To see itself as seen, whiteness would have to deny the imperial epistemological and ontological base from which it sees what it wants (or has been shaped historically) to see. Whiteness refuses to risk finding itself in exile, in unfamiliar territory, an unmapped space of uncertainty in the form of both knowing and being. It refuses the difficult process of alienation and return, that is, return to a different, antiwhiteness place of knowing and being. To refuse this process, whiteness denies its own potential to be Other (to be "the not-same"), to see through the web of white meaning that it has spun. Whiteness refuses to transcend an economy of white discourse and action that creates the illusion of a social world of natural, immutable arrangements, arrangements that get axiological assignments (black = bad, white = good) from within a rigid system of white totalization. Hence, the black, within the social space of whiteness, does not constitute a radical Otherness, but an always already preinterpreted *thing*. The black is held captive by the totalizing tendencies of whiteness. As such, the black falls short of the Levinasian notion of the infinite Otherness of the other; rather, the black constitutes a familiar and mundane sameness. From the omniscient pretensions of whiteness, the black, far from shattering the myth-making categories of whiteness, simply "confirms" them. Given the ubiquity of whiteness, there is no apparent position of externality from which the black is able to negotiate its identity.[7] Hence, the possibility for a radically new dynamic process of relationality (between whiteness and blackness) becomes difficult to establish. The social ontology of whiteness is totalizing. Encompassing. Terrorizing. Brutalizing. Denying. Whiteness inhabits a space of exclusivism. To be genuinely inclusive, however, whiteness must cast off its tendencies toward paternalism. Black people have never been the white man's burden; rather, *sustaining* whiteness is the burden. The idea that it was the white man's burden to make sure that nonwhites became "civilized" was born from the white imaginary. Seeing the Other through a prism of difference (contra-sameness that issues from whiteness's proclivity toward totalization) whereby the presence of the Other forces one to see his or her own (white) positionality as strange and alien will provide for the necessary paralogical context wherein the black voice is heard and is able to enter into a space of equally respectful discursive exchange and mutual influence. In this way, the nonwhite Other's Otherness does not become another mere instantiation of whiteness's sameness. Again, in this way, one avoids the totalizing tendencies of whiteness. It is only through the medium of "white understanding," though, that the black voice will be heard. This "white understanding," however, need not function as an insuperable barrier, but as an opportunity for the development of a porous horizon, one that responds positively to the Other in his or her difference, learns from the Other, and changes based upon an encounter with the Other. The Other would be recognized as both similar and different, a conjunction that involves overlap, expansion and deconstruction of aspects of the horizon of white ways of knowing and being.

The social ontology of whiteness is a species of racism. Whether racism is in the heart or necessarily consisting of a set of racist beliefs, whiteness continues to be a living, breathing historical construction, a social ontological performance that has profound, pervasive, and systemic oppressive consequences for nonwhite people.

Racism is predicated upon the notion that the category of "race" refers to a naturally occurring biological kind. It has been argued, however, that race is a fiction, a nonreferring term, that race is (as the mantra goes) a socially and politically constructed category that was created at a particular historical moment to justify and rationalize the subjugation of groups of people by other groups of people. It might be argued, then, that since whiteness is implicative of race, and since race is a fiction, an epistemologically and ontologically bankrupt concept, that whiteness is itself a fiction. This, of course, would be a glaring mistake. It simply does not follow. Although I reject the notion of racialized whiteness as an actual entity that constitutes an ontological substratum, a fixed essential thing that makes whites into naturally occurring racial kinds, it does not follow that whiteness is devoid of reference. Whiteness refers to a multitude of individual, collective, intentional, unintentional, isolated, systemic actions that synergistically work to sustain and constantly regenerate relationships of unequal power between whites and nonwhites. Those who are designated as "white" reap very significant psychosocial, political, cultural, and moral power vis-à-vis nonwhites. "White" actions get performed, ritualized, and calcified within the (social, political, economic, and interpersonal) transactional, dramaturgical space of the lived experience of both whites and nonwhites. Within such a context, the constructivity of whiteness recedes and various modes and manifestations of white supremacy (many subtle and many not so subtle) may come to represent the "natural" order of things.

Whiteness, then, falls within a social ontological domain, not a domain of ontological substances. And again, though its being is understood here within the framework of an antiessentialist hermeneutic, it does not follow that whiteness is somehow *unreal.* Whiteness embodies a difference that indeed makes a difference on the minds and bodies of both whites and nonwhites. Whiteness's *reality* gets concretized through complex systems of advantage that have accrued over time, systems of differential power (whites benefiting more than nonwhites) created and maintained by whites who see it as their natural (God-given) right to be at the apex of natural and historical evolution. In short, assuming that the concept of race is indeed empirically empty, though by no means an analytical concept, that race is as empirically based as the term "centaur," it does not follow from this that whiteness is devoid of social ontological import; for it is a mode of being that expresses itself, makes its reality known, through a process of world-making; its intelligibility and social ontological reality presupposes a functional, hegemonic axiological system.

Prior to any formal "scientific" theorizations regarding racial taxonomic distinctions among people, black people knew in their souls and bodies what it meant to suffer under the weight of whiteness. After all, black people of African descent were enslaved, owned, reduced to property, prior to any formal theoretical conceptualization of the notion of race. There was a time when black people knew all too well the potentially deadly consequences of something as simple as looking a white directly in the eyes. In the presence of whiteness, black folk had to show respect, had to acknowledge, in so many ways of humiliating genuflection, that they were not equal to white folk. Hence, white folk controlled the direction, and structure, of the gaze. For a black person to return the gaze would have meant, even for that brief moment, that whites had lost control on the direction of the emanation of power, the capacity to control what and how things are seen. Of course, it also would have meant that blacks refused to play the game—albeit a very serious and often deadly game—of whiteness.

Whiteness enjoyed (and enjoys) the power to represent, to engage in the representation and objectification of the Other. This power of white scopophilia, with all of its psychosexual overtones, raises significant issues regarding dehumanization, control, fear, anxiety, subjectivity, embodiment, relationality, and politicized social spaces, and different forms of psychological and bodily comportment. Black people, however, were always cognizant, perhaps even clairvoyant, regarding the souls of white folk. Such knowledge was important for survival. Even from the auction block, that site of pernicious white bidding for black flesh, where black people were examined like beasts of the field, having their bodies checked and poked as a means of assessing their mere utility value, enslaved blacks, believed devoid of subjectivity, looked upon the white crowd with perspicacity. As David R. Roediger notes: "The auction block gave flesh to questions of sexual exploitation and of gender. Its stark realities laid the urgent imperative for slaves to penetrate the psychologies of whites and their necessity to make distinctions even among white slave buyers."[8] Contrary to white lies, black people looked out upon the white crowd from a perspectival *here*, a location of embodied subjectivity and criticality.

Despite the insightful analyses done by whites within the field of critical whiteness studies, can black people afford to leave it to whites to *name* their own reality, their world? Although black people ought to praise the autocritical explorations of white people to figure out ways to disrupt aspects of their white hegemony, they cannot abandon the task to white people. Black social and economic powerlessness can and does continue in the very midst of white autocritique. Critical whiteness theorists can and do engage in powerful and insightful discourse regarding the deconstruction and dismantlement of whiteness, but it is black people who must live the reality of whiteness expressed in the form of black unemployment, inferior health care, inferior education, police brutality, ontological criminalization and driving while black, lower wages, higher incarceration rates, and so on. For black people, such conditions constitute a space of existential being-in-the-world; a space of being and suffering that is metadiscursive. After all, after a day of theorizing, the white theorist rides back to the suburbs, escapes being profiled, walks up and down the streets of all-white neighborhoods without fear of being harassed or labeled "a problem," and finds it easy to hail a cab if necessary. It is not enough that whites, with good intentions, thematize their whiteness and attempt to render it harmless. The white semiotic space within which whites move and have their being far exceeds their intentions. Hence, whites can have good intentions, but what is to be done when one's whiteness carries a surplus of significations over and above such intentions? For example, what would it mean for a white to fight against white supremacy and yet reap the material benefits of whiteness: easily obtaining bank loans, gaining meaningful employment, and so on? To rearticulate white identity, to render it nonhegemonic and nonsupremacist without renegotiating the actual redistribution of political, economic, and cultural power based upon whiteness leaves the coordinates of white power untouched. How does one "unbecome" white when white America, for example, is constantly making it beneficial for one to "become" or remain white? After all, no one wants to be black, Latino, Native American, or Asian in a society where such groups are marginalized and existentially derailed. To advocate the "abolition of whiteness" while structures created by whites to benefit whites still remain in place is a nominal position at best. Abolishing whiteness is not to be confined to the psychological sphere. It is not about feeling comfortable with one's whiteness. It is not about confession. An effective form of white abolition must involve the self-conscious deracination of interconnected and synergistic political, cultural, economic, semiotic, psychosocial, intra-psychological, and interpersonal sites of white supremacy. Once this occurs, perhaps there will emerge a completely harmless (for example, non-supremacist) form of white existence and white identity. Or, perhaps, the appellation "white" itself will prove needless and obsolete. After all, does it make sense to speak of a "post-white" form of *whiteness* when whiteness has become the antithesis of itself? What a "post-white" world would look like, a world in which whiteness ceases to possess and express hegemony, supremacy, and injustice, I cannot say. I can say, however, that it is not enough that liberal and progressive academic whites (and white politicians) seek the proliferation of differences, and white postmodern and poststructuralist theorists pontificate about the death of the modern subject; for whiteness is able to survive a process of ethnic showcasing and is capable of remaining intact as the modern self dissolves into an interplay of signs, an unstable site of multiple narratives, a site of multicultural hybridity, and an assemblage of shifting language-games. No matter how pastiche the postmodern subject may become, the power of capital appears to benefit most those who are nevertheless designated white. Critical whiteness studies is an important site of anti-white racist activity. It should be seen as an important site of liberatory discourse, but it must remain open to those nonwhite voices that continue to reveal the extent to which they actually suffer and feel terrorized by whiteness.

This raises the issue concerning the purpose of this text. One significant purpose is to call upon African-American philosophers to *name* with greater specificity the type of racism about which they often write. *Whiteness* is that object so named. The text is not designed to guilt whites, although guilt can be a potentially positive motivating force toward change. Guilt without paralysis can lead to possible change. Another significant point is that the text continues the African-American tradition (David Walker, Thomas N. Baker, Frederick Douglass, Nat Turner, W.E.B. Du Bois, Ralph Ellison, Harriet Jacobs, Ida B. Wells-Barnett, Richard Wright, James Baldwin, bell hooks, Toni Morrison) of critically engaging whiteness. Of course, I am told today that we are able to do this openly and without fear of white retaliation. It is important that the theoretical work done here be recognized as a continuation of a long tradition of critiquing whiteness. We never begin ex nihilo, but take our departure from preexisting historical discourse and praxis. This underscores the reality of the endurance of whiteness and its capacity to undergo metamorphosis, but it also underscores the long-standing liberatory efforts of African Americans from the past (and present) who fought (and fight) the good fight against white hegemony and injustice. Hence, the philosophers within this text inherit a discourse of black liberation from past historical forms of black resistance against the malignant tendencies of whiteness. Grounded within such a black space of resistance, the philosophers within this text explore various dimensions of whiteness, mapping its various forms of concealment, its pretense of universality, its existential threat to nonwhite people, its imperial nature as expressed in everyday life, political theory, and modern philosophy, the nature of its privilege, its addictive power, the dynamics of what it means to be a goodwill white, the possible rehabilitation of whiteness, the ontology of whiteness, and its constructivity.

In the first chapter, Charles W. Mills raises very significant and challenging questions regarding the silence (in American social and political theory, social and political philosophy, and even in orthodox left theory) on the issue of racial justice. Mills insightfully explores how this situation might be remedied through an accurate *naming* and characterization of the global dimensions of white supremacy. He then offers an analysis of a specifically racial form of exploitation, looks at the wages of whiteness, and then situates racial justice-seeking norms that have the potential to address racial injustice.

Next, Robert E. Birt explores whether or not a white person can live whiteness authentically. Working with Sartre's characterization of bad faith as a form of self-negation and lying to oneself, Birt goes on to develop Sartre's notion that the human being is freedom, but always already a situated freedom. From this Birt explores the notion that whiteness is a form of flight from situated facticity, and sees itself as possessing the property of *exclusive transcendence*. However, it is this exclusive transcendence that has profound negative existential implications for the reality of black transcendence. Birt's conclusion is that whiteness's supremacy and privilege are achieved at great existential risk and inauthenticity.

Moving between different discursive styles, Janine Jones provides a rigorous discussion of what it means to be a goodwill white. Jones philosophically attends to the fact that goodwill whites often fail to empathize with African Americans, despite their good intentions. Jones offers a very useful model of empathy: "Empathy occurs when we succeed in mapping the *structure* of an experience (where specific emotional content is part of the structure) onto the structure of an experience of the individual with whom we seek to empathize." After delineating the basic pattern of empathetic explanation of a person P's situation, Jones systematically shows (through the use of the Los Angeles riots of 1992 and the subsequent acquittal of the white officers who beat Rodney King) how empathy on the part of whites can fail because one fails, in part, to find a source analogue that corresponds to the emotions, goals, and situations of the person (in this case a black person) for whom one desires to show empathy or because a retrieved source does not correspond, and should be constructed. Jones reveals that there are very complex dynamics of denial at the heart of goodwill whites, even when empathy is achievable.

Clevis Headley draws upon Africana philosophy to explore whiteness. Distinguishing Africana philosophy from those directions in black thought that reject all things white, create inverse embodiments of whiteness (e.g., black essentialism), and deny black agency through the idea that blacks are helplessly seduced by whiteness, Headley correctly emphasizes the *critical confrontational* dimensions of Africana philosophy. He critically appropriates the notion of conjuring over traditional uses of the term "constructionism" when explaining "the phenomenon of making the world white." Using conjuring as a root metaphor for understanding the ontology of whiteness, Headley explores the many "economies" of metaphors of whiteness. He then concludes with an exploration of the future of whiteness, arguing that going beyond whiteness is not to be achieved through rational argument but through "a continuously affirmed refusal to prolong the ontological and existential project of whiteness."

In my own chapter, I provide a Foucauldian analysis of whiteness as a specific historically constructed standpoint, one that emerges as a universal value code. It is through a genealogical reading that whiteness is revealed as a kind of emergence, a reactive value-creating power that shapes how the black body/self is disciplined and how the black body/self comes to internalize a self-denigrating (white) episteme. I then provide a "textual genealogy" of Toni Morrison's *The Bluest Eye*, demonstrating how Pecola Breedlove, the young black tragic figure in the text, is the product of a world of historical, value-laden white sedimentation. Part of this sedimentation involves the pervasive supremacist, semiotic representation of whiteness in the everyday life of Pecola. I conclude with a discussion of the possibility of what it would mean to liberate Pecola from the (aesthetic, somatic, and psychological) debilitating weight of whiteness.

Arnold Farr picks up on the project of whiteness as expressed philosophically in the West. He highlights the limitations—reminiscent of Jones's chapter—of white ways of seeing the world, a form of seeing "whose entire epistemic grid for deciphering social data was *too white* to empathize with and comprehend the African-American experience." Instead of making blackness visible in philosophy, Farr takes it as his task to render whiteness visible in philosophy. He does this through an insightful discussion of the myth of color-blind philosophical inquiry, the whiteness of Geist, and Geist as racialized consciousness. He concludes that white forms of racialization have been historically destructive to nonwhites and that it is important that white philosophers engage in a process of self-reflexivity upon their own whiteness and racial locations, thus deconstructing whiteness as a view from nowhere.

Lucius T. Outlaw, after clearly establishing the historical project of whiteness, at least in terms of its project of nation-state building in the United States of America, critically welcomes the burgeoning field of critical whiteness studies. For he maintains that there can be no substantial renovative work vis-à-vis whiteness "without the willing embracing of such ongoing work and of its progress-spurring consequences by those identified and living as *white* folks." Outlaw would have us be done with condemning folks for being white, which does not mean that he fails to realize the history of white supremacy/white hegemony. Rather, he is interested in rehabilitating, reworking, and rearticulating whiteness in ways that will aid in the establishment of (normatively) just ways of being in America. Hence, Outlaw is interested in the transformational possibilities inherent in reimagining a genuine heterogeneous nation. He does not advocate the familiar "abolition of whiteness" thesis, for he recognizes pragmatic uses in such (bicultural) gathering or identifying terms as whiteness and blackness. However, he does acknowledge that the lived reality of whiteness as greed and fear must be dislodged from whiteness. Outlaw argues for a critical engagement with whiteness, the result of which ought to lead to a rehabilitated notion of whiteness freed from such notions as white supremacy and white hegemony.

Lewis R. Gordon offers critical reflections on three tropes that he finds problematical limitations in whiteness studies. Through insightful etymological examination of the term "privilege," which is one of the tropes, Gordon explores the problematicity involved in the notion of white privilege. Engaging in additional etymological exploration, Gordon explores the notion of "victimization" (the second trope) vis-à-vis whites and communities of color. The third trope that Gordon examines involves the idea that if race is not treated as a social construction, then epistemologically false and ethically misguided consequences obtain. He goes on to draw a very insightful distinction between normativity and normality, a distinction that is very important concerning questions of whiteness and its tendency to conflate normality with normativity. Not rejecting the notion that whiteness is an achievement within the space of social constructivity, Gordon does object to the reduction of the social world into "all there is." He argues for the importance of "intervening forces of reality." This clears space for his insightful theoretical stance on human evolution and its explanatory power for derailing racist subtextual questions regarding the "anomalous" emergence of black people.

Paget Henry sees the importance of critiquing whiteness to be linked to the potential of black nonbeing. Hence, it is so important that Africana philosophy, as a form of resistance and restoration of Black identity and survival, challenge whiteness. Like Gordon in his concern with whiteness as a trope, and Headley in his understanding of the metaphoricity of whiteness, Henry is interested in exploring how whiteness became a trope for power, "ownership of the earth," as Du Bois says, and for "the appropriation of the labor of those whose land had been taken." Henry goes on to discuss Hegel and the imperial self of whiteness, and the whiteness of the master self. Henry reserves Africana phenomenology as an important critical hermeneutic framework for understanding the impact of the (white) master self on black people of African descent. More specifically, Henry traces the various ways that "the dead seeing eye" of the Western master self evolves and how it creates a dialectic of nonrecognition of blackness (or nonwhiteness).

Like so many postmodern thinkers, John H. McClendon states his standpoint up front. His philosophical standpoint is dialectical materialism of the Marxist-Leninist type. Though the reader may assume that McClendon's analysis of whiteness/race will involve a reduction of sorts, this is far from the truth. His argument "is not that race is reducible to class relations; rather, it is grounded in the material conditions of capitalism." McClendon goes on to explore race as fact or fiction, critically discussing what he terms "the argument from illusion" and what the implications of this argument are for understanding the methodological aims of the natural/social sciences. Telescoping his Marxist-Leninist approach, he discusses the pragmatic function of phenotypic description that is linked to the dynamics of racialized relations. Such racialized relations, according to McClendon, are derived from "social relations of capitalist exploitation." Last, McClendon provides a very important and challenging discussion of the distinction between "whiteness" and "white supremacy."

Paul C. Taylor focuses on the implications of American philosopher John Dewey's racial identity as white. He frames the discussion of Dewey and whiteness within the context of Dewey's introductory remarks to Claude McKay's *Selected Poems*. Given Dewey's claim that the poems leave "white men able to express only 'humiliated sympathy,'" this leads Taylor, understandably, to question Dewey's response along lines of insight into the nature of whiteness offered by critical whiteness theorists. Taylor does not stay with Dewey. He uses Dewey as a point of embarkation for critically examining the discourse of critical whiteness studies, finding aspects of the field, indeed, the field itself, problematic. For example, can it be said that Dewey read McKay's poems "whitely"? Was Dewey's "silence" indicative of the typical lack of autocritique that is found in so many whites? Perhaps the motif of "white invisibility," that is, where whites apparently "fail" to see their whiteness as a site of hegemony and power, was operative in Dewey's response? After providing an overview of some of the tensions and contradictions in Dewey, deepening an appreciation for Dewey's *raced* identity and situation, Taylor provides toward the end of his chapter an intriguing interpretation of Dewey's "silence."

Blanche Radford Curry delves into the theme of whiteness and feminism. Her exploration is a three-pronged consideration. First, she considers feminism and racism and how whiteness formed the standpoint according to which white feminists, during the first wave of feminism, drew the line between themselves and the Other (black women). The point here is that despite feminist liberatory discourse vis-à-vis male hegemony, white feminists maintained their own form of (white) hegemony. Curry provides an insightful discussion of how whiteness shaped the identities and actions of white suffragists and white women abolitionists. Second, Curry explores how black women are marked (Othered) by their racial identity as black (or not-white). She draws insightfully from the work of Toni Morrison, Paula Giddings, Deborah K. King, bell hooks, Patricia Hill Collins, Angela Davis, and Elsa Brown. Third, Curry proposes a form of discourse, theory, and action that transcends both the white women/feminists' and the African-American women/womanists' embodiments of theory and praxis. An important motif of Curry's chapter involves the theoretical and "praxic" limitations accompanied by déjà vu experiences regarding white feminism and black womanism. Hence, she proposes a third level of theorization and recommendation, one that involves a new and transformational womanist/feminist ethics, engagement, and praxis.

Joy James writes a very interesting narrative account of what it means to be a recovering black white supremacist addict. Her chapter is both witty and sardonic, skillfully utilizing metaphor, innuendo, deep cultural and political excavation and critique. She confesses that she probably started out her "preacademic years in incremental dosages, sniffing rather than shooting" (whiteness). She correctly reveals that whiteness is indeed pervasive, plentiful, and free, but it comes at a high price, a price that could eventuate in death. She insightfully references Senator Trent Lott's apology while being fully cognizant that "this nation is incredibly strung out" (on whiteness). Reconfiguring the twelve-step program for alcoholics, James offers a five-step program for recovering white supremacy (WS) addicts.

NOTES

1. Alice McIntyre, *Making Meaning of Whiteness: Exploring Racial Identity with White Teachers* (Albany: State University of New York Press, 1997), p. 96.
2. Jessie Daniels, *White Lies: Race, Class, Gender, and Sexuality in White Supremacist Discourse* (New York: Routledge, 1997), p. 20.
3. Ibid., p. 24.
4. Ibid., pp. 24–25.
5. McIntyre, *Making Meaning of Whiteness*, p. 31.
6. Richard Delgado and Jean Stephancic, *Critical White Studies: Looking behind the Mirror* (Philadelphia: Temple University Press, 1997), pp. 291–99.
7. The point is to suggest how whiteness attempts to maintain its hegemony by rendering *merely reactionary* pro-black, pro-agential performativity.
8. David R. Roediger (ed.), *Black on White: Black Writers on What It Means to Be White* (New York: Schocken Books, 1998), p. 3.

1

RACIAL EXPLOITATION AND THE
WAGES OF WHITENESS

Charles W. Mills

DISCUSSIONS in the academy in general, and in philosophy in particular, of racial injustice have come a long way over the past decade or
two.[1] African-American philosophers such as Bernard Boxill and
Howard McGary can testify far better than I concerning how little interest there was in these matters only a few years ago, and how the
torch was kept burning by a few figures, mostly blacks such as themselves, but with a scattering of white progressives.[2] From being a
strictly fringe concern, the issue of reparations has become sufficiently
mainstream for city councils across the country to take a position on
the question, and for "white" universities to debate the matter. Unfortunately, very little of the credit for this development can go to mainstream white philosophy, despite the fact that philosophers are by their
calling supposed to be the group professionally concerned about justice as a concept and an ideal; indeed, the book regarded by many as the
fountainhead of the Western tradition, Plato's *Republic*, is focused single-
mindedly on that very subject. Instead, it is black intellectuals, black
activists such as Randall Robinson, and community groups such as the
National Coalition of Blacks for Reparations in America (N'COBRA)
who deserve the credit. Yet there is certainly enough blame to go
around—one would not want to pick just on one's own profession.
The indictment for (relative) historic silence on the question of racial
justice can be extended to American social and political theory in
general, not merely social and political philosophy, but mainstream

American sociology and mainstream American political science. (Depending on how one defines "mainstream"—and from the racial margins, pretty much everything else looks mainstream—this judgment also holds true for a lot of orthodox left theory in these fields, not just liberalism, since Marxists have tended to dissolve the specificities of these racial problems into the general oppression of capital, with socialism then being plugged as the universal panacea.)

How do we correct this situation? In this chapter, extrapolating the line of argument I have articulated elsewhere in my work,[3] I want to make some suggestions toward the development of a possible long-term theoretical strategy for remedying this deficiency. My recommendation is that we (1) retrieve and elaborate, as an alternative, a more accurate global sociopolitical paradigm, the concept of *white supremacy*; (2) develop an analysis of a specifically *racial* form of exploitation, in its manifold dimensions; (3) uncover and follow the trail of what W.E.B. Du Bois famously called the "wages of whiteness"; and then (4) locate normative demands for racial justice within this improved descriptive conceptual framework.

"WHITE SUPREMACY" AS ALTERNATIVE PARADIGM

At least since Marx's time, if not long before, it has been a cliché that major political battles are ideological battles also, struggles over rival understandings of the sociopolitical order and conflicting framings of the crucial issues. Normative debates about right and wrong, justice and injustice, typically involve not merely axiological clashes but rival pictures of the factual: competing narratives of what happened in the past and what is happening right now, alternative descriptive frameworks and interpretations. The ignoring of race as a global issue in American sociopolitical theory—I distinguish "global" from, say, "local" discussions of race in subsections of a field such as the sociology of race relations, urban politics, or affirmative action debates in applied ethics—is made possible by a certain conception of the American polity and social order. With appropriate disciplinary adjustments for the particular subject in question (whether sociology, or political science, or political philosophy), this picture provides the common overarching framework of debate in the field: the United States is conceptualized as basically an egalitarian (if a bit flawed) liberal democracy free of the hierarchical social structures of the Old World. This profoundly misleading picture is Eurocentric in at least two interesting ways: (i) it focuses on the Euro-American population, those we call "whites," and takes their experience as representative, as the raw material from which to construct theoretical generalizations; (ii) it draws on a set of theoretical paradigms drawn *from* European sociopolitical theory—the classic writings of the great figures in European sociology and modern political thought, centered on class as the primary social division, and either not recognizing race as an emergent structure in its own right or biologizing it. The New World is being intellectually grasped with the tools of the Old World, and with reference to the Old World's transplanted population, an operation thus doubly blinded to the possibility that the experience of expropriated reds, enslaved blacks, annexed browns, and excluded yellows may be sufficiently different as to warrant the development of a new tool kit and, accordingly, a new paradigm. To the extent that race is not ignored altogether, it is naturalized or marginalized, and the nonwhite non-nation is assimilated in theory to the white nation.

The results can be seen in the typical silences and evasions of these disciplines. In an article giving a historical overview of American sociology, for example, Stanford Lyman argues that from the very start the discipline had a "resistance to a civil rights orientation":

> Race relations has been conceived of as a social problem within the domain of sociology ever since that discipline gained prominence in the United States; however, the self-proclaimed science of society did not focus its attention on the problem of how the civil rights of racial minorities might be recognized, legitimated, and enforced. . . . Indeed, tracing the history of the race problem in sociology is tantamount to tracing the history and the central problem of the discipline itself—namely, its avoidance of the issue of the significance of civil rights for a democratic society. . . . The reformist solution to social problems . . . rests upon a rational approach to modifying the structures of a society that is regarded *a priori* as fundamentally sound with respect to its basic values and norms. . . . Sociology, in this respect, has been part of the problem and not part of the solution.[4]

In political science, similarly, Rogers Smith's recent important and prizewinning book, *Civic Ideals*, outlines the various ways in which the most important theorists of American political culture, Alexis de Tocqueville, Gunnar Myrdal, and Louis Hartz, have managed to represent racism as an "anomaly" within a polity conceived of as basically egalitarian:

> [W]hen restrictions on voting rights, naturalization, and immigration are taken into account, it turns out that for over 80 percent of U.S. history, American laws declared most people in the world legally ineligible to become full U.S. citizens solely because of their race, original nationality, or gender. For at least two-thirds of American history, the majority of the

domestic adult population was also ineligible for full citizenship for the same reasons. . . . Although such facts are hardly unknown, they have been ignored, minimized, or dismissed in several major interpretations of American civic identity that have massively influenced modern scholarship. . . . All these Tocquevillian accounts falter because they center on relationships among a minority of Americans—white men, largely of northern European ancestry—analyzed in terms of categories derived from the hierarchy of political and economic status such men held in Europe. . . . [Writers in the Tocquevillian tradition] believe . . . that the cause of human equality is best served by reading egalitarian principles as America's true principles, while treating the massive inequalities in American life as products of prejudice, not rival principles.[5]

Finally, in our own discipline, philosophy, it is notorious—at least among black philosophers—that racial justice has been a major theme or subtheme of hardly *a single one* of the numerous books on justice by white philosophers written in the three decades since the revival of political philosophy following John Rawls's work.[6] One must conclude either that racial justice is of no concern to them or that they think it has already been achieved.

How are such evasions possible in a country built on Native American expropriation and hundreds of years of African slavery, followed by 140 years of first de jure, and now de facto, segregation? An interesting essay, or even a whole book, in the sociology of knowledge (or here, more accurately, the sociology of ignorance) could certainly be written on this question, but briefly, one would need to highlight the role of historical amnesia (the suppression, or the downplaying of the significance, of certain facts), the group interests and nonrepresentative experience of the privileged race (what cognitive psychologists would identify respectively as hot and cold factors of cognitive distortion), and, crucially, a conceptual apparatus inherited, as I said, from European sociopolitical theory, for which race is marginal. Though the problem is by no means confined to philosophy, in philosophy (for home-team reasons, I want to make sure that we get the credit for something) it is worst of all, because of the much greater possibilities for abstracting away from reality provided by the nonempirical nature of the subject.

Consider our own discipline, then. In philosophy it becomes possible for what some see as the most important work in Anglo-American political philosophy of the twentieth century, or even the most important work in twentieth-century political theory period, *A Theory of Justice*, to be written by an American, John Rawls, and yet make next to no mention of the centrality of racial *injustice* to the American polity. Defenders will, of course, tell me—I have had these debates before—that that is because Rawls expressly set out to do a book in *ideal* theory. My response would be to ask why he chose to do this, considering that the role of normative inquiry is presumably ultimately to intervene in our own, manifestly *non*ideal world. I would also suggest, though I suppose this verges on the ad hominem, that only those whose experience is one of privilege would find it so natural to deal purely with "ideal" theory in the first place. After all, having mapped out the ideal theory, should not the natural next move be to *apply* this theory to social reality so as to generate concrete prescriptions for making it more just? Moreover, in the three decades since the publication of Rawls's book, why have so many white philosophers followed his lead? As my colleague Tony Laden has pointed out to me, having done an *Ethics* review essay on a five-volume collection of articles on Rawls's work that includes no less than 88 papers from the past three decades, only *one* of these essays—by the African-American philosopher Laurence Thomas—deals with race.[7] Why has nobody done for race what Susan Moller Okin did with Rawls's apparatus for gender[8] and imagined what kind of social structure you would prescribe from behind the veil if you knew how people of color were disadvantaged by white supremacy? For that matter, why are European imperialism, African slavery, Native American expropriation, Jim Crow, and so on not part of the "general facts" about society and history, knowledge of which you are supposed to take with you behind the veil? How is it that in a book that appeared in 1971 and whose chapters were being written and circulated in the 1960s, a time of national civil rights protest from the mainstream NAACP to the more radical Black Panthers, we get no whiff of these struggles, no consideration—over the span of 600 pages—of what the implications might be if the "basic structure" is itself unjust?

And from a black point of view, of course, Rawls's later work is even less helpful in that the focus has shifted from the distributive concerns that at least provided some opening for philosophers of color to what I think most of us feel to be a largely irrelevant, profoundly *non*urgent and sleep-inducing debate about whether a just and stable society is possible when citizens are divided by their adherence to reasonable but incompatible doctrines.[9] In a post–Cold War United States where liberalism (in the broad, antifeudal sense) is obviously hegemonic, this is hardly a pressing matter. Of far greater importance from the point of view of justice, one would think, are the growing divisions between rich and poor of all colors, and the decades' long retreat from whatever weak corrective measures had been implemented in the '70s and '80s to address the legacy of de jure racial domination, which many black intellectuals have seen as the betrayal of the "Second Reconstruction."

So there has been a debilitating "whiteness" to mainstream political philosophy in terms of its crucial assumptions, the issues it has typically taken up, and the mapping of what it has deemed to be appropriate and important subject matter. And my claim is that the transdisciplinary framing of the United States as an if-not-quite-ideal-then-pretty-damn-close-to-it liberal democracy, particularly in the exacerbatedly abstract form typical of philosophy, has facilitated and underwritten these massive evasions on the issue of racial injustice. Accordingly, I have suggested in my own work that to counter this framing we need to revive "white supremacy" (which is already being used by many people in critical race theory and critical white studies) as a descriptive concept.[10] Normative questions, as pointed out above, hinge not merely on clashes of values, but on rival factual claims, both with respect to specific incidents and events and with respect to determining and constraining social structures. And particularly when challenges are coming from the perspective of *radical* political theory (e.g., Marxism, feminism, critical race theory), it may well be the case that most or all of the work in claims about injustice is being done by the divergent factual picture put forward rather than different values. Marxism is famously associated with antimoralism, but for those Marxists who *have* sought to make a normative case for the superiority of socialism, the appeal has often been made with reference to standard liberal norms of equality and well-being. (Indeed, some Marxist theorists have argued that there are *no* distinctively socialist values—that insofar as Marxism has a normative critique of capitalism, it is basically parasitic on liberal-democratic values.) And while there are numerous varieties of feminism, the most important kind historically has obviously been mainstream liberal feminism, which has simply sought to extend liberal values across the gender divide. So the point is that one can utilize mainstream values to advance quite radical demands: the key thing is to contest the factual picture with which mainstream theorists are operating. With the feminist concept of *patriarchy* and the Marxist concept of *class society*, women and the left have been better able to intervene in mainstream discussions of justice, because they have also contested the factual picture that has framed these discussions.

My claim is, then, that African-American and other philosophers working on race, and critical race theorists more generally, should make a comparable theoretical move: challenge the mainstream liberal "anomaly" framing of race by developing the concept of white supremacy. Doing so would have several advantages.

(i) To begin with, just on the terminological level, this *is* the term that was traditionally used to denote white domination, so one would be drawing on a vocabulary already established and familiar.[11] Feminists appropriated an existing term ("patriarchy") but had to shift its meaning; Marx had to provide an analysis of class society not merely in terms of rich and poor but, more rigorously, in terms of ownership of the means of production. So both are being employed as terms of art. But in the case of race in the United States, "white supremacy" was the term standardly used. What would now be necessary, of course, would be to give it a more detailed theoretical specification than it has hitherto had, to map in detail its various dimensions, and to try to work out its typical dynamic.

(ii) More important, the term carries with it the connotation of systematicity. Unlike the currently more fashionable "white privilege," *white supremacy* implies the existence of a system that not only privileges whites but is run by whites, for white benefit. As such it is a global conception, including not just the socioeconomic, but also the juridical, political, cultural, and ideational realms. Thus it contests—paradigm versus paradigm—the liberal individualist framework of analysis that has played and continues to play such an important and pernicious role in obfuscating the real centrality of race and racial subordination to the polity's history.

(iii) Finally, by shifting the focus from the individual and attitudinal (the discourse of "racism") to the realm of structures and power, it helps highlight the most important thing from the perspective of justice, which is how the white population benefits illicitly from its social location. Current debates about "racism" are hindered by the fact that the term is used in such a confusingly diverse range of ways that it is difficult to find a stable semantic core. Moreover, the dominant interpretation of white racism in the white population is probably individual beliefs about innate nonwhite (particularly black) biological inferiority, and individual hostility toward people of color (especially blacks). Given this conception, most whites think of themselves as nonracist—one positive thing about the present period is that nobody wants to be a racist, though this has also motivated a shift in how the term is defined—while continuing to hold antiblack stereotypes. But in any case, with the decline in overt racism in the white population, the real issue for a long time has not been individual racism but, far more important, the reproduction of white advantage and black disadvantage through the workings of racialized social structures. The idea of white supremacy is intended, in part, to capture the crucial reality that the *normal* workings of the social system continue to disadvantage blacks in large measure *independently* of racist feeling. Insofar as, since Rawls, our attention as philosophers concerned about justice is supposed to be on the "basic structure" of society and its workings, the concept of "white supremacy" then forces us to confront the possibility that the basic structure is itself systemically unjust. Corrective measures to end racial injustice would thus need to begin here.

However, the term also has one major and, some might argue, insuperable disadvantage. Apart from sounding "extremist" to whites, and perhaps to some blacks, it will just seem flagrantly inaccurate, a description that (if this much is conceded) may once have been true but is no longer so. White supremacy for most people will be identified with slavery, the hoods of the Ku Klux Klan, "Colored" signs, legal segregation and discrimination, police dogs attacking black demonstrators, and so forth. So considerable spadework will have to be done in arguing that the key referent of the term is white domination, and in demonstrating that white domination can persist in the absence of overt nonwhite subordination, white terrorism, and legal persecution. But there is a sense in which such spadework would have to be done regardless of the term chosen, inasmuch as individualist analyses of the sociopolitical order, which deny the existence of structures of domination (not just for race, but in general), are hegemonic in the popular mind. So this would be an ideological obstacle to be overcome no matter what term were chosen. And in the case of race, by contrast with class and gender, one should in theory at least face a somewhat easier task in convincing people, since although the society is routinely thought of as classless, and gender domination is seen as natural, it cannot (one would think) be denied that people of color were long legally suppressed. So even if whites are reluctant to concede the *continuing* existence of white supremacy, the concession that it *once* existed provides at least some theoretical foothold, since one can then make an argument (if no more than this) that it would have to have left some legacy.

Finally, I would claim that philosophers have a distinctive role to play in analyzing white supremacy.[12] Obviously, crucial work would have to be done at the empirical level, in sociology and political science. But investigations and formulations at a higher level of abstraction would be invaluable also. My model here, of course, is Marx's analysis of capitalism, which as we recall moved back and forth between the empirical and the philosophical. Think of all the articles and books there have been in Marxist theory over the past hundred years, looking at such issues as philosophical anthropology, class exploitation, the role of class ideology, the influence on cognition of class division, fetishism, naturalistic mystification, and so forth. My belief is that white supremacy has been sufficiently important as a social reality over the past few hundred years, and has been sufficiently influential in shaping human beings, that a parallel abstract philosophical investigation on race will turn out to be equally fruitful. The loftily metatheoretical vantage point of philosophy could then provide the insights about human existence, value theory, and cognition that are peculiar to the discipline, but informed (unlike the ostensibly colorless "view from nowhere") by the realities of white domination.

RACIAL EXPLOITATION

I now want to turn specifically to the idea of racial exploitation and draw a comparison between racial and class exploitation, since it will be illuminating for us to consider both their similarities and their differences. Exploitation is, of course, central to Marxist theory, since what distinguishes his analysis of capitalism from that of liberal theorists is that for him it is necessarily an exploitative system. Exploitation is not a matter of low wages or poor working conditions, though these will, of course, make it worse. Rather, exploitation has to do with the transfer of surplus value from the workers to the capitalists. To the extent that there is a normative critique in Marxism, then, it relies centrally on the claim that this relation is an exploitative one. Moreover, it is not just capitalism but class society in general that is exploitative, which is why we need to move toward a classless society. Finally, the exploitative nature of the system does not reside in class prejudice, in hostile views of the workers, but rather in their systemic disadvantaging by this transfer of surplus value through the wage relation. If Marx is right, class exploitation is *normal*, not requiring extraordinary measures, but flowing out of the routine functioning of the system.

Now the claim that capitalism is necessarily exploitative historically rested on the labor theory of value, and with the discrediting of this theory it has become harder to defend. The left-wing economist John Roemer has for many years been developing a revisionist view of exploitation,[13] but his development of the notion is quite far from traditional conceptions. For Marx exploitation was a real relationship, not merely an artifact of mathematical manipulation, and was linked with proletarian agency: it was in part precisely because of their exploitation that the workers were supposed to develop class consciousness, form trade unions, and ultimately participate in a movement to overthrow capitalism. So exploitation provides both an explanation for the logic of domination and a potential basis for its political overcoming. Marxism's pretensions to being a social science hinge in part on claims about the centrality of exploitation and how it organizes bourgeois and proletarian interests, thus generating behavioral uniformities that Marx thought could be expressed in social laws. And his theory is not merely a holistic, social-systemic one that opposes the "Robinsonades" of liberal theory, but famously a *materialist*, and thus a realist, one. (Note that [i] analyses of a social-systemic kind need not be materialist, since they can be idealist, for example seeing everything in terms of language or discourses, and [ii] materialism is a species of realism rather than coextensive with it, since while political realists claim that determination by group interests is crucial, they do not necessarily identify those interests as material ones. For Marx, though, what are supposed to make the sociopolitical wheels go round are class interests of a material kind, tied to economic advantage.)

The case I want to make is that racial exploitation can provide a parallel, even superior, illumination, and that it is greatly advantaged over the Marxist concept by not being tied to a dubious economic theory. Comparatively little work has been done on the concept of racial exploitation. I think this is because it has fallen between theoretical and political stools in an interesting way. In his recent book on "mutually advantageous and consensual exploitation," Alan Wertheimer points out that though the term is routinely tossed around, mainstream liberal theorists have had surprisingly little to say about it: "Exploitation has not been a central concern for contemporary political and moral philosophy." He suggests that there are at least three reasons for this silence: the concept's guilt-by-association with Marxism, the post-Rawlsian focus on ideal theory, and the fact that whereas exploitation is typically a "micro-level wrong" characterizing individual transactions, "much of the best contemporary political philosophy tends to focus on macro-level questions, such as the just distribution of resources and basic liberties and rights."[14] (The presumptive contrast in this last point arguably vindicates my earlier claim about the racially sanitized picture of the United States dominant in mainstream normative political theory. Don't *macro*-level questions about the unjust "distribution of resources and basic liberties and rights" arise from the history of American white supremacy? Can't it be argued that racial exploitation has been *national*?)

On the other hand, when Marxists have looked at race, as another author, Gary Dymski, points out in a left-wing anthology on exploitation, they have typically reduced it to a variant of class exploitation: "Race has been virtually ignored in Marxian theorizing about exploitation. Race is assumed to enter in only at a level of abstraction lower than exploitation; and anyway, since minorities are disproportionately workers, racial inequality is simply a special case readily accounted for by a racially neutral exploitation theory."[15] And this, of course, is part of a larger problematic pattern of Marxist theory: its failure to recognize race as a system of domination in itself.[16] Indeed, this is well illustrated by one of the classic texts of Marxism, Lenin's *Imperialism: The Highest Stage of Capitalism*.[17] Someone from the Third World (someone like me!) who had never read this pamphlet might come to it thinking from its title that Lenin is going to talk about the role of race and racism in First World imperialist exploitation of its colonies. But in fact Lenin barely refers to race at all. For him the populations in the colonial world suffer the exploitation of finance capital, which is merely an exacerbated variant of the exploitation typical of wage labor. So what one has is a "quantitative" change—it is the same thing, but worse. The idea that racial exploitation could have qualitatively distinct dimensions, that racial exploitation could crucially involve the active participation of white workers both in the metropolis and the colonies, is not envisaged by Lenin. Racial domination is subsumed under capitalist domination, and no separate theorization of its distinctive features is recognized as necessary. If we utilize the orthodox base-superstructure taxonomy, then the materialist region of society, which is the most important, "determining" part, is the base, the relations of production that encapsulate class relations of domination. Insofar as race is recognized, then, race would be at best part of the superstructure, a set of ideological relations. Even when race is cashed out in terms of superexploitation, the process is still assimilated to class exploitation in that the "race" in question is thought of as a differentially subordinated section of the working class, and the exploitative relation involves getting extra value for the bourgeoisie.

So neither in mainstream liberal theory nor in oppositional Marxist theory has racial exploitation been properly recognized and theorized. And I am suggesting that we redress this theoretical deficiency, and follow up on the insight expressed by W.E.B. Du Bois 70 years ago in his now-classic *Black Reconstruction in America* when he coined the phrase "the wages of whiteness."[18] The phrase represents a conceptual breakthrough, since at a time (even more than now) when Marxist theories effectively monopolized accounts of exploitation, and of course long before what we now know as "critical white studies" had come into existence, Du Bois was arguing that whiteness needed to be recognized as a system of exploitation in itself, and that *whiteness paid.* In keeping with the shift in the radical academy over the past two decades from Marxism to poststructuralism, much of the recent literature on whiteness, as Ashley Doane and Margaret Andersen complain in a new anthology, *White Out,* focuses on the discursive, the cultural, and the personal testimonial.[19] This is not to deny, of course, that whiteness has numerous aspects, and that the orthodox left of the past was deficient (following Marx's own footsteps) in its handling of what were dismissed as "superstructural" issues. But Du Bois's own insight was in terms of political economy, and the discussion arguably needs to be brought back to these fundamentals. The concept of "white privilege," Cheryl Harris's notion (following Derrick Bell) of whiteness as "property,"[20] and George Lipsitz's notion of a "possessive investment" in whiteness[21] can all be seen as indebted to Du Bois's original insight. Yet though this subsection of the field is well established, comparatively little has been done, so far as I know, to develop and articulate the conceptual mapping of the structure they presuppose. And within the African-American scholarly community, Du Bois's concept of "double consciousness" from *The Souls of Black Folk* has received far more attention than his "wages of whiteness."[22] So I am arguing that we need to redress this imbalance.

Before getting into the analysis, though, we have to deal with some preliminary objections.

It might be objected, to begin with, that racial exploitation cannot exist because races do not exist. If, as the growing scholarly consensus in anthropology on the question agrees, races have no biological existence, then how can they be involved in relations of exploitation, or for that matter any other relations? And here, of course, the standard answer from critical race theorists is that races can have a reality that, though social rather than biological, is nonetheless causally efficacious within our racialized world. From the fact that race is socially constructed, it does not follow that it is unreal.[23]

However, it might be claimed that insofar as it *is* socially constructed, then it is to the constructing agent that causality and agency really have to be attributed. In historical materialist versions of this claim, for example, it might be insisted that class forces, and ultimately the ruling class, the bourgeoisie, are the real actors. (So we could think of these as two Marxist reasons [though they come in other theoretical varieties also], apart from simple myopia, to deny racial exploitation: races do not exist in the first place, or if their social reality is grudgingly conceded, then, as a fallback position, this reality is reduced to an underlying class reality.) But even if Y is created by X, so that there is generating causation, it does not follow that Y continues to be moved, either wholly or at all, by X, so that there may not be sustaining and ongoing causation. In other words, even if we concede (and an argument would be necessary to prove this) that race is originally created by a class dynamic, this does not mean that race cannot attain what used to be called, in Marxist theory, at least a "relative autonomy" (if not more), an intrinsic dynamic of its own. One of the key books in initiating the current flood of "whiteness" literature was David Roediger's study of white American workers, *The Wages of Whiteness*,[24] and the significance of his paying tribute to Du Bois in his title was precisely because his conclusion was that these workers' whiteness *was* a real social fact about them, one that played a crucial role in their motivations and actions. So social "whiteness," the belief that one is a member of the privileged race, and the institutional reflections of these beliefs are causally efficacious.

Finally, it might be objected that "whites" come in all classes, different genders, and divergent nationalities, that there are power relations and great power differences among them, and that they also are exploited. But the claim that racial exploitation exists does not commit one to the claim that its benefits are all necessarily distributed *equally*, so if some whites get more than others this is still consistent with the thesis. Nor does it require that all whites be equally active in the processes of racial exploitation—some may be both actors and beneficiaries, while others are just beneficiaries. Finally, claiming that racial exploitation exists does not (it should be obvious) imply that it is the *only* form of exploitation. All of us will have different hats, and so it will be not merely possible but routinely the case that people are simultaneously the beneficiaries of one system of exploitation while being the victims of another, as with white women, for example. Society can be thought of as a complex of interlocking and overlapping systems of domination and exploitation, and I am by no means asserting that race is the only one. My claim rather is that it is an undertheorized one and that it has repercussions for holding the overall system together that are not generally recognized.

Let us contrast race and class exploitation, then. To begin with, assuming that the dominant position on the origins of race is correct, race is a product of the modern period, so that racial exploitation is limited to the last few hundred years, and so is much younger than class exploitation, and even more so by comparison with gender exploitation. Moreover, it is a historically contingent form of exploitation: while it is almost impossible to imagine the development of human society having taken place without class and gender hierarchy and exploitation, the fact that race might never have existed at all implies that racial exploitation might never have existed.

Suppose we use the terms R1 and R2 for the races involved, respectively dominant and subordinate. (Obviously, it is possible to have more than two races involved—think of apartheid South Africa, and the role of "Coloreds"—but we will make this simplifying assumption.) To begin with, it needs to be pointed out that the mere fact that two races are involved in relations of exploitation does not mean it is a relationship of *racial* exploitation. Racial exploitation is, as emphasized, just one variety of exploitation, and if it is a necessary condition that races be involved in the transaction, it is not a sufficient one. For it could be that the relations between R1 and R2 are simply standard capitalist relations. Imagine, say, that a group of capitalists from one racial group hires a group of workers from another racial group, but race plays no role in the establishment, or particular character, or reproduction of the relations of exploitation established. What is also required is that the relations of race play a role in the nature and degree of the exploitation itself. What makes racial exploitation *racial* exploitation, then, is not merely that the parties to the transaction are races, but that race determines, or significantly modifies, the nature of the relation between them.[25]

In what does this determination or modification consist? We are a bit handicapped here by the fact that the transaction has to be described in suitably general terms, encompassing (as I will soon argue) such a wide range of possibilities. But I suggest that the paradigm case of racial exploitation is one in which the moral/ontological/civic status of the subordinate race makes possible the transaction in the first place (i.e., the transaction would have been morally or legally prohibited had the R2s been R1s), or makes the terms significantly worse than they would have been (i.e., the R2s get a much poorer deal than if they had been R1s). And the term "transactions" is being used broadly to encompass not merely cases in which R2s are directly involved but also (and this is another significant difference from classic class exploitation) cases in which they are *excluded*. In Marx's vision of class exploitation, surplus value is extracted through the expenditure of the labor power of the working class, so obviously the workers have to be actually working for this transfer to take place. But I want to include scenarios in which R2s are kept out of the transaction but are nonetheless exploited because R1s benefit from their exclusion (for example, in the case of racial restrictions on hiring). For me, then, racial exploitation is being conceptualized so as to accommodate both differential and inferior treatment of R2s (e.g., lower wages) and their exclusion where they should legitimately have been included (e.g., the denial of the job in the first place).

Now it needs to be noted that the role of R2 normative inequality is in sharp contrast to Marx's vision of class exploitation under capitalism. In the class systems of antiquity and the Middle Ages, the subordinate classes do indeed have a lower normative status. But capitalism, as the class system of modernity, is distinguished by the fact that these distinctions of ascriptive hierarchy are leveled. So in Marx's discussion of capitalism, the whole point of his analysis—what made capitalism different from slave and feudal modes of production—was that the workers nominally had *equal* moral status. Hence his sarcasm in *Capital* about the freedom and equality boasted of by liberals obtaining only on the level of the relations of exchange, since they are systematically undercut at the level of the relations of production. But at least juridically, that freedom and equality are real. So it is not (as with the slave or the serf) that the subordinated are overtly forced to labor for the capitalist class, since such coercion would be inconsistent with liberal capitalism. Rather, it is the economic structure that (according to Marx anyway) coerces them, reduces their options, and forces them to sell their labor-power.

But in what I suggest is the paradigm case of racial exploitation, the R2s do *not* have equal status, which implies that bourgeois-democratic norms either do not apply to them at all, or do not apply fully. In both liberal and many Marxist theories of racism, this has usually been represented as a return to the *premodern*. But as various theorists, including myself, have argued, it is better thought of in terms of the modern, but within the framework of a revised narrative and conceptual framework which denies that egalitarianism is in fact the universal norm of modernity.[26] In other words, to represent racism as a throwback to previous class systems accepts the mystificatory representation of the modern as the epoch in which equality became the globally hegemonic norm, when in fact we need to reject this characterization and see the modern as bringing about white (male) equality while establishing nonwhite inequality as an accompanying norm. In Rogers Smith's language, racism is not an anomaly in the global system, but a norm in its own right. What justifies African slavery and colonial forced labor, for example, is the lesser moral status of the people involved—they are not seen as full humans in the first place. If in the colonies blacks, browns, and yellows are coerced by the colonial state to work, while in the metropolis, according to Marxist theory, white workers are compelled by the market to work, this is not a minor but a major and qualitative difference.

One of the straightforward implications of this inequality is that, by contrast with class exploitation, racial exploitation is in its paradigm form uncontroversially unjust by deracialized liberal democratic standards. By contrast, in the Marxist tradition, as is well known, there has been a general leeriness about appealing to morality and a specific leeriness about appealing to justice because of the dominant metaethical interpretation of Marx as a theorist disdainful of ethical norms in general and hostile to justice in particular as a supposedly transhistorical value. So some Marxists have repudiated moral argument in toto as a return to a supposedly discredited "ethical" (as against "scientific") socialism. But if one does want to make a moral case for socialism, then, some theorists have argued, one has to appeal to freedom rather than justice, or to social welfare, or to Aristotelian self-realization. A discourse of rights is not amenable to prosecuting the proletarian case insofar as bourgeois rights *are* being respected. (One can, of course, appeal to positive "welfare" rights, but these are far more controversial in the liberal tradition.) And such an argument would have to rely on factual and conceptual claims obviously highly controversial even then, and far more so now in a post-Marxist world, about capitalist economic constraint undermining substantive freedoms, or people as a whole doing better under socialism. By contrast, the striking feature of demands for racial justice in the paradigm cases of racial injustice is that they can be straightforwardly made in terms of the dominant discourse, since the whole point of racial exploitation is that (at least in its paradigm form) it trades on the differential status of the R2s to legitimate its relations. Contrast the proletarian struggle with the black struggle, for example in the United States. The banner under which the latter has been organized has typically been the banner of equal rights: for civil rights—indeed for human rights—and for first-class rather than second-class citizenship. But it would be far more difficult to represent the struggle for socialism as a struggle for equal rights, since it would, of course, be denied that capitalism *is* a violation of workers' rights.

So in the first instance (in the period of overt white supremacy), what justifies racial exploitation is that the R2s are seen of lesser human worth, or zero worth. They have fewer rights or no rights. A certain normative characterization of the R2s is central to racial exploitation in a way that it is not to class exploitation in the modern period.

But apart from this paradigm form, there is also a secondary derivative form, which becomes more important over time (so there is a periodization of varieties of racial exploitation, with the different salience of different kinds shifting over time), and which arises from the legacy of the first kind. Here the inequity does not arise from the R2s' being stigmatized as of inferior status, or at least such stigmatization is not essential to the process. White supremacy is no longer overt, and the statuses of R1s and R2s have been formally equalized (for example, through legislative change). Of course the perception of R2s as inferior, as not quite of equal standing, may continue to play a role in tacitly underwriting their differential treatment. But it is no longer essential to it. Rather, what obtains here is that the R2s inherit a disadvantaged material position which—by comparison with what, counterfactually, would have been the case if they had been R1s— handicaps them in the bargaining process or the competition in question. At this stage, then, it *is* possible for them to be treated "fairly," by the same norms that apply to the R1 population. Nonetheless, it is still appropriate to speak of racial exploitation, because they bring to the table a thinner package of assets than they otherwise would have had, and so they will be in a weaker bargaining position than they otherwise would have been. Whites are differentially benefited by this history insofar as they have a competitive advantage that is not the result, or not completely the result, of innate ability and effort but rather of the legacy they have inherited. So unfairness here is manifest in the failure to redress this legacy, which makes the perpetuation of domination the most likely outcome.

I would also claim, and will elaborate in the next section, that another crucial difference between class and racial exploitation is that the latter takes place much more broadly than at the point of production. (Here, of course, I am referring to Marx's classic conceptualization; in Roemer's revisionist view, this contrast will no longer be as sharp.) For insofar as racial exploitation in its paradigm form requires only that the R2s receive differential and inferior treatment, this can be manifested in a much wider variety of transactions than proletarian wage labor. Society is characterized by economic transactions of all kinds, and if race becomes a normative dividing line running through all or most of these transactions, then racial exploitation can pervade the whole economic order. Moreover, it is not just the market that is involved, but the active role of the state, not merely in writing the laws and fostering the moral economy that makes racial exploitation normatively and juridically acceptable, but in creating opportunities for the R1s that are not extended to the R2s and in making transfer payments on a racially differentiated basis.

Another important difference is that whereas Marx's analysis of class exploitation focused on economic benefit, the transfer of surplus value from worker to capitalist, I would claim that racial exploitation has crucial dimensions beyond the economic. Indeed, this is encapsulated in Du Bois's phrase itself, since the whole point he was making was that whiteness garners wages other than the straightforwardly economic. The peculiar character of race as a social structure and its perceived intimate link with what one essentially, biologically *is* makes possible a variety of benefits greater than those typical of class exploitation.

Finally, whereas it is, of course, Marx's famous claim that capitalism needs to be abolished to achieve the end of class exploitation (since a capitalism that did not extract surplus value would liquidate itself), racial exploitation is at least in theory eliminable within a capitalist framework. That is, it is possible to have a nonracial capitalism, either because races do not exist as social entities within the system, or because though they do exist, there is no additional racial exploitation on top of class exploitation. Since we live in a postcommunist world in which Marx's vision seems increasingly unrealizable, with no attractive socialist models to point to, this conclusion is welcome because it implies that the struggle for racial justice need not be anticapitalist. Particularly in the United States, of course, such an ideological designation has historically been a heavy handicap—see Seymour Lipset and Gary Marks's *It Didn't Happen Here: Why Socialism Failed in the United States*[27]—and in the present time period more so than ever before. The long-entrenched hostility to black demands need not, then, be compounded and redoubled (or some far greater multiple) by the additional antipathy to communism, to black and red together. One simple formulation of the political project would be the demand for a nonracial or non–white supremacist capitalism. (Representing white supremacy as a system in its own right, with its distinctive modes of exploitation, has the virtue of clarifying what the real target is.)

However, I qualified the "eliminable" above with "in theory." The counterargument that needs to be borne in mind, coming from the left in particular, is that while a nonracial capitalism could certainly have developed in another world, the fact that the capitalism in *our* world has been so thoroughly racialized from its inception means that racial inequality has long been crucial to its reproduction *as* a particular kind of capitalist formation. Logical distinctions in theory between U.S. capitalism and white supremacy are all very well, but their fusion in reality into the composite entity of white supremacist capitalism makes any political project attempting to separate them a nonstarter, in part because of the reciprocal imbrication of class and race, class being racialized, race being classed. I will not say anything more about this counterargument, but it should be noted as an important objection to the whole project.

To summarize, then. By comparison with class exploitation, racial exploitation (i) benefits R1s generally, not just the capitalist class of the R1s; (ii) involves the causality and agency (albeit to different extents) of R1s generally, not merely those of the capitalist class; (iii) is in its paradigmatic form straightforwardly wrong by (deracialized) liberal norms; (iv) includes economic transactions other than labor; (v) typically involves the intervention and/or collusion of the state; (vi) extends to spheres of society besides the economic; and (vii) could in theory be eliminated within a capitalist framework.

THE WAGES OF WHITENESS

The discussion so far has been very abstract. Let us now move to the level of the concrete.

In the United States, the privileged race, the R1s, are, of course, whites. There will be a core whiteness that is relatively clear-cut and a penumbral whiteness that is fuzzier. A significant part of the burden of the whiteness literature over the past decade has, of course, been the emphasis on the historically variant character of whiteness, and various books—most famously Noel Ignatiev's *How the Irish Became White* but also Karen Brodkin's *How Jews Became White Folks*, and Matthew Frye Jacobson's *Whiteness of a Different Color*—have tracked the shifting boundaries of the white population.[28] And part of the motivation for aspiring to and becoming white is precisely so that one can benefit from this exploitation.

Now Du Bois's phrase is a bit misleading insofar as it is limited, if taken literally, to "wages" and the white working class. But one could also speak illuminatingly, focusing on different kinds of relationships, of whiteness as property, whiteness as a joint-stock company, the interest on whiteness, the rent on whiteness, the profit on whiteness, the residuals on whiteness, the returns on whiteness, and so on. The point is that racial exploitation is manifest in many more economic relations than just that of wage labor. So if we retain the phrase for the sake of convenience and its historic resonances, we must remind ourselves that we are not talking just about wages.

Let us now go through some concrete examples, to put some flesh on these abstractions.[29]

Native Americans were cheated out of their land. (They were not given a fair price in the first place, or the original deal was reneged upon, or their understanding of what they were signing away was mistaken because of deliberate deceit, etc.)

Africans were enslaved at a time when slavery was dead or dying out in the West. (Obviously if Africans were enslaved in the ancient world, as they were, there is nothing *racial* about this, since race played no role in their enslavement—indeed, at the time they did not even have a race).

Blacks freed from slavery were conscripted into "debt servitude" as sharecroppers, from which they could never get free because the plantation owner forced them to buy goods he provided, at higher prices, and weighed the cotton they produced himself, so that at the end of each year they owed more than before.

Blacks were not permitted, or were permitted only to a far lesser extent, to stake their claim on lands opened up by the settling of the West. (This illustrates the complexities of racial exploitation since had they been allowed to do so, they would, of course, have been participating in the exploitation of Native Americans.)

Male Chinese immigrants were forced to pay a head tax for admission into the United States, at a time when no such tax was imposed on white immigrants.

Black children were given an inferior education by state governments, with most of the resources going to white children.

Blacks were given higher sentences than whites for comparable crimes, so that they could supply a population of convict lease labor in the South.

Black enterprises were not permitted access to white markets.

Black enterprises were burned down, or otherwise illicitly driven out of business, by white competitors.

Blacks pay higher rent in the ghettoes for housing.

Blacks pay more for inferior goods in the ghettoes.

White workers refuse to admit blacks into their unions.

Blacks, Mexican Americans, and Asian immigrants hired in jobs are paid less than white workers would be.

Blacks, Mexican Americans, and Asian immigrants hired in jobs are not promoted, or are promoted at differential rates and to lower levels, than whites with comparable credentials.

Black candidates with superior credentials are turned down in favor of white candidates.

Black candidates with inferior credentials are turned down in favor of white candidates, though the reason the credentials of the black candidates are inferior is that they have had poorer schooling and poorer opportunities at every step of the way than they would have had if they were white.

Black performers are forced to sign contracts on worse terms than white performers because they have no alternative company to give them a better deal.

Black performers sign contracts with worse terms because they are not sufficiently well educated to know better, and racism explains their inferior knowledge.

Blacks don't get a chance to hear about and compete for certain jobs in the first place, because racially exclusionary word-of-mouth networks restrict notice of them to white candidates.

Federal money earmarked for Native Americans ends up in white hands instead.

Transfer payments from the state (e.g., unemployment benefits, welfare) are not extended equally to the black population, either through overt racial exclusion or because the terms are carefully designed to exclude certain jobs in which blacks are differentially concentrated. The Federal Housing Agency, established under the New Deal, discriminates against would-be black homeowners, thereby denying them access to the main route to wealth accumulation by the middle class. The Wagner Act and the Social Security Act "excluded farm workers and domestics from coverage, effectively denying those disproportionately minority sectors of the work force protections and benefits routinely afforded to whites."[30]

Several things about this (very short) list should be striking.

One is the diversity of examples of racial exploitation. Even focusing just on the economic aspect, we can see how many ways there are for racial exploitation to manifest itself. Thus there is a sense in which, far from being a theoretical appendage or minor codicil to Marxism's view of class exploitation, racial exploitation is *much broader* and should long ago have received the theoretical attention it deserves. Marx's focus was on just one relation, because he was working within a framework in which it was assumed (since he was really talking about the white population) that normative status differentials had been eliminated, so that exploitation had to take place in a framework of the transaction of equals. Once one rejects this assumption, one comes to recognize that the relation can manifest itself in *any* economic transaction or transaction with economic effects and thus is ubiquitous. And this is one of the very important ways in which Marxism is Eurocentric, in its failure to conceptualize how broadly exploitation as a concept can be shown to apply once one takes the focus off the white population.

Second, notice the cumulative and negatively synergistic effect of these transactions. It is not merely that blacks (for example) are exploited serially in different transactions, but that the different forms of exploitation interact with one another, exacerbating the situation. For example: blacks receive inferior education, thereby losing an equal opportunity to build human capital, thereby losing out in competition with white candidates, thereby having to take inferior jobs, thereby having less money, thereby being disadvantaged in dealings with banks (which, additionally, already follow patterns of discrimination), thereby being forced to live in inferior neighborhoods, thereby having homes of lesser value, thereby providing a lower tax base for schooling, thereby being unable to pass on to their children advantages comparable to whites, and so on. It is not a matter of a single transaction, or even a series, but a *multiply interacting set* with repercussions continually compounding and feeding back in a destructive way.

But what has been negative for blacks has been very beneficial for whites. The point of utilizing the political-economy category of "exploitation," as against just talking with a liberal vocabulary about the "unfairness" of discrimination against nonwhites, is, as emphasized at the start, to shift the discussion from the personal to the social-structural, so that we can start seeing white supremacy as itself a *system* for which this "wage" is the motivation. Melvin Oliver and Thomas Shapiro's prizewinning *Black Wealth/White Wealth*, judged by many to be one of the most important books on race of the last two decades, argues that to understand racial inequality, its origins and its reproduction, wealth is a far better investigative tool than income. As they point out:

> Whites in general, but well-off whites in particular, were able to amass assets and use their secure economic status to pass their wealth from generation to generation. What is often not acknowledged is that the accumulation of wealth for some whites is intimately tied to the poverty of wealth for most blacks. Just as blacks have had "cumulative disadvantages," whites have had "cumulative advantages." Practically, every circumstance of bias and discrimination against blacks has produced a circumstance and opportunity of positive gain for whites. When black workers were paid less than white workers, white workers gained a benefit; when black businesses were confined to the segregated black market, white businesses received the benefit of diminished competition; when FHA policies denied loans to blacks, whites were the beneficiaries of the spectacular growth of good housing and housing equity in the suburbs. The cumulative effect of such a process has been to sediment blacks at the bottom of the social hierarchy and to artificially raise the relative position of some whites in society.[31]

And if one were to go back to slavery and Native American expropriation, of course, and track the financial consequences of these institutions and processes for the respectively racialized populations, the size and ubiquity of the white wage would be even greater. Whites sometimes receive the wage directly, by themselves participating in these transactions, but far more often indirectly—from their parents, from the state and federal governments, from the general advantage of being the privileged race in a system of racial subordination. The transparency of the connection between race and social advantage or disadvantage will also have implications for social consciousness. Marx famously claimed that capitalism was differentiated from slave and feudal modes of production by the seemingly egalitarian nature of the transactions involved: a "fair exchange" between worker and capitalist that requires conceptual labor to be revealed as (allegedly) inequitable. As a result, the subordinated workers often do not recognize their subordination—capitalism is the classless class society. By contrast, the transparency of racial exploitation, certainly in its paradigmatic form, means that the R2s will usually have little difficulty seeing the unfairness of their situation. If Marxist "class consciousness" has been more often dreamed of by the left than found in actual workers, "racial consciousness" in the subordinated has been far more evident historically.

In conclusion, I should also briefly say something about noneconomic varieties of racial exploitation. One will be cultural. What I am thinking of here is the representation of some important cultural innovation or breakthrough as owing to the R1s when it really comes from the R2s. In other words, I don't just mean that the R1s differentially and unfairly profit from it in material terms, but that, in addition, they *claim it as their own.* Native Americans, for example, often point out that many agricultural products that are worldwide staples were originally developed through their farming techniques, but without their getting credit for them. The controversy over the relation between ancient Egypt and ancient Greece remains unresolved, with Martin Bernal's claims about a "black Athena" (who was once recognized but later written out of the record with the rise of racist scholarship) being subjected to fierce and unyielding criticisms by the scholarly establishment in classical studies.[32] The payoff from cultural exploitation is, of course, the positioning of one's race as superior, as differentially endowed with talents and abilities.

There are also specific gendered dimensions to racial exploitation, where racism intersects with sexism. The sexual exploitation of black women under slavery and into the post-Emancipation period is well known. Black women were differentially forced into prostitution because of the lack of available opportunities for them. Some feminists have argued for a distinct form of exploitation of the affective labor of women. Insofar as generations of white children in the South were raised by black "mammies," one could see this as a distinctively racialized form of affective labor exploitation.

Finally, I would like to suggest, admittedly more fancifully (but what else is philosophy for?), that we could also talk about "ontological" exploitation. In Marx's *1844 Manuscripts*, his representation of the relation between worker and capitalist is not merely in terms of the growing wealth of the latter and the growing poverty of the former, but also in terms of their respective "beings": "So much does labour's realisation appear as loss of realisation that the worker loses realisation to the point of starving to death. . . . Whatever the product of his labour is, he is not. Therefore the greater this product, the less is he himself. . . . the more values he creates, the more valueless, the more unworthy he becomes."[33] I would claim that this exploitative transfer of being moves from the metaphorical to the (almost) literal in the case of paradigmatic racial exploitation, since in this period non-whites, particularly blacks, were thought of as having lesser—close to zero—human worth. They were, in the vocabulary I have used elsewhere, "sub-persons" rather than persons. And this sub-personhood, as a result of racial exploitation, increasingly became *materially grounded*—that is, it was not merely a matter of stigmatized representations of blacks, but of the literal destruction of black being by slavery and colonial forced labor, regimes in which people were often worked to death and were at all times reduced to a condition beneath the human. Thus it is not only that whites are depicted as the superior race, beings of a higher order, but that this depiction begins to seem *true* in a world in which they dominate the planet and become the exemplars of the human.

RACIAL JUSTICE

The articulation of such a framework would, I claim, greatly assist discussions about racial justice. Instead of focusing exclusively on "racism," our attention would shift to *illicit white benefit*. The ideal for racial justice would, quite simply, be the end to current racial exploitation, and the equitable redistribution of the benefits of past racial exploitation. Obviously working out the details would be hugely complicated, and in fine points impossible, but at least on the level of an ideal to be simply stated, and by which present-day society can be measured, it would give us something to shoot for. In talking with the white majority, the imperative task has usually been to convince them that, independently of whether or not they are "racist" (however that term is to be understood), they are the beneficiaries of a system of racial domination and that *this* is the real issue, not whether they have goodwill toward people of color or whether they owned any slaves. The concept of racial exploitation is designed to bring out this central reality. Relying not on dubious claims about surplus value, it derives its legitimacy from the simple appeal to the very normative values (albeit in their inclusive race-neutral incarnation) to which the white majority already nominally subscribes. And because it encompasses a derivative as well as primary form (exploitation inhering not in the assumption of unequal normative status, but in the continuing impact of the unfair distribution of assets resulting *from* that original normative inequality), it can handle transactions seemingly just but actually inequitable because of the legacy of the past. That is not to say that it will not be very controversial; obviously it *will* be very controversial and will be militantly and furiously opposed. But such hostility goes with the territory, and will greet *all* attempts to prosecute the struggle for racial justice, no matter what conceptual banner is chosen to fly over it. At least the advantage of selecting this framework is that it appeals to norms central to the American tradition (if not normally extended to blacks) and a factual picture for which massive documentation, at least in broad outline, can be provided. In addition, the macro, big-picture, social-systemic analysis—the emphasis on the structural dynamic—locates it in the same conceptual space as the famous "basic structure," which, since Rawls, has been the central focus of discussions of social justice. Thus we would be better positioned, as I emphasized at the start, to pose the simple and crucial challenge to mainstream white theorists: But what if the basic structure is itself unjust because it is predicated on racial exploitation? Both from the mainstream liberal perspective, then, with its normative focus on the justice of foundational institutions, and from the nonmainstream left perspective—the political economy of a system of exploitation and how it shapes political, juridical, and ideological realms—we are considerably advantaged by developing the concept of white supremacy as a theoretical framework intended to compete with liberal individualism and (though of lesser importance) orthodox Marxist class theory.

Moreover, another signal virtue of approaching things this way is that it would provide a more realistic sense of the *obstacles* to achieving racial justice. It is a standard criticism of normative political philosophy, especially from nonphilosophers, that the authors of these inspiring works give us no indication at all as to how these admirable ideals are to be *realized*, of how we are to get from A to Z. By contrast, in the left tradition—at least the non-amoralist strain of it—the claim has always been that the strength of a materialist approach is that it not only articulates ideals but shows how they can be made real, that it unites description and prescription by identifying both the barriers to a more just social order and the possible vehicles for overcoming those barriers. If race and racism are thought of in the standard individualistic terms of irrational prejudice, lack of education, and so on, then their endurance over so many years becomes puzzling. Once one understands that they are tied to benefit, on the other hand, the mystery evaporates: racial discrimination is, in one uncontroversial sense of the word, "rational," linked to interest. Studies have shown that the major determinant of both white and black attitudes on issues related to race is their respective perceptions of their *collective group interests*, of how, in other words, their group will be affected by whatever public policy matter is up for debate.[34] (To repeat an earlier point of comparison with class: the role of group interests in determining consciousness, which was Marx's hoped-for engine of proletarian revolution, is *far more* convincingly borne out, at least in the United States, for race than it is for class.) Rational white perception of a vested group interest in the established racial status quo can then be understood as the primary reason for whites' resistance to change.

But as with orthodox left theory, a materialist, or at least realist, privileging of group interests as the engine of the social dynamic also opens up the possibility of progressive social change. The natural constituency is, of course, the population of color, who would be the obvious beneficiaries of the end or considerable diminution of white supremacy. But given their minority status both in straightforward quantitative terms, and, more important, the qualitative dimension of access to social sources of power, they will clearly not be able to do it on their own. I suggest there are two main political strategies for recruiting a smaller or larger section of the white population to the struggle. The left strategy, which comes in a classic Marxist version as well as a milder, left-liberal/social-democratic version, would seek to split off those whites who benefit less from white supremacy and try to persuade them that they, or perhaps they and their children (the appeal might be more convincing in terms of long-term outcomes) would be better off in an alternative nonracial social order, socialism for Marx, social-democratic redistributivist capitalism for liberals. So the strategy would be to appeal to group interests as well as justice, the latter, alas, not having historically proven itself to be that efficacious as a social prime mover. White workers, for example, would be asked to compare their present situation not to that of blacks in this actual system, RS, but to what their situation would be in a counterfactual nonracial system, ~RS, the presumption being that a convincing case can be made that though they do gain in this present order, they lose by comparison to an alternative one. Indeed, with the massive upward transfer of wealth in the booming '90s, followed by the collapse of the last two years, some theorists might argue for increasing interracial class convergence.[35] The other, more centrist political strategy would try to appeal to the white population as a *whole*, the argument this time being that in a sense racism hurts everybody, given the costs of racial exclusion (the expenses of incarcerating the huge prison population, the untapped resources of marginalized racial groups), and that from an efficiency point of view, the overall GDP would be greater in a nonracist USA.

It might be felt, understandably enough, that there is something ignoble, perhaps even demeaning, about such arguments, and that the case for racial justice should be made on moral grounds alone. I am in sympathy with such a feeling, but I want to differentiate two ways of presenting these arguments: (i) the demand for racial justice cannot be justified on purely moral grounds, or (ii) the motivation for the white majority to implement racial justice cannot be activated on purely moral grounds. Endorsing the second does not commit one to endorsing the first. The struggle for racial justice is indeed a noble struggle, and on moral grounds alone its completion is indeed justifiable. But unfortunately—whether as a general truth about human beings, or a more contingent truth about human beings socialized by racial privilege—I don't think the historical evidence supports the view that many whites will be effectively motivated purely by such considerations. Philip Klinkner and Rogers Smith's important recent book, *The Unsteady March*, for example, makes what is to my mind a convincing historical case that major racial progress in the United States has depended, whether in the Revolutionary War, the Civil War, or the Cold War, on the contingent convergence of a white elite or white majoritarian agenda with black interests, and in the present time period, absent such convergence, we are in for more rollback.[36]

Finally, I want to conclude by pointing out a possible obstacle to interest-based theoretical optimism about the possibilities for the realization of a nonracial social order—that is, an obstacle apart from the obvious ones (familiar from the 1980s discussions of proletarian rationality) of transition costs as a factor in one's calculations, the temptations of free-riding, and the simple preference for the comfortable familiar rather than the dangerous unknown. The multidimensionality of the wages of whiteness means that it is possible for the benefits to come apart and be in opposition to one another in a way not found in straightforward working-class computations of gain under socialism. Material benefit does not necessarily include any relational aspect to others, but benefits of a political or status or cultural or "ontological" kind do. In other words, if it has become important to whites that they be politically dominant, have higher racial status, enjoy the hegemonic culture, and be positioned "ontologically" as the superior race, then the threatened loss of these perks of whiteness may well outweigh for them the gains they will be able to make in straight financial terms in a deracialized system. One can only be white in relation to nonwhites. So some or many whites may calculate, consciously or unconsciously, that by this particular metric of value they gain more by retaining the present system than trying to alter it, even if by conventional measures they would be better off in the alternative one. It may well be, then, that apart from all the other problems to be overcome, this simple fact alone may be powerful enough to derail the whole project.

Nonetheless, the important thing is obviously to get the debate going, so discussion of these issues in an increasingly nonwhite USA can move from the margins to the mainstream. Facing up to the historically white supremacist character of the polity will be an important conceptual move in facilitating this debate, and philosophy, committed by its disciplinary pretensions to both Truth (getting it right) and Justice (making it right), can and should play an important role in bringing about this paradigm shift, even if—or rather especially since—it has been culpably absent so far.

NOTES

1. This chapter was originally presented as a paper at a conference, "The Moral Legacy of Slavery: Repairing Injustice," sponsored by the Department of Philosophy, Bowling Green State University, October 18–19, 2002. I would like to thank the organizers, particularly David Copp, Marina Oshana, and Carolyn Council, for the invitation. The paper was subsequently published in *America's Unpaid Debt: Slavery and Racial Justice*, ed. Michael T. Martin and Marilyn Yaquinto, Bowling Green State University Department of Ethnic Studies Working Papers Series on Historical Systems, Peoples, and Cultures, nos. 14–16 (May 2003), pp. 49–77.

2. See Bernard Boxill, *Blacks and Social Justice*, rev. ed. (Lanham, MD: Rowman & Littlefield, 1992), and Howard McGary Jr., *Race and Social Justice* (Malden, MA: Blackwell, 1999).

3. Charles W. Mills, *The Racial Contract* (Ithaca, NY: Cornell University Press, 1997), and *Blackness Visible: Essays on Philosophy and Race* (Ithaca, NY: Cornell University Press, 1998).

4. Stanford M. Lyman, "Race Relations as Social Process: Sociology's Resistance to a Civil Rights Orientation," in *Race in America: The Struggle for Equality*, ed.,

Herbert Hill and James E. Jones Jr. (Madison: University of Wisconsin Press, 1993), pp. 370–71, 397.

5. Rogers M. Smith, *Civic Ideals: Conflicting Visions of Citizenship in U.S. History* (New Haven, CT: Yale University Press, 1997), pp. 15, 17, 27.

6. John Rawls, *A Theory of Justice* (Cambridge, MA: Harvard University Press, 1971).

7. Anthony Simon Laden, "The House That Jack Built: Thirty Years of Reading Rawls," *Ethics* 113, no. 2 (January 2003): 367–90. The collection is Henry Richardson and Paul Weithman, eds., *The Philosophy of Rawls: A Collection of Essays* (New York: Garland, 1999), 5 volumes.

8. Susan Moller Okin, *Justice, Gender, and the Family* (New York: Basic Books, 1989).

9. John Rawls, *Political Liberalism* (New York: Columbia University Press, 1993).

10. Charles W. Mills, "White Supremacy and Racial Justice, Here and Now," in *Social and Political Philosophy: Contemporary Perspectives* ed. James P. Sterba (New York: Routledge, 2001), pp. 321–37.

11. See, for example, George Fredrickson, *White Supremacy: A Comparative Study in American and South African History* (New York: Oxford University Press, 1981).

12. See my "White Supremacy as Socio-Political System: A Philosophical Perspective," in *White Out: The Continuing Significance of Racism*, ed. Ashley W. Doane and Eduardo Bonilla-Silva (Routledge, 2003), pp. 35–48.

13. See, for example, John Roemer, *A General Theory of Exploitation and Class* (Cambridge, MA: Harvard University Press, 1982).

14. Alan Wertheimer, *Exploitation* (Princeton, NJ: Princeton University Press, 1996), pp. ix, 8.

15. Gary A. Dymski, "Racial Inequality and Capitalist Exploitation," in *Exploitation*, ed. Kai Nielsen and Robert Ware (Atlantic Highlands, NJ: Humanities Press, 1997), pp. 335–47.

16. For a classic discussion, see Cedric Robinson's *Black Marxism: The Making of the Black Radical Tradition* (1983; Chapel Hill: University of North Carolina Press, 2000). I explore these problems in my *From Class to Race: Essays in White Marxism and Black Radicalism* (Rowman & Littlefield, forthcoming).

17. V. I. Lenin, *Imperialism: The Highest Stage of Capitalism* (1916; Chicago: Pluto Press, 1996).

18. W.E.B. Du Bois, *Black Reconstruction in America, 1860–1880* (1935; New York: Free Press, 1998).

19. See the introductory essays by Ashley Doane and Margaret Andersen in Doane and Bonilla-Silva, *White Out*.

20. See Cheryl Harris's classic essay "Whiteness as Property," *Harvard Law Review* 106 (1993): 1709–91.

21. George Lipsitz, *The Possessive Investment in Whiteness: How White People Profit from Identity Politics* (Philadelphia: Temple University Press, 1998).

22. W.E.B. Du Bois, *The Souls of Black Folk* (1903; New York: Penguin, 1996).

23. See my "'But What Are You *Really?*' The Metaphysics of Race," in *Blackness Visible*, pp. 41–66, and Ronald R. Sundstrom, "'Racial' Nominalism," *Journal of Social Philosophy* 33, no. 2 (2002): 193–210.

24. David Roediger, *The Wages of Whiteness: Race and the Making of the American Working Class* (London: Verso, 1991).

25. Note that it is *not* necessary for racial exploitation that the parties in *every* transaction be of different races, for it could be that the overall social structure of R1/R2 domination allows for a few R2s to participate in exploitation of their fellow R2s, as in the case of the small number of black slaveholders in the South.

26. Charles W. Mills, "European Spectres," *Journal of Ethics*, 3, no. 2, Special Issue: Marx and Marxism (1999): 133–55.

27. Seymour Martin Lipset and Gary Marks, *It Didn't Happen Here: Why Socialism Failed in the United States* (New York: W. W. Norton, 2000).

28. Noel Ignatiev, *How the Irish Became White* (New York: Routledge, 1995); Karen Brodkin, *How Jews Became White Folks and What That Says about Race in America* (New Brunswick, NJ: Rutgers University Press, 1998); Matthew Frye Jacobson, *Whiteness of a Different Color: European Immigrants and the Alchemy of Race* (Cambridge, MA: Harvard University Press, 1998).

29. For two very useful sources of information on these matters, from which most of the following list comes, see Melvin L. Oliver and Thomas M. Shapiro, *Black Wealth/White Wealth: A New Perspective on Racial Inequality* (New York: Routledge, 1995), and Lipsitz, *Possessive Investment*, esp. the title chapter.

30. Lipsitz, *Possessive Investment*, p. 5.

31. Oliver and Shapiro, *Black Wealth/White Wealth*, p. 51.

32. Martin Bernal, *Black Athena: The Afroasiatic Roots of Classical Civilization*, Vol. 1: *The Fabrication of Ancient Greece, 1785–1985* (New Brunswick, NJ: Rutgers University Press, 1987); Mary R. Lefkowitz and Guy MacLean Rogers, eds., *Black Athena Revisited* (Chapel Hill: University of North Carolina Press, 1996); Martin Bernal, *Black Athena Writes Back: Martin Bernal Responds to His Critics*, ed. David Chioni Moore (Durham, NC: Duke University Press, 2001).

33. Karl Marx and Frederick Engels, *Collected Works*, Vol. 3 (New York: International Publishers, 1975), pp. 272–73.

34. See, in this regard, the highly instructive work of Donald R. Kinder and Lynn M. Sanders, *Divided by Color: Racial Politics and Democratic Ideals* (Chicago: University of Chicago Press, 1996).

35. See, for example, William Julius Wilson, *The Bridge over the Racial Divide: Rising Inequality and Coalition Politics* (Berkeley: University of California Press, 1999).

36. Philip A. Klinkner with Rogers M. Smith, *The Unsteady March: The Rise and Decline of Racial Equality in America* (Chicago: University of Chicago Press, 1999).

2

THE BAD FAITH OF WHITENESS

Robert E. Birt

[T]he white man has enjoyed, the privilege of seeing without being seen; he was only a look. . . . The white man—white because he was man, white like daylight, white like truth, white like virtue—lighted up creation like a torch and unveiled the secret white essence of beings.

—Jean-Paul Sartre, *Black Orpheus*

I am overdetermined from without. I am the slave not of the "idea" that others have of me but of my own appearance. I am being dissected under white eyes, the only real eyes. I am fixed.

—Frantz Fanon, *Black Skins, White Masks*

CAN A WHITE PERSON BE authentic? Or must his whiteness condemn him inexorably to the prisons of bad faith? Of course, our primary concern is not with "physical" whiteness or skin color. Rather, our concern is with a structure of values, a worldview and way of life. Whiteness is a chosen (though socially conditioned) way of being-in-the-world. But can one *live* whiteness authentically?

As a form of identity and consciousness, whiteness is a species of bad faith. There is no authentic existence in the kingdom of whiteness. While this is easier to say than to show, some reflection on the origin and character of whiteness may lend credence to my claim. But first we must briefly explicate the notion of bad faith.

I speak of bad faith in the sense classically described by Sartre in *Being and Nothingness* and further developed by him and others in later works. The human being, according to Sartre, is "the one who can take negative attitudes with respect to himself."[1] This is a possibility inherent to human consciousness. Consciousness may direct its negation toward others, as in the form of resentment or lying. But there is also the perpetual possibility that "consciousness, instead of directing its negation outward turns it toward itself."[2] This attitude of self-negation is bad faith.

But what form does this self-negation take? Bad faith is self-deception, a lie to the self. Sartre sharply distinguishes it from "lying in general" (i.e., to others). In normal lying there is a duality of deceiver and deceived, distinct existents that do not constitute a single consciousness. The "liar actually is in complete possession of the truth which he is hiding."[3] It is the Other, not himself, who is deceived. For the "liar intends to deceive and he does not seek to hide this intention from himself."[4] But the intent of bad faith is precisely to deceive oneself while also denying that intention. The person "who practices bad faith," Sartre writes, "is hiding a displeasing truth or presenting as truth a pleasing untruth." In bad faith "it is from myself that I am hiding the truth."[5]

But how does whiteness fit this description of bad faith? To address this question we must acknowledge that bad faith has an inherently social dimension.[6] This fact may be obscured by Sartre's sharp distinction in *Being and Nothingness* between the lie to others (which alone is *overtly* other-directed) and the lie to oneself. One is easily left with the impression that bad faith is purely inward and void of a social aspect. Philosopher Robert V. Stone surmises that bad faith "need not be an act in which one operates *only* on oneself."[7] Even when it is, the aim is to circumnavigate problems in the social world. Sartre's famous description of the waiter who attempts to be *merely* a waiter depicts a choice of bad faith in response to a situation of social repression. Sartre himself notes that bad faith "can even be *the normal aspect of life* for a very great number of people," that a "person can live in bad faith," and that this "implies a constant and particular style of life."[8] This is of no small importance here since we have indicated that whiteness is a worldview and a way of life that is lived in bad faith. A way of life "for a great number of people" cannot be purely inward, and a notion of bad faith as purely inward would be of little value in our effort to understand whiteness.

But even if bad faith is not purely inward, and whatever its social basis, as a chosen way of life it is clearly self-deception. If "it is from myself that I am hiding the truth," then what is this truth that I am hiding? A truth that one hides from oneself is a truth concerning the self; it is from some aspect of one's own being that one flees. But we must recognize that the self is not a monad or self-contained essence. It is in relations with others that one becomes a self. Hence a "hiding" from oneself also implies a hiding from others. If I conceal from myself some truth concerning my own being, it is at least implicitly a truth concerning the human condition (though individual particularities may vary). The person in bad faith ultimately flees the truths and perplexities of human existence; in short, he flees himself and alienates himself from his fellows.

For Sartre, freedom is the most fundamental truth of human existence, and it is ultimately freedom that one flees in a spirit of bad faith. Central to the whole of existential thought is the thesis that freedom constitutes the very being of the human, the structure of existence. Sartre surmises that in the absence of a fixed nature or predetermined essence "man is freedom,"[9] that "freedom is impossible to distinguish from the *being* of human reality."[10] But this also means that our be*ing* is *becoming*, that we humans can exist only through the self-invention of our choices and actions. Our capacity for self-creation is indeed the most unique manifestation of human freedom.

Yet human freedom is always *situated* freedom, and we are beings in situation. Our freedom is transcendence and possibility, but not the pure transcendence of a disembodied spirit. We humans create ourselves, but only through actions and choices conditioned by our social existence. To say that the human being is situated freedom or being-in-situation means that one exists within an ensemble of limitations (e.g., class, race, physical attributes, culture, one's past, and so forth) that one does not choose, but by which one is conditioned. Human existence, human freedom, is not only irrepressible *transcendence* and possibility, but also the inescapable *facticity* of situation. Indeed, there is no freedom without facticity. And yet the very meaning of situation is not a given, but arises from the free choice of oneself in situation. A situation must be *lived*. And it is always lived in relation to others, these relations being an inseparable aspect of my situation and of my becoming the human being whom I become. And just as "there is no difference between the being of man and his *being-free*," there is for humans no sense in which being is distinguishable from being-in-situation. I *am* my situation, which shapes and limits me; but I also transcend my situation through choices and attitudes that decide its meaning. My existence is at once both transcendence and facticity.

Yet it is precisely because of our freedom, because our being is becoming, that bad faith is possible. Moreover, it is precisely the ambiguities of existence as transcendence and facticity that one seeks to escape through the self-deceptions of bad faith. And we may note here Thomas Martin's interesting insight that there are two types of bad faith that seeks to escape the ambiguity of our existence as situated freedom, as transcendence and facticity. One may deny one's transcendence and/or try to identify oneself totally with one's facticity (e.g.,

Sartre's waiter), or one may deny one's facticity and try to identify oneself as pure transcendence.[11] As we shall see, whiteness inclines toward the latter. But since real human freedom is situated freedom, transcendence *and* facticity, both types are vain efforts to flee from freedom and from one's own being, which that freedom *is*.

Of course, we humans *can* embrace our freedom and the exalting privilege of responsibility that accompanies it. We can refuse to deceive ourselves. We can embrace the ambiguities of our existence. In relations between self and others we could recognize that "the existence of others as a freedom defines my situation and is even the condition of my own freedom."[12] Yet many humans flee the burden of freedom, and the self-deceptions of bad faith often originate in a project of denying the freedom of others. As Robert Stone observes, the choice of bad faith "may originate in the social world" and may sometimes be "an internalization of a negation initiated in the social world."[13] This is certainly the case with whiteness, since it is a social relation. Stone's analysis, however, alluded to the bad faith of the oppressed (e.g., proletarians like the waiter) whose self-deceptions are responses to domination by others. Our own focus on whiteness draws our attention to the bad faith of the privileged.

This distinction is important. For one can ponder the ways in which the bad faith of oppressor and oppressed resemble and differ. Even if the bad faith of each originates in the social world, it cannot originate in the same way. The "internalization of negation initiated in the social world" must be experienced differently by people differently positioned in the social world. Perhaps, as a proletarian, Sartre's waiter is, in Simone de Beauvoir's words, "congealed in his immanence, cut off from his future, deprived of his transcendence" which is then "condemned to fall uselessly back upon itself."[14] It is quite likely that he abandons a transcendence whose realization is denied, and tries to make of himself a pure facticity. He seeks to be *merely* a waiter. His bad faith is surrender to the overwhelming power of others.

Such cannot be the case when we consider whiteness. Whiteness is the bad faith identity of the racially dominant. The bad faith of whiteness is the self-deception of the privileged, the inauthenticity of dominant people within a racialized social hierarchy.[15] To embrace whiteness is to embrace the bad faith of privilege. Whiteness is the privilege of *exclusive transcendence*. But it can live as such only through the denial of the transcendence of an Other, the reduction of that Other to an object, to pure facticity. At least in America, that Other has been primarily the black. Whiteness could not exist without that Other. Whiteness is a parasitic identity.

In this respect, whiteness resembles the inauthentic Aryan identity of the anti-Semite which Sartre has so insightfully examined. A privileged Aryan identity or collectivity could not exist without a degraded Jewish Other. Indeed, the anti-Semite "finds the existence of the Jew absolutely necessary. Otherwise to whom would he be superior?"[16] Similarly, it was through the creation of an inferior "Negro" identity that a superior white identity emerged; and one can imagine that even today if blacks did not exist many whites would feel compelled to create them.

However, Sartre's description of the anti-Semitic Aryan identity suggests the practice of bad faith through a flight from transcendence and embracing of facticity.[17] This superior Aryan is said to be "afraid of reasoning," to flee his own consciousness, and to choose "for his personality the permanence of a rock."[18] He has no trouble attributing transcendence to the Jew in the form of freedom and intelligence, but he essentializes that transcendence as evil will and sinister intelligence inherent to an unalterably evil Jewish nature. By contrast, it is precisely exclusive (sometimes *pure*) transcendence that is the mark of white identity. Intelligence, freedom, consciousness, and all the intellectual and moral virtues traditionally thought to be marks of a transcendent human subject are presumed to be quintessentially white within the milieu of a Negro-phobic culture. To be a subject is be white; otherwise one is an object. It is the black, even more than Sartre's waiter, who is "congealed in his immanence" and "reduced to pure facticity."[19] Traditionally, not even an evil intelligence has been attributed to the blacks, who have more often been associated with the bestial. Whiteness is predicated upon the denial of transcendence to the Other.

But that whiteness is predicated on denying the transcendence of the Other suggests that whiteness is also a flight from facticity. It is the black who is congealed in facticity. But a flight from facticity is as much an expression of bad faith as a flight from transcendence. Thus, as Lewis Gordon once surmised, bad faith can be "shown to be an effort to deny the blackness within by way of asserting the supremacy of whiteness."[20] In the truncated dialectic of whiteness and blackness, whiteness alone is mind—or at least the *essence* of mind. By contrast, the "blacks, as a cultural group, are most associated with their bodies."[21] But given the metaphysical dualism prevalent in Western culture and its insidious mind/body dichotomies, an exaggerated association with the body implies dissociation from mind—from the center of transcendence and humanity in the prevailing cultural and philosophical tradition. Thus, transcendence becomes the property of whites, while blacks suffer "the misfortune of being situated in a *what* mode of being."[22] The *who* are always white.

Historically, whiteness originates in racism and even today has no real life apart from it. Its social origin was slavery; it was in that maleficent crucible that racism and whiteness were born. Alexis de Tocqueville writes in the 1830s that "first in enlightenment, power, and happiness, is the white man, the European, *man par excellence*; below him come the Negro and the Indian."[23] The whites—man par excellence—are already given as the prototype of the human, while "in one blow oppression has deprived the descendants of Africans of almost all the privileges of humanity." Indeed, the French author even wonders (in light of the fates of blacks and Native Americans) whether the "European is to men of other races what man is to animals."[24] White humanity seems predicated on the subhumanity of Others, and enlightenment (a cultural expression of transcendence) is the exclusive property of whites.

Even cherished ideals of liberty were predicated upon an exclusively white transcendence. The "rights of man," Toni Morrison argues, "is permanently allied with another seductive concept: the hierarchy of race." American notions of liberty did not emerge in a vacuum. Morrison comments that nothing highlighted freedom (if not actually creating it) like slavery. "For in that construction of freedom *and* enslavement could be found not only the not-free but also, with the dramatic polarity created by skin color, the projection of the *not-me*."[25] One is the free white "me" only in contradistinction to the unfree "not-me" who makes the free white me possible.

Of course, economic exploitation was the initial intent of slavery. But the practice entailed reducing the enslaved Other to a subhuman status; and once the system became racialized—indeed racist—it was simply a matter of time before whites became "man par excellence," while others were numbered among the beasts. The human reality of the slave's transcendence was simply not acceptable to the masters. There lies the contradiction in one's relation to the oppressed Other that gives rise to the self-deceptions of bad faith. The lie of a pure or exclusive white transcendence is parasitic upon the lie of an Other who is pure facticity void of transcendence. Whiteness is born of this lie.

In the *Critique of Dialectical Reason*, Sartre argues that oppression "consists . . . in treating the Other as an *animal*." But "the slave acquires his animality, through the master, only *after* his humanity is recognized." The contradiction lies in the fact that "to *treat a man like a dog*, one must first recognize him as a man. The concealed discomfort of the master is that he always has to consider the *human reality* of his slaves."[26] He must consider this human reality at least prereflectively even while denying its existence or pretending not to see it. He must implicitly acknowledge the humanity he denies if only to better dominate his victim.

Of course this humanity is rendered invisible as part of the process by which the masters invented an inferior race called Negroes. Indeed, it was the racists who invented the Negro, who transformed varied African peoples into the Negro. But it should be noted too that it was also themselves whom the whites were inventing in and through their invention of the Negro. It was through the invention of the Negro as a degraded race that whites invented themselves as an exalted race. Through the relegation of blacks to bestiality they affirmed the elevation of whites to divinity. From this process arose a common white identity (whether openly asserted or prereflectively assumed) and the illusion of an egalitarian community of whites with mutual interests and common freedom.

Sartre notes the rise of "the myth of the equality of the higher classes" (should he not have called them "castes"?) that is sustained "to the point that poor Whites do not perceive the exploitation of which they are victims."[27] Rather, they think of themselves (by virtue of their whiteness) as privileged members of the ruling aristocracy. Of course, this allows the poor white to conceal from himself the realities of his own degradation. Not surprisingly, this self-deception of poor whites is encouraged by the planter elite, who, as Frederick Douglass writes, "by encouraging the enmity of the poor laboring white man against the blacks, succeeded in making the said white man almost as much of a slave as the black."[28] Consequently, the "white slave" (as Douglass calls him) has "taken from him by indirection" what the black slave has "taken from him directly and without ceremony. Both are plundered, and by the same plunderers."[29] So even whites must pay for the delusions of whiteness.

Still, the myth of a white aristocracy inclusive even of poor whites inclined the poor to identify with the plunderers and conceal from themselves their own servitude. It generated a type of relation among whites which Sartre called "the recognition of one master by another."[30] Every greeting "indicates that one is a man by divine right and that one belongs to the privileged race."[31] Even the poor laid claim to this divine right of masters of the privileged race. The peculiar relations developed among whites which entailed a perverse form of respect whereby "each master recognizes the other's freedom as a master's freedom. And does so *against* the slave." For "the value of being white," Sartre infers, "comes from the fact that he is not treated as a Black."[32]

Has this not always been the value of whiteness? Without the degradation of blackness (or some form of Otherness), whiteness would have no value—or would even be impossible. Implicit in whiteness are Manichean social relations and values. The valorizing of whiteness entails the devaluation of blackness. It was in the context of slavery that there began a polarizing of the world into exclusive black and white realms, with the white realm as exclusively human and the locus of all values. This has not ended with slavery and de jure segregation. Nor is it merely the perversity of extreme racists (who exhibit what Gordon calls "strong bad faith") or the neoconservative right. In *Black Looks*, bell hooks takes note of the surprise expressed by many of her "liberal" or "progressive" students upon learning that black people critically assess white people. Their "amazement that black people watch white people with a critical "ethnographic gaze," hooks surmises, "is itself an expression of racism."[33] They had prereflectively assumed themselves to be the sole possessors of the Look, and are shocked by the presence of an insurgent black transcendence. Moreover, an independent black perspective offends their liberal sensibilities. These enlightened *antiracist* whites wish to believe in "a universal subjectivity (we are all just people) that they think will make racism disappear."[34] They resemble the French democrat whom Sartre criticizes for recognizing "neither Jew, nor Arab, nor Negro, nor bourgeois, nor worker, but only man."[35] Hooks surmises that they "have a deep emotional investment in the myth of "sameness," even as their actions reflect the primacy of whiteness as a sign informing who they are and how they think."[36] For the inauthentic identity of whiteness, of pure and exclusive transcendence, is wedded to "the fantasy the Other who is subjugated, who is subhuman, lacks the ability to understand, to comprehend, to see the working of the powerful."[37]

According to Robert Westley, "whiteness has always been seen as a norm constitutive of full humanity. . . . White normativity persists, rearticulated as a social ideal of colorblindness and equality of opportunity."[38] Notice that the privilege of whiteness persists while concealing itself behind the façade of colorless humanity. Whiteness is hegemonic. As it is the norm it can be taken as simply human (or the "Individual"). But whiteness remains predicated on racism, which taints even antiracist whites to the extent that they choose to accept whiteness (even prereflectively) as their identity and way of life. Racism has been defined by Lewis Gordon as "the self-deceiving choice to believe either that one's race is the only one qualified to be considered human or that one's race is superior to other races."[39] Of course, most whites today do not explicitly claim racial superiority. Some deny that races exist.[40] Yet whiteness is based on a racialized social order that privileges whites both materially and in terms of honor and respect accorded to them as human beings. To live uncritically in a universe of whiteness is to embrace the privileges thereof, and to embrace a legacy and way of life permeated with the poison of bad faith.

NOTES

1. Jean-Paul Sartre, *Being and Nothingness* (New York: Pocket Books, 1956), p. 84.
2. Ibid., p. 87.
3. Ibid.
4. Ibid., p. 88.
5. Ibid., p. 89.
6. My reflections here are informed by Robert V. Stone's "Sartre on Bad Faith and Authenticity" in *The Philosophy of Jean-Paul Sartre*, ed. Paul Arthur Schilpp, (La Salle, IL: Open Court, 1981), pp. 246–56.
7. Stone, "Sartre on Bad Faith," p. 246. Emphasis is mine.
8. Sartre, *Being and Nothingness*, p. 90.
9. Jean-Paul Sartre, *Existentialism and Human Emotions* (Secaucus, NJ: Citadel Press, 1957), p. 23.
10. Sartre, *Being and Nothingness*, p. 60.
11. Thomas Martin, *Oppression and the Human Condition* (Lanham, MD: Rowman & Littlefield), pp. 1–21. See especially chapters 3 and 5 for an analysis of how oppressors can make use of either style of bad faith.
12. Simone de Beauvoir, *The Ethics of Ambiguity* (Secaucus, NJ: Citadel Press, 1991), p. 91.
13. Stone, "Sartre on Bad Faith," p. 248.
14. De Beauvoir, *Ethics of Ambiguity*, pp. 81, 100.
15. We are aware that among whites there are oppressed strata. White poor, workers, women, and others are dominated groups. But it is not *as whites* that they are dominated, though it is often their *whiteness* that obscures their awareness of their own subjugation.
16. Jean-Paul Sartre, *Anti-Semite and Jew* (New York: Schocken Books, 1948), p. 28.
17. See chapter 3 of Martin's *Oppression*.
18. Sartre, *Anti-Semite and Jew*, pp. 19, 27.
19. De Beauvoir, *Ethics of Ambiguity*, p. 100.
20. Lewis Gordon, *Bad Faith and Antiblack Racism* (Atlantic Highlands, NJ: Humanities Press, 1995), p. 6.
21. Robert Westley, "White Normativity and the Rhetoric of Equal Protection," in, *Existence in Black: An Anthology of Black Existential Philosophy*, ed. Lewis Gordon (New York: Routledge, 1997), p. 95.
22. Gordon, *Bad Faith and Antiblack Racism*, p. 6.
23. Alexis de Tocqueville, *Democracy in America* (New York: Harper & Row, 1969), p. 317.
24. Ibid.
25. Toni Morrison, *Playing in the Dark: Whiteness and the Literary Imagination* (Cambridge, MA: Harvard University Press, 1992), p. 38.
26. Jean-Paul Sartre, *Critique of Dialectical Reason* (London: New Left Books, 1976), pp. 110–11.
27. Jean-Paul Sartre, *Notebooks for an Ethics* (Chicago: University of Chicago Press, 1992), p. 569.
28. Frederick Douglass, *Life and Times of Frederick Douglass* (New York: Macmillan Publishing Company, 1962), p. 179.
29. Ibid., pp. 179–80.
30. Sartre, *Notebooks*, p. 569.
31. Ibid.

32. Ibid.
33. bell hooks, *Black Looks: Race and Representation* (Boston: South End Press, 1992), p. 167.
34. Ibid.
35. Sartre, *Antisemite and Jew*, p. 55.
36. hooks, *Black Looks*, p. 167.
37. Ibid., p. 167–68.
38. Westley, "White Normativity," p. 92.
39. Gordon, *Bad Faith and Antiblack Racism*, p. 2.
40. Yet more whites than one wishes to believe hold to such biases prereflectively (or even explicitly). As late as the mid-1990s, polls and surveys indicated that as many as three-quarters of American whites believe that blacks and Latinos are less intelligent, less virtuous, less hardworking, less patriotic, and more inclined to violence than whites. The great popularity of that abstruse racist polemic *The Bell Curve* suggests that racism and the privileges of whiteness appeal to the white intelligentsia as well as to popular culture.

3

THE IMPAIRMENT OF EMPATHY IN GOODWILL WHITES FOR AFRICAN AMERICANS

Janine Jones

FRANTZ FANON IS KNOWN TO HAVE thought that when blacks walk in the door Reason walks out.[1] Perhaps Fanon had observed something many African Americans, throughout history, have observed: whites do not seem to apply the same rules to whites and blacks in similar circumstances.[2] However, contrary to Fanon's conclusion, we might think that if a white person applies rules in some special way when it comes to blacks it is because his reason *is* well intact. For his way of reasoning may help him achieve his practical goals, which are of primary interest to him, even if it falls short of his ideals.

In *Living across the Color Line*, Sharon Rush, the white, adoptive mother of an African-American child, Mary, cites her child as asking her, after an afternoon of experiencing [more] avoidance behavior from whites: "Don't they know everyone can get hurt feelings even if they aren't White? I have a heart with feelings too!"[3]

On the face of it, Mary is not calling into question the rationality of whites. Her question might suggest no more than puzzlement and dismay at the manifest lack of knowledge on the part of whites in a particular realm. But we do not say that someone is irrational simply because he lacks knowledge.

However, if we dig a little deeper, more than what whites know or do not know may be at issue. Their capacity for a certain type of *understanding* may be what Mary is inquiring about—a type of understanding we believe that most "normally" constituted human beings possess at a certain age: the type of understanding necessary for navigating a world that includes more members than one's self.[4] What could it possibly mean that whites would possess this type of understanding when it comes to other whites, but not where blacks are concerned? What could account for this kind of impairment of their understanding? Is this type of impairment a kind of irrationality?

These are the questions I will address. I proceed with one caveat. My discussion will focus, for the most part, on what I call "goodwill whites," a term I coined after reading the work of Rush. In the beginning of her book she recalls a scene in which her daughter, Mary, raced with a little white girl. Twice the two girls tied. The coach, against the parents' better judgment, insisted (for some reason) that the girls race a third time. The third time, which was the last time, the little white girl won. While the winner was being congratulated on her victory, Mary said to the coach: "Why did you hold me that way?" certain that she could have tied the other girl a third time if she had not been held back.

The scene continued. First the coach asked Mary's mother, "But *why* should I hold your daughter back?" He then became defensive and denied the accusation, while the other parents, all white, looked at Rush in a way that suggested that she should control her child (who had begun to cry while maintaining her accusation) and make her apologize for *her* "insulting" behavior. Rush commented on this episode, saying:

> Six or seven years ago, I would have shared this sentiment, even though I was a White liberal who believed in racial equality. My commitment to the Black Civil Rights movement came at a very young age. I share this bit of my background in an attempt to express how deep my feelings are about the "wrongness" of racism and also it illustrates that notwithstanding this, it was not until my daughter came into my life that I truly began to *understand* how profound and persistent racism is in our society.[5]

Rush went on to confess that at one time she suspected that she shared with the coach and other parents a common view: "We fashioned ourselves people of goodwill and people of good will would *never* lay a White hand of oppression on a Black child."[6] Thus, we see the provenance of my use of the term "goodwill white." But my interest in this type of white person predates my reading of Rush (she only confirmed for me that goodwill whites should be the focus of my attention). The white person who knows that she means to harm blacks may not suffer from the kind of impairment that I'm interested in investigating.

Indeed, the white who *means* to harm a black, who knows it and *acknowledges* it, may possess an empathetic understanding of blacks equal to that which Iago possessed with respect to Othello. But the goodwill white, like Rush in her past life, simply may not *want to believe* or simply *cannot believe*—evidence to the contrary—that race is relevant to the kind of situation that arose with the coach.[7] The kind of person who means a black person harm, on the other hand—the kind of person I encountered daily as a child in the American school system during the '60s—had no trouble believing this kind of thing and thinking well of themselves at the same time.[8]

A good place to begin a philosophical discussion of empathy or of putting oneself in another's shoes—an expression I will sometimes use though I find it misleading[9]—is with Thomas Nagel's seminal paper "What Is It Like to Be a Bat?"[10] In this paper, Nagel argued that because bats experience the world through echolocation, a way of experiencing the world unavailable to us through any sensory modality we possess, we (humans) cannot imagine what it is like to be a bat, for it is impossible for us to imagine how a bat experiences the world *from a bat's subjective point of view.* Put more plainly, we cannot put ourselves in a bat's shoes, as it were.

Though Nagel observes that problems may also arise with respect to how one human being can imagine what it is like to be another human being, because each human has a different subjective perspective on the world, the problem he finds insurmountable emerges when we consider the kinds of boundaries that can exist between members of different species. For when species are as different as bats and human beings, the sensory experience of the one cannot be mapped onto that of the other.

But I take Nagel's claim only as a starting point, for we may have no more reason for believing that we can imagine what it is like to be a cow than we have for believing that we can imagine what it is like to be a bat, even though cows have the same sensory organs we do. In other words, sameness of sensory organs between species is not enough to guarantee that their *perceptions* of the world share the kind of structural similarity that would allow the perceptual experience of the one to be mapped onto the perceptual experience of the other.[11]

This doesn't mean, of course, that we cannot have *sympathy* for members of other species. But it may mean that we cannot have empathy for them. Following the definitions of empathy and sympathy that Paul Thagard and Allison Barnes employ in their paper "Empathy and Analogy," we can have sympathy for cows, where sympathy refers to our awareness and participation in the suffering of another. Empathy, by contrast, is "the attempt to *comprehend* either positive or negative [mental] states of another."[12]

One of the fascinating observations Barnes and Thagard make is that, in spite of what I say above, it may be easier to achieve empathy with members of another species than to achieve it with some members of our own species, such as autistic people. Barnes and Thagard cite the work of Cheny and Seyfarth, *How Monkeys See the World*,[13] which advances the view that "the features and structures of human family relations are analogous in many respects to those of Vervets."[14] Cheney and Seyfarth illustrate their point through a simple example: "A human mother's *emotional need* to nurture and protect her enfant is *easily mapped* to the Vervet mother's defense of infants, who show signs of distress."[15]

Let us assume that Cheny and Seyfarth are correct. My question—reminiscent of that posed by Mary (above)—is this: If we perform this task so easily, why should it have been so difficult for some whites—Thomas Jefferson, for example—to empathize with the plight of the slave mother whose child was sold? Could he not *see* that black slave women had hearts with feelings too, feelings for their children?

Notwithstanding the fact that Jefferson has been called "the greatest champion of liberty this country has ever had," and notwithstanding the fact that this apostle of liberty "could never reconcile the ideals of freedom expressed in the Declaration of Independence and his other writings with the reality of his ownership of men and women and his leadership of a slaveholding society,"[16] we can still ask: What made it possible for Jefferson to believe or what compelled him to believe (to borrow a phrase from Lillian Smith)[17] that breaking up the families of his slaves was of little consequence—that the slaves would get over it fairly quickly?[18] Even if Jefferson believed, as he seems to have—if we trust his words—that the griefs of blacks are transient, why would he be unable to anthropomorphize African Americans to the same degree that all kinds of people today seem to be able to do with respect to vervet monkeys?[19] Why couldn't he *map* the experience of the loss of family members in white people onto the experience of loss of family members in black people? How is it possible that whites can understand how vervets feel but not how blacks feel? Certainly a pervasive occurrence of autism in the African-American community cannot account for this bizarre state of affairs.

Ultimately, my concern is not with Thomas Jefferson. But I speak of him first, for he is the moral father of those whom I've called goodwill whites. The father and his legitimate offspring have a great deal in common. Goodwill whites, like Jefferson, cherish the *idea* of life, liberty, and the pursuit of happiness for all. Father and progeny alike believe in justice for all. Goodwill whites want to be *or to be seen as being* (perhaps especially in their own eyes) champions of liberty, much as they perceive their founding father to have been.

Unlike Jefferson, however, goodwill whites are not slave owners and are not typically viewed as advocating harsh, criminal punishment for blacks.[20] But like Jefferson, who throughout his life sought to avoid discussions of slavery,[21] goodwill whites attempt to avoid discussions about racism. Like their ideological father, they seek to avoid confrontation and friction, especially of an internal nature.

Like Jefferson, who restricted the application of the supposedly self-evident truth that "all persons are created equal, that they are endowed by their creator with certain unalienable Rights, that among these are Life, Liberty, and the pursuit of Happiness," many goodwill whites restrict the application of the concept of racism to acts carried out by Klansmen (or to white people they sometimes unabashedly refer to as "trailer trash" and "rednecks") in blatant, intentional acts of racial bigotry and discrimination.[22]

In short, goodwill whites define racism simply as racial prejudice. By not understanding racism as a system of advantage based on race, the goodwill white avoids the considerable pain, guilt, and shame that might be elicited by a definition of racism that clarifies how she benefits from racism and perhaps serves as an active, intentional, though unconscious, participant in it.[23]

In *The Life of Thomas Jefferson, Third President of the United States,* James Parton wrote: "I think that the best chance for Republican America is an adherence to the general line of politics of which [Jefferson] was the embodiment." He further asserted, "If Jefferson was wrong, America is wrong. If America is right, Jefferson was right."[24] A century later, Merrill D. Peterson argued that "the historians' obligation to historical truth is compromised, in some degree, by his sense of obligation to Jefferson's symbol. . . . Objectivity *must not be allowed* to empty the symbol of meaning for 'Jefferson's children.'"[25] As Paul Finkelman observes, Peterson's point is clear: "Jefferson personifies an 'image,' a 'vision' of America. Tamper with Jefferson, and you tamper with that image."[26]

What is being recommended here? It would seem that historians are being enjoined to create certain kinds of images of America and its founding fathers in order that Americans form certain beliefs about America that allow them to construct the *meanings* deemed necessary for specific purposes, perhaps praiseworthy ones. But out of this *concern* for the construction of meanings and values, truth takes a hit. Of course, if history is just myth, as some claim it is, then everything would seem to be as it should be. And that's fine, as long as we apprise the schoolchildren of the fact that they will be reading mythology when we hand out the history books.[27]

Now many philosophers tend to put a premium on truth: it's something that we either seek or should be seeking. But insofar as humans are seeking something as grand as truth, our investigations are often carried out for truth's instrumental value. People often seek truth in order to *navigate* their world, not for truth's own sake.

Possessing good evidence that our beliefs are true (i.e., that they allow us to map our beliefs onto the world) may aid our navigation, not to mention manipulation, of the world. Possessing the true belief that fast-moving cars can cause me great bodily harm if they hit me is useful in my avoidance of this kind of injury, assuming that I desire not to be harmed in this way. Very small children may not possess such a belief. We try to inculcate it in them so they can avoid injury.

But once we get away from the idea of truth for truth's sake and focus on the *usefulness* of possessing true beliefs, the door is open for us to explore the idea that where certain realms of the world are at issue—certain socially constructed ones, for example—possessing an impressive array of select falsehoods may be thought to be far superior to truth in attaining some of our goals.

One problem, then, goodwill whites must face if they are to empathize with blacks, or even with themselves, is the problem of articulating what they are and what they desire. Jefferson *believed* that he was white, and the last thing he wanted to see was a free class of blacks *roaming* freely in the state of Virginia or any other places inhabited by whites. But many of Jefferson's children are unwilling or unable to say that they are white. Indeed, some of them seem to find it difficult to *believe* that they are white. Race is something that others possess. Whites are just "normal." Whites' inability to form the belief that they are white skews the nature of the relationships that exist between whites and blacks. It affects their ability to empathize because they are unable to import an ingredient essential to empathy: an appreciation of their own situation.

Goodwill whites' desire not to see themselves as whites may partly explain their desire not to see blacks as blacks,[28] for an essential part of the meaning of being black in the United States has had to do (and has to do) with the existence of whites whose *white* identity (and hence position) depended on white constructions of people of African descent living in the United States.

In addition to not understanding who they are, goodwill whites seem unable to state what they desire. Do the majority of goodwill whites *really* want to see blacks—many blacks, not just the one imaginary black that equals one hundred blacks in their minds—occupy the same *places* they do? By place I include positions in society, neighborhoods (not just the same *kinds* of neighborhoods), gifted children's programs where blacks and white children are sitting side by side, and so forth? Do they really want the world to be one in which *their* CEO or *their* professor of physics is as likely to be a black person as a white one?

If Jefferson was wrong, then America was wrong. But if America is wrong and goodwill whites find their ideal of the American Way in the Jeffersonian *way* rather than in Jeffersonian declarations, then in spite of themselves goodwill whites may be wrong about what their goals and values are with respect to African Americans. At the very least they seem to be extremely confused about these things. But confusion about one's goals, values, and emotions can lead to confusion about the beliefs one holds and one's reasons for action. In some cases it may even lead to an individual's being unable to see what actions he's performing or even what he is (affectively) experiencing.

Recognizing that goodwill whites are often ignorant of their own whiteness and their own desires is important in understanding why they often fail to empathize with African Americans. But in order to see how failures in empathy can occur I will introduce a model of empathy, which explains failures of empathy in general.

Building on the work of Oatley,[29] who maintains that basic human emotions are all connected with goals, Barnes and Thagard explain our ability to empathize with a person as requiring our being able to produce a system of mapping between that person's life and some aspect of our own.[30] Thus, empathetic understanding *begins* with an appreciation of that person's situation.

Barnes and Thagard use Hamlet's situation to illustrate this idea. Hamlet's uncle has killed his father and married his mother. Now we need not have an uncle who has killed our father and married our mother to appreciate or understand Hamlet's situation. It is enough that we retrieve from memory potential source analogues of varying degrees of similarity; analogues of situations in which loss made us sad, betrayal made us angry, and difficult situations made us indecisive.[31]

Thus, empathy occurs when we succeed in mapping the *structure* of an experience (where specific emotional content is part of the structure) onto the structure of an experience of the individual with whom we seek to empathize. Or as Barnes and Thagard put it, empathy is possible when "there is a system of mapping that draws correspondences between two persons' situations, goals, and emotions."[32] Empathy involves an understanding of another person not only in the sense that it allows us to infer the other person's emotions. It also enables us to predict or explain the other person's behavior based on the emotion we've attributed to the person.

This model of empathy reveals why it can fail to go through. Consider the basic pattern of empathetic explanation of a person P's situation:

> The person P is in situation S, which is like your situation S_1.
> P has goals G, which are like your goals G_1.
> When faced with situation S_1, which affected your goals G_1, you felt emotion E_1.
> (S_1 and G_1 caused E_1.)
> So P is probably feeling emotion E, which is like your E_1, caused by S and G.[33]

Empathy can easily fail "either because you do not find a source analog that corresponds to the goals, situations, and emotions of the other person, or because a retrieved source does not in fact correspond and should be constructed instead."[34] It will be weak to the extent that the source analogue of the empathizer:

1. has disparate goals, situations, and emotions to those in the target analog (i.e., those of the person who is the object of an empathetic response);
2. has causal relation with different structure than those in the target analogy;
3. does not contribute to the cognitive purposes of the empathizer.[35]

Let's first consider an example in which a white empathetic response failed dismally along the lines spelled out in (1). On the eve of the Los Angeles riots of 1992, I sat in on a course for which I was a teaching assistant: Philosophy in Literature. Throughout the semester the professor had led discussions on the *randomness*—the arbitrary nature—of justice through an examination of various literary texts. Given that things were heating up in L.A. the professor thought it opportune to talk about the Simi Valley Trial, in which the white officers implicated in the beating of Rodney King, a black man, were all acquitted.

First, the professor asked students for their response to the acquittal of the policemen. I will not venture to say whether these were whites of goodwill, but here are some of their responses. "Well, it is true that they beat him worst than they would a dog." "We keep talking about the beating, but was he (King) really guilty of speeding?" The last student comment was spoken by a young woman, whose face became red with anger: "I'm tired of talking about these people. They don't work. All they do is use drugs and steal."[36]

Now, as if the extraordinary comments of these young white adults were not enough, the professor—a prime example of a goodwill white, in my opinion—imparted his special brand of wisdom to the class. What he instructed his students to understand was that we were witnessing, firsthand, a real live example of the randomness of justice and reactions to that randomness.

Now let's cast this professor's construction of the situation in Los Angeles in terms of the Barnes-Thagard model. First we state a purported source *goal:* to attain justice. The source *situation* is that of failing to receive justice because of the arbitrary, random workings of the justice system. The source *emotion* is anger and frustration.

But this source analogue fails to map onto the target analogue representing the experience of Rodney King and blacks all over America. The goal and the emotion *may* be the same. The causal structure may even be the same (i.e., failures in the justice system causes anger and frustration). But the *situations* are simply not the same, and it actually frightens me that this professor of *law* could have seen them as such. Did he not know the history of the United States? Did he not know the recent history of the relationship between the LAPD and the African-American community? Did he not know that a white judge, Joyce Karlin, had only a few months prior let a Korean-American woman, Soon Ja Du, go scot-free (with community service) after she shot an African-American girl *in the back*—as the store videotape showed—as the girl, with whom she had an altercation, was leaving her store? The girl died, and the woman served absolutely no time. Did this UCLA professor not understand that there was nothing random or arbitrary about the *pattern* of injustice toward African Americans in this proud country, whose motto is justice for all?[37]

In fact, if we consider that a pattern of injustice was at the root of the riots, the emotion that blacks felt may be so different from the anger a white feels when there's a failure in the justice system as to warrant our saying that the emotions felt in the two cases are not the same, even if we do not have a word to express what blacks felt. Or maybe we do: *black rage.*[38]

Further consideration of the Rodney King case will allow us to see how empathy can fail along the lines of (2). During the riots a white truck driver, Reginald Denny, was attacked by several rioters, who left him bleeding on the sidewalk. The beating of Reginald Denny, like the

Rodney King beating, was captured on videotape. One of Denny's attackers, Damian Williams, could be seen on videotape hitting Denny in the head with a brick. Williams was tried on charges of attempted murder and aggravated mayhem, and on charges of assaulting other people. The jury acquitted him of aggravated mayhem and attempted murder, finding him guilty of the lesser crimes of simple mayhem (an unpremeditated violation) and of four misdemeanor assaults. Another black man who participated in the assault, Henry Watson, was acquitted of attempted murder and found guilty only of a misdemeanor assault. The racially mixed jury (four blacks, four Latinos, two Asian Americans, and two whites) apparently agreed with the argument advanced by the defense, namely, that Williams and Watson were caught up in the rage and mob hysteria of the rioting. Most whites were not pleased with the jury's verdict. White media commentators across the nation condemned both the jury and the verdicts. Samuel Francis, a syndicated columnist for the *Washington Times*, spoke of a "racially rigged case," indicating that whites "no longer enjoy the same legal rights . . . as non-Whites."[39]

After the riots, various community groups came together to discuss what had happened and to rethink how Los Angeles might be rebuilt so that this kind of thing would never happen again. In a Frontline documentary, the viewer sees a racially mixed group of concerned citizens from various communities come together for a discussion about the riot.[40] One of the hot topics was the beating of Reginald Denny and how the community should feel about it. Two of the whites (I believe it is safe to say that these were goodwill whites, given their voluntary participation in such a conversation) questioned the African Americans on this point with a great deal of energy. How did African Americans feel about *that* occurrence of racism? Wasn't it just as bad as the Rodney King beating? Finally, one black woman got a white man to finally admit that there was a critical difference between the two cases. Watching this, however, I got the distinct impression that this white man would rather not have admitted a critical dissimilarity between the two cases, and when he did so, a smile (a smirk?) slipped from his lips.

The black woman was right. The Denny and King cases do not map onto one another. As Feagin, Batur, and Hernán point out, the context was different:

> The police officers were not participating in an event that takes place every decade or two at most. . . . [T]he King beating took place in a department, as the Christopher Commission and others have noted, with a *historical* problem of police violence targeting Blacks and Latino citizens.

[Moreover,] the beating of King was carried out by government agents *trained and sworn to protect all citizens equally.* In contrast, the assault on Denny was carried out by rioters with no government authority in the midst of an explosion of community rage. Significantly, even in the midst of this collective rage several Black residents rescued Denny and helped him get to a hospital. In contrast, however, numerous White officers watched the violence against King without making serious efforts to stop it or to give him first aid once it was over.[41]

The *causal* dissimilarity in this case is striking because the nature of the cause is so very different. On the one hand, you have *officers of the law* beating a citizen, subsequently being fully acquitted at the Simi Valley trials. These events (along with a pattern of such events) caused or led to rioting and anger in black and Latino communities. On the other hand, you have *rioters, some of them known gang members*, who beat a citizen, which led to anger in white and black communities. The rioters were found guilty of a misdemeanor assault—something not even the cops received at the Simi Valley trial! They did not, however, get prosecuted for attempted murder.

Now perhaps the goodwill whites involved in this discussion had not been fully apprised of these facts. That's a possibility. Assuming they were, we have a case of a gross mismapping of one situation onto another, with the result that the whites could not *understand* the reaction of the blacks. They could not understand why the blacks did not perceive the two situations as being the same, and they may have assumed, as did a majority of the white public and the white media, that the problem in perception—in judgment, that is—lay with the blacks.

Interestingly, David B. Oppenheimer, a white professor of law, wrote regarding the attack on Reginald Denny, which he viewed on videotape: "There, I thought, but for the grace of God, go I." Regarding the videotape of the Rodney King beating he remarked that he was "horrified, but not afraid. For King I had sympathy; for Denny, empathy."[42] This suggests two things. First, that sympathy for others is not the panacea that some white liberals (and some blacks ones) would like to make it out to be. Second, we must seriously consider the possibility that in addition to appreciating the situation someone is in and trying to construct or to retrieve through memory an analogue experience to match it, the successful empathizer must *believe* that the situation that the other is in is such that it is structurally similar to some situation that is really possible for him. Otherwise, he will not even seek to construct or to retrieve an analogue experience. Here, it wouldn't be a lack of *motivation* that would prompt the putative empathizer not to seek an analogue experience. Rather, his belief would indicate to him that it is beside the point to look for or construct such an experience.

But the problem may run deeper. Above, the issue has to do with what kinds of experiences are *really* possible for a white person. But we must also consider the case in which a white person believes that it is *conceptually* impossible that he be in some situation S analogous to that of a black person. The latter is perhaps more problematic, for if an allegedly white person in this country gave the matter some thought (two seconds of thought might suffice) she might see that what happened to Rodney King *could* happen to her. All she has to do is imagine the situation in which it is discovered that she is in fact black. The existential conditions for being black in the United States make such discoveries live epistemic possibilities! But if an allegedly white person is thinking of herself *under the concept of white*, then she may believe it is impossible to find herself in a situation structurally similar to that in which Rodney King found himself. That being said, insofar as a goodwill white is unable to see herself as white, she would not think of herself under the concept of white. But in this case we may be left in the situation described above, in which goodwill whites—not perceiving any important differences between the King and Denny cases—believe that they can empathize with blacks because they have (supposedly) experienced a similar kind of thing through the Reginald Denny situation. Or, perhaps more to the point: Blacks should be able to empathize with *them*.

Regarding failures in empathy along the lines presented in (3), Barnes and Thagard write: "Empathy is particularly likely to fail if you are not motivated to go to the effort of *constructing* an appropriate source analog when simple retrieval produces inaccuracy."[43] Examples of this kind abound. We might consider the example of a Labor Day parade in Queens in September 1998, which included a float mocking James Byrd's dragging death in Jasper, Texas, on June 7, 1998: "The float included White men in Blackface wearing dreadlock wigs standing under a sign that read 'Blacks to the Future, 2098.' One man—one of six firefighters and police officers on the float—said they did not originally intend to parody the killing in Texas, but *somebody* just 'did it.'"[44]

As if this were not enough, Mayor Giuliani described what happened as the action of a few individuals. (I suppose in the way that the attack on Rodney King and the Simi Valley Trial acquittals were just the arbitrary, random actions of a few individuals.) This is a case where we might say that these firefighters were unmotivated—as opposed to being unable—to appreciate how African Americans would feel knowing that such a float would be used to celebrate Labor Day, a quintessentially *American* holiday.[45] They simply did not care, and the reaction of Giuliani only confirmed for them, and all Americans, that they *need* not care.

But let us return one last time to the Rodney King case, where we see a shocking example of what can happen when a white person is not motivated to empathize with a black person. Or perhaps I should say when a white person is motivated *not* to empathize with a black person. Here is one juror's version of how the jury in Simi Valley approached the videotape of the King beating: "We all agreed that it was a bad beating. But we had to kind of leave the emotional impact of the evidence behind, and just weigh things on the physical evidence." Another jury member agreed, saying, "Maybe that's the reason why we got the verdicts we did. I wasn't into it emotionally."[46]

It is not clear to me how one accomplishes the task of leaving the emotional impact of the evidence behind in a case of this kind.[47] For the belief or judgment that the beating was a *bad* one might be thought, in part, to be constituted by the felt evaluation that it was bad.[48] This is a view held by Bennett Helm. But, in addition, we might suppose that we learn our emotional repertoire. Martha Nussbaum discusses this view (which was Samuel Beckett's) in "Narrative Emotions: Beckett's Genealogy of Love." In that piece she explores the idea that we learn emotions primarily through stories or narratives. The thought goes that narratives embody forms of human life and desire and that certain types of human understanding are irreducibly narrative in form.[49]

Several different accounts of emotion can be given within this general cognitive picture: (1) belief is a necessary cause of the emotion but no part of what the emotion is; (2) whether an external cause or a component part, the belief is sufficient for the emotion; and (3) emotion is itself identical with the full acceptance of, or recognition of, a belief. What is common to all these views is the idea that if emotions rest upon beliefs then they can be modified by a modification of belief, and they can be assessed as beliefs are assessed: "as rational or irrational (in respect of their manner of acquisition), as helpful and noxious, even as true and false." [50]

These views of human emotion share an affinity with Helm's in that they view emotions as having cognitive content. Nussbaum says of emotions that "they are intimately related to beliefs or judgments about the world in such a way that the removal of the relevant belief will remove not only the reason for the emotion but also the emotion itself."[51] But Helm's view or the exposition of his view focuses on the direction of emotion to belief rather than belief to emotion. So instead of asking what happens to an emotion if you remove the belief that caused it or that is a component of it, we might ask what happens to a belief when you remove the emotion that caused it or that is a component of it. If the emotion is a necessary component of the belief then the coherence of the claim that the Rodney King beating was bad but I don't *feel* it as bad must be called into question.[52] Furthermore, supposing the felt evaluation to be a part of the full evaluation that the beating was bad, then a method of determining the goodness or badness of the act that proceeds by first "removing" the felt evaluation in order to reach a conclusion would be irrational, rather than "objective" as the jury members seemed to be suggesting.[53] And if the Simi Valley jury members, whatever else they were doing, succeeded in removing the emotional impact of the beating, then they failed to empathize with Rodney King. For as we have seen, empathy is a mapping of one's experience onto the situations, goals, and *emotions* of another. Hence, they could not but have failed.

I would like to conclude with a response to little Mary, who may still be wondering whether whites can see in her heart. I would say that in some instances they may not be able to do so because they do not possess a retrievable source analogue to match your experience. Moreover, unable to appreciate either your situation or their own, they are unable to map a *constructed* source analogue of their experience onto yours. And yet in some cases I think they can see in your heart. They can empathize with you because as human beings living in a society with at least some important shared lived experiences and shared stories, they can either retrieve or construct experiences that map onto some of your experiences.

However, the goodwill white may not choose to look for a mappable experience if she is not motivated to do so. Sometimes when she *must* or *should* do so she *may* see how you feel, for a moment. But then she might (somehow) remove the feeling or pretend to do so, and, consequently, no longer be able to see how things are with you. Indeed, she may no longer see you at all. And without seeing you, seeing what you feel, she may make a judgment about you. Or if she doesn't make a judgment explicitly, she may treat you in a way that is in line with the felt evaluation (a part of her inheritance she hadn't counted on) that she pretends not to feel.

If we are to say that the goodwill white is irrational in such cases, her irrationality will consist in having behaved as though this were the correct way to go about understanding another person. In such circumstances we cannot claim that the goodwill white is rational by arguing that her way of *not* understanding you is, after all, serving her practical purposes. For it cannot serve her practical purposes to deliberately *misunderstand* the people around her, as long as they really do exist independently of her and have goals and values and emotions of their own. In other words, this kind of falsehood will not help a white person, of good or bad will, navigate her world.

Mary asked one question of whites. I ask another. What does a heart of whiteness *really* desire? What does goodwill value?

AFTERWORD

We were playing a wartime game—ring around the roses. Before we could fall down, dead presumably, we had to be united. For that, we had to all hold hands. I took Célia's hand on my left and Eduard's on my right. We began:

"Ring around the roses a pocket full of posies—"

"Wait, wait," I said.

Eduard's right hand dangled at his side like an amputated limb.

"Hold Lucien's hand, Eduard. Go ahead."

When I spoke to Eduard I often thought I sounded like a big mouse talking to a small mouse. My voice became squeaky when normally it never was.

Eduard's body became stiff. I felt his left hand freeze, become lifeless in mine. He looked straight ahead; his eyes grew larger. What could he see? The tall black bars of the gate that closed in the schoolyard. The sidewalk beyond it. People rushing by, hugging baguettes, clenching briefcases, dodging dog shit on the sidewalk.

I stooped down in front of Eduard, made him bigger than me. I took his right hand and tried to put it in Lucien's hand.

"He's black all over. I don't want to hold his hand."

What?

My head jerked left, to where the words had come from. Looking straight at their source, I continued to search for their source. Lucien couldn't have uttered those words. Not my Lucien! It must have been some other little boy who looked just like him.

The boy I looked down on (I was back on my feet, towering over all those little bodies) was a puny-looking white boy with dirty blond hair, brown eyes, and a ruddy face made ugly by a thick pug nose still scrunched up in Eduard's direction. I'd seen this face before. All my life.

I switched places with Eduard. His right hand would go in mine, his left in Célia's. I began the game again.

"Ring around the roses, a pocket full of posies—"

"Hey, wait Janine! Hold my hand!"

I whipped my right hand behind my back, where it would remain. You would have thought that I smelled the dog shit emanating from the sidewalks beyond the black gates, or perhaps that I had inadvertently stepped in a pile of that *ca ca boudin* (doo-doo pudding), as the children called it, their faces a mixture of disgust and mockery—kind of the way my face probably looked at the moment, my nose crunched up, my nostrils flaring, but a laugh on my face all the same. After all, we *were* in the middle of playing a game.

I hadn't stepped in anything. My feet firmly planted on the asphalt, I was merely looking at Lucien.

"I don't wanna hold your hand. You're white all over," I said.

And the game went on.

"Ashes, ashes, we all fall down!"

I rolled on the ground with the children, laughing and shrieking. Eduard sat cross-legged, smiling to himself the way he did when he was amused.

Only Lucien remained standing in place. Frozen. White-faced. Devastated. I could just make out my tears burning in his eyes.[54]

NOTES

1. See Lewis Gordon, *Her Majesty's Children* (Lanham, MD: Rowman & Littlefield, 1997), p. 29.

2. Here is what the Fourth edition of the *American Heritage Dictionary* (Houghton Mifflin Co., 2000) says about the terms "black" and "white." "Black is sometimes capitalized in its racial sense, especially in the African-American press, though the lowercase form is still widely used by authors of all races. The capitalization of Black does raise ancillary problems for the treatment of the term white. Orthographic evenhandedness would seem to require the use of uppercase White, but this form might be taken to imply that whites constitute a single ethnic group, an issue that is certainly debatable. Uppercase White is also sometimes associated with the writings of white supremacist groups, a sufficient reason of itself for many to dismiss it. On the other hand, the use of lowercase white in the same context as uppercase Black will obviously raise questions as to how and why the writer has distinguished between the two groups. There is no entirely happy solution to this problem. In all likelihood, uncertainty as to the mode of styling of white has dissuaded many publications from adopting the capitalized form Black." In this chapter, I follow the style for this book as a whole, with "black" and "white" in lowercase.

3. Sharon Rush, *Living across the Color Line: A White Adoptive Mother Learns about Race* (Lanham, MD: Rowman & Littlefield, 2001), p. 82.

4. See Debra Van Ausdale and Joe R. Feagin's account of children as young as three and a half years of age learning and applying racial concepts in preschool in *The First R: How Children Learn Race and Racism* (Lanham, MD: Rowman & Littlefield, 2001), pp. 2–12. Ausdale and Feagin's research calls into question a view held by those who remain in the grip of Piaget's model of childhood development; namely, that very young children are incapable of the kind of empathetic responses required for understanding the use of racial concepts. The accounts that Van Ausdale and Feagin provide show

young white children using racial concepts to control the resources in the classroom, such as the teacher's lap, wagons, and other desired objects.

5. Rush, *Color Line*, p. 4. Emphasis mine.

6. Ibid., p. 5.

7. See Rush, *Color Line*, p. 69, where she speaks of *not having been able to believe* or not *wanting* to believe that race is relevant to certain kinds of situations.

8. In a piece of creative nonfiction titled "What I Learned in First Grade," I recount my parting with my first-grade teacher, whose classroom I transferred out of because of her racism:

> Shortly after this incident [of mistreatment] I transferred out of Mrs. Stock's Class. But I couldn't go without first speaking to her. I wanted things to be clear. I didn't want to pass her in the hall and have her look at me with some surprised I-don't-know-what-happened look stretched across her saccharine smile and pasty white cheeks. So I took her out into the hall at the end of my last day in her class . . . and told her that I had to leave her class because she was prejudiced. "Yes dear," she said, her hard-edged smile seizing my curious face. The last I heard of Mrs. Stock was the swish of her nylon stockings rubbing together at the thighs as she turned and walked away from me. But at least we had come to an understanding, and that must be a beginning.

9. It is misleading because it suggests that we are to put ourselves, with *our* histories and *our* stories, in someone else's situation (their shoes). But the idea is that we are to simulate others' minds by trying to understand how *they* are in their shoes. We do this by trying to find similarities between our histories and stories and those of the person with whom we are seeking to empathize in such a way that via the mapping of our experiences onto theirs, imagining ourselves in the other person's shoes would be to imagine that other person in his or her own shoes.

10. Thomas Nagel, "What Is It Like to Be a Bat?" *Philosophical Review* Vol. 83, No. 4. (Ithaca, NY: Cornell University Press, 1974), pp. 435–50.

11. I have argued for this view in an unpublished paper, "No Body No Mind." We find a similar view in Fred Dretske's *Naturalizing the Mind* (Cambridge: MIT Press, 1995) p. 95.

12. Paul Thagard and Allison Barnes, "Empathy and Analogy," *Canadian Philosophical Review* 36: 705–20. I used the online version, which can be retrieved at http://cogsci.uwaterloo.ca/Articles/Pages/Empathy.html. References to pages numbers are in accordance with the online version (p. 3, emphasis mine).

13. Dorothy L. Cheney and Robert M. Seyfarth, *How Monkeys See the World* (Chicago: University of Chicago Press, 1990).

14. Thagard and Barnes, "Empathy and Analogy," p. 11.

15. Ibid. Emphasis mine.

16. Paul Finkelman, *Slavery and the Founders* (Armonk, NY : M. E. Sharpe, 2001), p. 129.

17. In *Killers of the Dream* (New York: W. W. Norton, 1949), Lillian Smith writes that after perceiving the incompatibility of her parent's racist views with the Christian ideals they professed to believe in, "I felt compelled to believe they were right. It was the only way my world could be held together" (p. 29). This way of holding a belief—which is not uncommon—may be responsible for some of the barriers a goodwill white faces when she tries to empathize with an African American.

18. Finkelman, *Slavery*, p. 191.

19. This becomes especially puzzling given the connections that whites have historically made between blacks and apes, where blacks were supposed, I take it, to be the higher primate of the two. Not that empathy is necessarily a transitive relation, but still, there is something particularly troubling here. See Tommy Lott's "King Kong

Lives: Racist Discourse and the Negro-Ape Metaphor" in *Next of Kin: Looking at the Great Apes* (Cambridge: MIT List Visual Arts Center, 1995), pp. 37–43.

20. One might have to dig beneath the surface of words and ideals in order to see what policies goodwill whites support and oppose when it comes to environmental problems in black communities (e.g., do they oppose using poor black communities as places where chemical and other plants can dump their waste, as vociferously as they support the cause of trees and wildlife in general and some nonhuman animals?). We can raise similar questions regarding goodwill whites' support or opposition to policies regarding other issues. What are goodwill whites' views on capital punishment, assuming they know that more blacks will be executed than whites, as the system currently operates? Should it come to the attention of goodwill whites that rich white kids are as likely to be drug users as black kids, poor and otherwise, would they then support a policy of profiling them? Would they support a policy that would put Ivy League universities under constant patrol because of the *likelihood* of a large portion of their populations being drug users? Do *they* really think they would?

    If our findings should reveal substantial differences between the policies that goodwill whites actively support when blacks (especially poor blacks) are the target population and policies that they actively oppose when whites are the population that would be affected, then like it or not, we will have unearthed the bones of their father in their very own bodies: for they, like Jefferson, would be (perhaps unbeknownst to them) engaged in a system of discrimination based on *preference* for whites and nonpreference for blacks, with degree of preference and nonpreference also determined by social-economic background. Further, it would be interesting to see what actions goodwill whites would support and oppose regarding poor whites, members of the group that they usually hold responsible for most of the racism. For the specific kind of whiteness I am targeting usually comes along with distinct economic privileges. While all Americans may in some sense be the offspring of Jefferson, the whites I am concerned with are his legitimate heirs, and poor whites are not that.

21. Finkelman, *Slavery*, p. 130. "The public Jefferson avoided the problem of slavery, forgoing opportunities to undermine the institution and its growing stranglehold on national politics. Throughout his life, Jefferson tried to dodge discussion of slavery. . . . When unable to evade the issue, Jefferson sought to avoid confrontation and friction."

22. Here the analogy with Jefferson doesn't fully work. Jefferson did not pretend to be color-blind. Consequently, he did not pretend to be blind to how a system of advantage was supposed to work in favor of whites. Jefferson's concept of liberty and justice *is* wide, wide enough, it would seem, to include blacks. That's the problem for Jefferson: he had to restrict a concept he knew to have wide application. It is the restriction that signals the role and place of whites in a system of advantage based on race.

    The goodwill white, color-blind and perhaps not as enlightened as his father, begins with Jefferson's wide concept of liberty and justice but takes himself to also desire the wide application of those concepts. On the other hand, he possesses a *narrow* concept of racism, one that fails to capture the system set in motion through the laws passed by his forefathers to benefit whites throughout the ages. The goodwill white's concept of racism does not capture the realities created through images and narratives constructed by his forefathers that depicted blacks as inferior physically, intellectually, and morally inferior even as to the *kind* of beings they are supposed to be. See Elise Lemire's *Miscegenation: Making Race in America* (Philadelphia: University of Pennsylvania Press, 2002) for an excellent discussion of how abolitionists, along with Jefferson, created—through narratives and imagery about miscegenation—a system of aesthetic value that not only placed whites at the top and blacks at the bottom of a hierarchy of beauty. It functioned in such a way that the evaluations whites made of blacks would be strongly *felt* negative evaluations. The narratives and imagery concerning blacks and the resulting felt evaluations then served to provide whites with valuable information about themselves, including whether their aesthetic sensibilities and values were as they *should* be, whether they were the right kind of white persons, or even stronger, whether they were whites at all!

It is because the goodwill white's concept of racism does not truly capture his role and place in a system of advantage based on race that he is not obliged, as his forefathers and mothers were, to explicitly *restrict* the application of concepts such as liberty and justice and freedom.

23. Beverly Daniel Tatum, *Why Are All the Black Kids Sitting Together in the Cafeteria?* (New York: Basic Books, 1997), p. 9.

24. Merrill D. Peterson, *The Jefferson Image in the American Mind* (New York: Oxford University Press), 447.

25. Ibid. Emphasis mine.

26. Finkelman, *Slavery*, p. 172. If this is the way we ought to go about things, then we are being asked to behave very much like the young Lillian Smith, who was compelled to hold certain beliefs in order for her world to have a certain meaning, a certain kind of coherence.

27. The schoolchildren must also learn about the value of myth: how it is used and abused.

28. Here I am referring to the malady of color blindness, which afflicts many goodwill whites. Color-blind whites claim not to see that black people are blacks, while nevertheless succeeding in treating blacks as though they can see that they are black. This is quite disturbing for the black child who must deal with a color-blind white adult. Most young white children have not become what I call goodwill whites. They often seem quite proud of their ability to navigate their little kindergarten and preschool worlds by using racial concepts that they've seen applied in other spheres to control desired resources. But the white goodwill adults do not teach them not to use racist concepts. Rather, they indicate that certain things are not *said*. "Don't use hurting words" is one nice, vague recommendation a goodwill white used after Carla, a three-year-old white child, said as she prepared for resting time to Nicole, a four-year-old black child on a nearby cot: "Niggers are stinky. I can't sleep next to one." Apparently Carla looked amused with her teacher's weak response. See Van Ausdale and Feagin's *The First R: How Children Learn Race and Racism*, for more accounts of very young children wielding racial concepts. Also see Patricia Williams's *Seeing a Color-Blind Future* (New York: Noonday, 1998), p. 3, where she recounts the story of her son, who was thought to have a vision problem. After visits to the ophthalmologist, Williams discovered that nothing was wrong with her child's eyes, but she became suspicious that something might be wrong with his teacher's eyes when her son claimed not to know the color of grass and remarked that it made no difference anyway. As it turned out, his goodwill white teacher had told the children that color didn't matter after some of the children had fought about whether black people could play "good guys." Perhaps this teacher should have asked the children why they thought blacks couldn't play good guys. But then, of course, she would have been forced to hear that the world she lived in and was a part of represented blacks, for the most part, as not being good guys. Then she would have been left without the resources to insist that color did not matter. For the children would have told her precisely one of the ways in which it does matter, probably with amused looks on their faces; that is, if they dared to have this kind of conversation with an authority, which children usually do not. Why amused? Imagine the children's position. They are taught to obey and respect adults, but the adults are indicating that *they* do not know what the world looks like, how it works. Of course, there is another alternative—the adults are simply lying. And, yes, catching an adult in this kind of lie might make a child smile.

29. Keith Oatley, *Best Laid Schemes: The Psychology of Emotions* (Cambridge, UK: Cambridge University Press, 1992).

30. Barnes and Thagard, "Empathy and Analogy," p. 5.

31. Ibid., p. 6.

32. Ibid., p. 7.

33. Ibid.

34. Ibid., p. 8. Source analogues are constructed using a folk theory of psychology. But using such a theory will be difficult for an empathizer to the extent that he fails to see the person with whom he is trying to empathize as being as fully human as he is.

35. Barnes and Thagard, "Empathy and Analogy,"p. 8.

36. Incidentally, I don't think that this young woman of 18 or so was a goodwill white. On the other hand, I would not be surprised to find that she denied that racism still exists.

37. It's important that America takes itself to value justice for all. For I take it that an occurrence of what we call injustice in a system where it is clear that justice is not supposed to be for all creates yet another kind of situation. Those who are treated unjustly may feel anger and resentment. But would it make sense to say that they feel *betrayed?* The mixture of these emotions creates highly specific emotions, for which we may not have names. But that does not mean that we cannot analyze these situations and distill from them the kinds of emotions that would go into the making of unnamed emotions.

38. In talking about what blacks *felt* I am not referring to nonintentional bodily processes, such as trembling or throbbing, or the feeling that one is boiling. Rather, I am referring to blacks' emotions being directed toward their important goals and projects. So above we might understand black rage as occurring not when justice fails to go through in some particular case, but when there is a pattern that suggests that justice is something that blacks are not to obtain, where this failure of justice is just one symptom that blacks have a different societal *value* than their white counterparts.

39. Samuel Francis, "Black Civil Rights, White Civil Rights," *Washington Times*, October 22, 1993, p. A27.

40. Frontline PBS Video, "L.A. is Burning: Five Reports from a Divided City" (documentary consortium of public television stations: KCTS Seattle, WGBH Boston, WNET New York, WPBT Miami, WTVS Detroit, 1992).

41. Joe R. Feagin, Hernán Vera, and Pinar Batur, *White Racism* (New York: Routledge, 2001), p. 142. Not only was Rodney King not aided, a videotape shows him being put into an ambulance *hog-tied*. Hence, even those in the business of saving lives participated in injuring and humiliating this man, demonstrating to the black population an important component of their emotional response: that black people are not valued in the same way as whites in this society.

42. Feagin, Hernán, and Batur, *White Racism*, p. 142.

43. Barnes and Thagard, "Empathy and Analogy," p. 10. Emphasis mine.

44. Feagin, Hernán, and Batur, *White Racism*, p. 111.

45. The public officials involved were Joseph Locurto (police officer) and Robert Steiner and Jonathan Walters (firefighters). After being fired by Giuliani, they sued to get their jobs back, claiming that there had been no racist intent in their action—perhaps they are low-grade goodwill whites—and that, in any case, they were protected by the First Amendment, since the float was just a parody. Apparently, the original intention was to parody Italian Americans. According to Locurto, this intention was changed at the last moment. A "spontaneous mistake," Lucarto called it. (See www.tabloid.net) Supposing this to be true, we might ask: Was it really a spontaneous mistake? Or was it that Lucarto was able to see (perhaps with such speed that

his judgment seemed to him to be spontaneous) that it would be a mistake to mock Italian Americans in certain kinds of ways? Suppose they had parodied Italian Americans by mocking how they had been treated and depicted after their arrival on Ellis Island. Did Lucarto get a sense of how the Italian American community (his community?) might *feel* about such mockery and how members of his community might have responded to such mockery? Considerations of this kind are what lead me to believe that Lucarto and his friends could have constructed a source analogue to map onto that of African Americans, if they had desired to do so.

46. Feagin, Vera, and Batur, *White Racism*, p. 132.

47. I can imagine an empathizer trying to leave the emotional impact of a case behind when the empathizer has an emotional response to a type of situation S that she assumes people normally do not have. For example, suppose that I enjoy being beaten, especially when the beatings are dealt out by authority figures on random occasions. When I see such a beating, I might call up what I feel on such occasions. That is, not only pleasure, but through that pleasure, the felt evaluation that such experiences are wonderful and extremely valuable. If I am to try to understand what Rodney King felt, I will have to put my particular idiosyncratic emotional response behind me. And if I live in a society and am in the least attuned to its workings, I will know that my viewpoint is idiosyncratic. I take it, however, that the jury members were not putting behind them the kind of emotional response I am describing here. A problem, however, remains regarding when we *should* leave our felt evaluations behind. Transport the Rodney King case to the '30s. I am a white person on the jury that has charged the white policemen. I watch the videotape of the beating, but then again I'm someone who sends postcards of black people being lynched to my loved ones. I see the beating and *feel* that it was the right thing to do. Moreover, my felt evaluation is not idiosyncratic. Not only my community but the larger community—with its system of laws and practices—supports this felt evaluation. Many upstanding white members of the community have the same emotional response. This might be a marker of their really being white. Well, as we've seen in the 1990s version of the Rodney King case, removing the felt evaluation and simply watching what happened didn't deliver the right result. So there's no reason to think that it would do so in the 1930s version. Still, one might have the sense (the illusion) that if the felt evaluation were removed, there would be some chance of bringing in the right verdict. When the victim in question is viewed as a human being, this might be what would happen. But when the person in question is viewed and imagined to be a *nigger*, then he occupies a territory between man and animal, and thus marks specificity even as he is denied it. And the specificity that marks him will depend on context, which is to be determined on white perceptions, needs, and desires. If the victim is seen and felt to be a savage, a nonhuman, then the act of controlling him, beating him, may be understood to be as innocent as cultivating the land. Many people still feel that the way they thoughtlessly and greedily destroy land is innocent. See Tony Morrison's *Playing in the Dark* (Cambridge, MA: Harvard University Press, 1992) for a discussion of how African Americans have been imagined in America.

48. This would be the case on a theory of emotion such as that of Bennett Helm, who argues in *Emotional Reason* (Cambridge, UK: Cambridge University Press, 2001) that the cognitive-conative divide is misguided, and that evaluative judgment, desire, and emotion are each essentially both cognitive and conative in a way that cannot be analyzed into separable components.

49. Martha Nussbaum, "Narrative Emotions: Beckett's Genealogy of Love," *Ethics I* 98, no. 2 (January 1988): 225–54.

50. Ibid., p. 232.

51. Ibid., p. 231.

52. Removing the emotional evaluation in effect reveals what many blacks suspected: that the object of the beating was of little value to the jury members. Or one might think that the object is of great value, great symbolic value. It is the kind of object to be treated in this way, and when this type of object—a black—is treated in this way we get a clear picture of who we are and how we are situated with respect to one another.

53. The jurors, in saying that they focused on the physical evidence, were unwittingly showing their allegiance to a view that purely physical evidence is so-called objective evidence.

54. Excerpt from an unpublished piece of creative nonfiction, "And We All Fall Down." My last question: What would I have seen in Lucien's eyes had I said, "Don't use hurting words"? My tears or his smile?

4

DELEGITIMIZING THE NORMATIVITY OF "WHITENESS"

A Critical Africana Philosophical Study of the Metaphoricity of "Whiteness"

Clevis Headley

THIS CHAPTER CRITICALLY EXAMINES WHITENESS from an Africana philosophical perspective, but resists the temptation to establish ontological symmetry between whiteness and blackness. In this regard, it differs from new scholarship that, despite its critical investigations of whiteness, falls prey to the tendency to treat whiteness as one identity among others.[1] This move to establish ontological parity between whiteness and blackness mistakenly interrogates whiteness without focusing on the power and privilege intimately connected to white identity.

Because of the tendency of some to construe immediately any approach to an understanding of whiteness from a black perspective as a form of extreme black nationalism, it is important to dissociate Africana philosophy from ideologically tainted construals of black nationalism. Though certain black cultural nationalists recommend a total repudiation of all things white, ranging from white aesthetics to white history, Africana philosophy eschews rigid ideological stances and, instead, pursues a course of critical confrontation.

On the other hand, there exists the tendency to interpret the responses of African peoples to whiteness in pathological terms. Blacks, according to this view, suffer from self-hatred and low self-esteem precisely because they have been conditioned to value whiteness over blackness and, since they are identified as black, they unfortunately must hate themselves even as they value whiteness.[2] This position is as unreasonable and misleading as the first for, in attributing collective self-hatred to blacks, it robs them of their human agency.

Finally, there is the view that whiteness serves as an object of desire for blacks, indeed, as the object of their ultimate concern. Here the alleged desire for whiteness is not pathological self-hatred. Instead, according to this view, blacks assume that even if denied the benefits of whiteness, they still can fabricate their own version of white reality. If the real thing is beyond the reach of blacks, then the next best thing is to create a black version of whiteness, ranging from black nationalism to black movie stars.

In this chapter, I resist the temptation both of acting out and of denial. Pursuing this task requires that I not simply react by denouncing the idea of whiteness. Indeed, to uncritically denounce whiteness would expose one to the risk of becoming a victim of whiteness, repeating its mistakes by appropriating its various essentialist tendencies, blindly embracing an inversion of whiteness in the form of an ontological blackness. Similarly, I avoid responding by means of denial, namely, unproductively engaging in the imaginary hope of believing that it is possible to think away the reality of whiteness simply by believing in its nonexistence. Rather, the task at hand is to work through whiteness, actively pursuing a close, careful, and critical engagement with whiteness. Working through means, among other things, struggling with whiteness to achieve cognitive integrity.

The Africana philosophical study of whiteness executed in this chapter does not take the form of a deduction of the concept of whiteness. In other words, there is no Kantian attempt to deduce the concept of whiteness by establishing its internal logical coherence and then illustrating its possible applicability. Here there is no attempt to demonstrate how one should think of the concept of whiteness without contradiction or to establish its internal incoherence by means of a logical dismantling. Nevertheless, in pursuing the task of investigating whiteness from the perspective of Africana philosophy, there should be no confusion about what precisely constitutes an Africana philosophical perspective.

DEFINING AFRICANA PHILOSOPHY

Lucius Outlaw recommends treating Africana philosophy as "an 'umbrella' notion under which can be gathered a potentially large collection of traditions of practices, agendas, and literatures of African and

African-descended peoples."[3] Consistent with his preference for employing "Africana philosophy" as a label or as a tag for purposes of classification, he states that "'Africana philosophy' is the phrase I use as a 'gathering' notion under which to situate the articulations (writings, speeches, etc.) and traditions of the same, of Africans and peoples of African descent collectively, as well as the subdiscipline or field-forming, tradition-defining, tradition-organizing reconstructive efforts which are (to be) regarded as philosophy."[4] Despite Outlaw's admirable efforts to connect the panorama of elements one can classify under the term "Africana philosophy," there is also the need to offer a more substantive take on Africana philosophy. Consequently, for purposes of this chapter, I suggest understanding Africana philosophy as also referring to the various metaphors and narratives employed by Africans and peoples of African descent to read and interpret the world. On this view, then, Africana philosophy must be attentive to the root metaphors characteristic of and constitutive of the African-based cognitive systems that African and African-descent peoples utilize in structuring and making sense of their existence.

In searching for the multiple metaphors of whiteness, we should be attentive to the various styles of thinking that make whiteness possible. Framing the issue as one of styles of thinking reinforces the significance of the role of metaphor. Here I am not suggesting the radical thesis that all thinking is metaphorical or that all concepts are metaphorical. The aim, rather, is to call attention to the permanence of metaphor in structuring our initial cognitive grasp of things. As Mark Johnson reminds us:

> [O]ur commonsense . . . understanding is deeply and pervasively metaphoric on two levels: (1) our fundamental concepts . . . are metaphorically defined, typically by more than one metaphorical structuring of each concept. (2) The conceptual frames in terms of which we understand concrete situations often involve systems of conventional metaphor. . . . Neither at the level of our most important . . . concepts, nor at the level of our framing of situations, can we eliminate metaphor. We can replace one metaphorical system with another, but we cannot get out of *some* set of metaphorical concepts.[5]

We should note that an Africana perspective on whiteness constitutes a confrontation of the Same by the Other. For whereas whiteness survives as the Same in the sense of seeking to reduce the Other to its own categories and principles, a form of epistemological violence, Africana philosophy, while occupying the role of the Other, seeks to challenge and call into question the epistemic imperialism of the Same, namely, the dominance of whiteness and its colonization of being. Consequently,

Africana philosophy does not claim any symmetrical status with whiteness but, instead, presents itself as the Other of whiteness. Thereby, it assumes an asymmetrical consciousness by challenging whiteness to listen to the voice of the Other, the voice of Africana philosophy, a voice long marginalized by the oppressive reign of whiteness.

In pursuing an Africana investigation of whiteness, questions of the lived reality of whiteness must be bracketed, since the focus of the inquiry will not center on a first-person phenomenological account of white identity. Nevertheless, it should be noted that blacks have been astute observers of whites precisely because, as Toni Morrison noted in *Playing in the Dark*, they understood that their cultural and physical survival depended upon knowing the internal, as well as external, factors motivating whites.[6] Ignorance of the reality of whiteness could result in the literal nonbeing of a black person.

Focusing on the social reality of whiteness, on its historical, political, social, and economic significance, need not commit us to an essentialist notion of whiteness. "Whiteness" does not name a real essence precisely because it is not a natural kind, and this is precisely the point that should not be taken lightly. At the same time, we should also not be seduced into a dogmatic realist treatment of "whiteness" as an empty and meaningless semantic term.

Consistent with my Africana philosophical perspective on whiteness, I argue that understanding whiteness requires investigating the metaphorical environment of whiteness. Hence, Africana philosophy's task of making whiteness cognitively visible means denouncing its chameleonic tendencies by exposing the various metaphorical disguises that, like the Klansman's hood, have served as camouflages for whiteness.

AFRICANA ROOT METAPHOR OF CONJURING AND WHITENESS

I want to begin accounting for the ontological reality of whiteness by situating it within the scope of a root metaphor. From an Africana philosophical perspective, the grammar of conjuring, unlike the discourse of constructionism,[7] connotes not only the sense of the making of reality but also the idea of the radical transformation of social reality through immaterial means. Furthermore, I do not intend to view conjuring as being totally incompatible with constructionism. Both conjuring and construction support the idea of reality as a human creation. However, constructionism is modeled upon an architectural metaphor, which connotes the idea of physical construction. But conjuring, unlike constructionism, is more closely associated with the phenomenon of human consciousness as a constitutive, meaning-giving activity. Consciousness is not a mere passive reflection on the world but, rather, it constitutes realities by endowing objects and situations with meaning. Hence, conjuring is more closely connected to immaterial transformations of the world, a notion not always captured in the metaphor of construction to the extent that the latter connotes fabricating artifacts. Furthermore, while "construction" implies that there is no world until it is constituted, "conjuring" on the other hand suggests a double implication. It implies both that we conjure up the world in the sense of constituting it, but also that we transform a previously constituted world. I will say more about the difference between conjuring and construction shortly.

Theophus Smith argues that one root metaphor of African and African-American culture is the metaphor of conjuration. Smith specifically underscores the idea of conjuring as the phenomenon of the transformation of reality. "Conjure" or "conjuration," according to him, can be variously understood as:

> a metaphor that circumscribes black people's ritual, figural, and therapeutic transformations of culture. But conjure phenomena are treated not only as literary or cultural metaphor. Conjure is fundamentally magic. It is first in consideration the magical folk tradition of black North Americans. Its practices have traditionally performed their craft in order to heal or harm others by the operation and invocation of extraordinary powers and processes. More concisely and comprehensively stated: Conjure is a magical means of transforming reality. Here the term "magic" is best understood as one system, among humanity's more primal cognitive systems, for mapping and managing the world in the form of signs.[8]

In embracing the notion of conjuring both as metaphor and as ritual practices, Smith considers three meanings of "conjure" pertinent to his project: "(1) to invoke or summon (up) a spirit, as in sorcery; (2) to effect by the use of 'magical' arts; and finally (3) to summon up an image or an idea as an act of imagination."[9] In stressing the creative and active aspects of conjuring activity, Smith seeks mainly to underscore the social transformative potential of conjuring activity. Commenting on the use of "the Bible as varieties of conjurational performances," Smith writes: "Conjure is construed . . . as a pharmacopeic (or healing-harming) practice and features a performative use of speech and ritually patterned or imitative behaviors. [C]onjurational performances at the level of social history employ biblical figures with a curative intention, [. . .] and for the purpose of reenvisioning and transforming lived experience and social reality through mimetic or imitative operations."[10]

It is my contention that we can employ the idea of conjuring, as one means of transforming social reality, to explain the ontological reality of whiteness. The metaphor of conjuring enables us to gain a more comprehensive understanding of the phenomenon of making the world white. The grammar of conjuration, unlike the language of construction, supports discourse about the phenomenon of calling into being or summoning whiteness into the world. And, as Smith states, such summoning or calling of whiteness into being can be alternatively understood as a whitening of the world, a "magical" transformation of the world, for making the world white oppositionally entails making blackness the diabolical other, subject to marginalization or even elimination.

Indeed, consistent with Smith's idea of conjurational practices being healing-harming, we can effectively understand why whiteness can be a source of existential healing, in the sense that it makes power available to one group while, simultaneously, being a source of harm to those who do not share in the power of whiteness. As a historical note, it is interesting to note efforts to invoke and appeal to symbols and images of white supremacy precisely during times of economic and political crises, when whites perceived their interests to be threatened. Conjuring whiteness at these times functions to reinforce structures of feeling that sustain certain ways of understanding social reality and that leave the reality of whiteness unquestioned.

Many may very well question the effectiveness of the metaphor of conjuring relative to the notion of constructionism. Let us briefly examine the difference. There are cognitive limitations to the architectural metaphor of constructionism. My apprehension concerning the idea of construction deals less with the original ontological insights of constructionism than with the threat of cognitive inertia. This inertia is made possible by the claim that "X is a social construction." The original insightfulness of this thesis weakened essentialism and underscored the role of human practices and intentions in creating social reality. To the extent that constructionism undermines unproductive attempts to view social reality as something discovered rather than created by human beings, such efforts are indeed commendable. However, we risk compromising clarity if we automatically and unimaginatively treat all social phenomena as enjoying ontological parity, without critically distinguishing between different kinds of constructions. For example, whiteness is not a noumena, an entity existing in itself, totally independent of human beings. It has no noumenal mystery that is inaccessible to human thinking. But viewing whiteness as an invention, in the sense of its being ontologically secondary to our concepts, should not lead us to settle for a strictly constructionist account of it. Doing so has led some advocates of constructionism to claim that the concept of "whiteness" is meaningless since it does not refer to a natural kind. In turn, this constructionist account too often fails to account for the existential role that the concept of whiteness plays in the lives of all people and how it profoundly affects these lives. As Jean Alsatian states, while endorsing a position espoused by Iris Marion Young, "relentless repetition of a short menu of metaphors stifles energetic and diverse discourse. Locutions that may at first enable us to see the world in new and startling ways (for example, 'the personal is political'), as 'they become worn, too familiar to be visible,' go on to 'assume a constraining power.'"[11] It is this possibility for constraining thinking, that I seek to resist by substituting conjuring for the metaphor of construction.

Furthermore, the radicalism of the constructionist thesis fades when we come to see that constructionism is oppositionally dependent upon realism and positivism. I would say that the constructivist embraces the same positivist theory of meaning that realism does. Roughly construed, realism is the belief in a mind-independent reality. In positing a mind-independent reality, realists embrace a certain view about the relation of correspondence between language and the world. Realism, on this view, holds that there is a direct referential relation between language and the world. Consistent with this word-world relationship, language is meaningful to the extent that words refer or name objects or entities. It follows, at least from this realist view of the relation between language and the world, that a legitimate concept when applied to an object must generate either a determinately true or false judgment. This requires that a legitimate concept, in the words of Gottlob Frege, have sharp boundaries. So, on the realist view, concepts that are ontologically committed to the existence of races are illegitimate because there are no races in the world, in the same way that there are no unicorns. Statements about race are similar to statements about unicorns. Since "race" and "unicorn" do not refer to natural kinds, they are not meaningful concepts.

What is characteristic of both realism and positivism is the demand that concepts be logically valid, rather than vague or fuzzy. Now it would seem to follow that rejecting realism and positivism would lead to some form of constructionism, i.e., the idea that social reality is not mind-independent but, rather, is a social construction.

I think it would be better to start with a perspective beyond realism or positivism on the one hand and beyond certain forms of constructionism on the other. Accordingly, instead of starting with the assumptions of realism and positivism, we should start with the assumption of the ontologically barrenness of the world, and then proceed to give an account of how the world comes alive ontologically through human intervention, that is, through consciousness bringing the social world into being. Concurrent with this ontological world-making is a certain view of language that is not premised on scientific concepts as the paradigm of semantic validity but, instead, on sociocultural concepts as the paradigm of meaning. Instead of exiling fuzziness and vagueness, the idea here is to acknowledge that these are general features of language and that they allow language to accommodate the flux of the social world. Concepts, far from having sharp boundaries, are contested. This contestability is a primary rather than a secondary reaction to the failure of either realism or positivism. So, all of the above should lead us to conclude that contestability is the transcendental ground of sociocultural concepts and not a second-best alternative to the failure of scientific concepts to apply to sociocultural realities. Our natural position should be a dynamic nominalism, a view espoused by Ian Hacking that holds that categories of people come into being before there are people who fall under these categories.[12] For example, the racial identification with whiteness was, among other things, contingent upon the constitutional category of whiteness.[13] One thing we can learn from an Africana philosophical study of whiteness is to question realist and positivist assumptions about meaning and reference.

We have successfully set the stage for a more penetrating examination of the metaphors of whiteness. According to our Africana philosophical perspective, conjuring serves as the root metaphor for understanding the reality of whiteness, its being in the world. Now, we will investigate the many ways of conjuring whiteness by critically examining its "economies" of metaphors.

METAPHORS OF WHITENESS: WHITENESS AS NORMATIVITY

First of all, whiteness masquerades as normativity, and there are various senses of normativity connected to it. From a sociological perspective, whiteness serves as the norm for social acceptability or what is considered to be naturally human. Since whites define acceptable standards of public behavior, normal behavior is behavior that conforms to white standards of decency, while abnormal behavior is behavior that deviates from these standards. Consequently, blacks are seen as pathological to the extent that they engage in styles of speaking, walking, and dressing and embrace attitudes toward intimacy and social interaction that deviate from white standards. Oftentimes, what many neglect to underscore is that ironically, although whites predominantly shape mainstream attitudes and behaviors, there is the tendency to treat these attitudes and behaviors as being universally characteristic of any rational being. In other words, these attitudes and behaviors enjoy the status of being those qualities characteristically attributed to abstract individualism. When mainstream attitudes and behaviors are thus viewed, whiteness becomes normative and deviation from this norm is seen as pathological.

Closely associated with the sociological sense of normativity is a second sense of normativity, that of civic normativity. Here, whiteness functions as a form of consciousness beyond race, which means then that social interaction cannot be limited by concerns of race. For example, racial integration is premised upon the idea that ending racism requires the rejection of race. Integration, according to this view, embraces the notions of equality, rationality, objectivity, and these values take focus away from the arbitrary characteristics of an individual such as his or her race. To the extent that integration advocates the integration of blacks into the mainstream, there is the presumption that full participation in mainstream institutions by blacks represents the fulfillment of the vision of a society beyond race and racism. What escapes notice is the fact that the institutions of mainstream society were historically structured on the basis of white privilege and black exclusion. Here, "whiteness" functions as a normativity only because predominantly *white* institutions are seen as institutions beyond race, grounded on rational Enlightenment principles of equality, rationality, and objectivity. As such, these institutions can readily accommodate any group, regardless of its cultural heritage.

A third instance of whiteness functioning as normativity is found in the law: legal normativity. The critical focus on the role of whiteness in law has been pioneered by critical race theorists.[14] This group of black and minority scholars, identifying themselves as speaking in the voice of color, expose the law as complicit in maintaining hegemony through cultural practices and beliefs which reinforce exploitative social and political structures that are partial to whiteness. To be more specific, "the legal legitimation of expectations of power and control that enshrine the status quo as a neutral baseline, . . . masking the maintenance of white privilege and domination"[15] conspires in promoting whiteness as normativity. In particular, whiteness functions as normativity with regard to the opposition to race-specific policies targeted at compensating historical victims for the harms of racial discrimination. The normativity of whiteness, in this context, takes the form of advocating color blindness, the notion that society should not "see" race. In other words, race should not play any significant role in how society treats individuals. This emphasis on color blindness sanctions equal treatment regardless of race. In addition to this strong emphasis on equal treatment and color blindness, there is also the reigning sentiment that equality is, roughly speaking, simply a matter of formal equality of opportunity. This formalistic spin on equality, the product of a formalistic analytic[16] that essentially reduces equality of opportunity to political equality, which, in turn, leads to a construal of equality of opportunity as the removal of legal impediments to competition, does not acknowledge that inequalities in wealth and power significantly affect and distort conditions of equality of opportunity. The consequence of the rhetoric of color blindness is that whites and blacks are seen as being in a symmetrical relation. In this view, whites are not seen as having benefited from any historical advantages over blacks. Furthermore, since the advocates of color blindness see no need for race-specific policies, they assume that current distributive shares are the fair outcome of individual initiatives. Therefore, the fact that whites have benefited and continue to benefit from institutional racism is not acknowledged. The result is that "the rhetoric of equal treatment and color blindness operates to normalize whiteness. White is not considered a color, and equal treatment is used to cover up important and relevant differences between people, a cover-up that leads to unjust treatment."[17] Whiteness functions as normativity in that it wraps itself in the progressive liberal cloak of equality, impartiality, and equal treatment. Robyn Wiegman recently commented on this aspect of whiteness, writing about "liberal whiteness," namely, "a color-blind moral sameness whose reinvestment in 'America' rehabilitates the national narrative of democratic progress in the aftermath of social dissent and crisis."[18]

WHITENESS AS ECONOMIC METAPHORS

In addition to the notion of the normativity of whiteness, there is also the mediation of whiteness in economic metaphors. Cheryl Harris, a critical race scholar, acknowledges a diverse understanding of property in the history of political thought: Property in the sense of rights, property as the ownership of things, property as self-ownership, and property as physical (biological) characteristics.[19] The import of Harris's analysis of "whiteness" as property underscores the extent to which the dominant understanding of the notions of rights, property, race, and even affirmative action are not neutral and impartial definitions but have been skewed by the historical coding of the metaphor of whiteness as property. Because of the effectiveness of Harris's metaphor of whiteness as property, it will be examined in greater detail.

Harris traces the various installations of whiteness through an exploitation of the metaphor of property. She describes the discursive structuring of whiteness as follows: (1) whiteness "as treasured property";[20] (2) whiteness as something in which American law recognizes "a property interest"; [21] and, finally, (3) whiteness as something that has evolved "from color to race to status to property as progression historically rooted in white supremacy."[22] The oppositional dynamics of whiteness and blackness means that "white identity and whiteness were sources of privilege and protection; their absence meant being the object of property."[23] So whereas blacks were objects of property and were prevented from being owners of property, "whiteness was the characteristic, the attribute, the property of free human beings."[24] The precondition for possession of property was defined in terms of the "cultural practices of whites."[25] In making whiteness a condition for property ownership, the foundation was laid for the "idea that whiteness—that which whites alone possess—is valuable and is property."[26] Whiteness is both a property, something valuable to possess, and a precondition for the right to own property. Indeed, rules of first possession, according to Harris, were defined totally in terms of having the property of whiteness, namely, of being white. According to her, "[t]his fact infused whiteness with significance and value because it was solely through being white that property could be acquired and secured under law. Only whites possessed whiteness, a highly valued and exclusive form of property."[27] Whiteness functioned as identity, self-identity, status, and as property. And when it achieved legal status, this process "converted an aspect of identity into an external object of property, moving whiteness from privileged identity to a vested interest."[28] This conversion of whiteness into vested interest explains the almost fanatical obsession with legal and constitutional definitions of whiteness. "The law's construction of whiteness defined and affirmed critical aspects of identity (who is white); of privilege (what benefits accrue to that status); and, of property (what *legal* entitlements arise from that status)."[29]

Closely related to Harris's analysis of whiteness as property is George Lipsitz's framing of whiteness as "possessive investment." Utilizing certain economic metaphors, he shows whiteness to be a construction disconnected from issues surrounding the biological validity of race. Whiteness, properly construed, is connected to the social distribution and accumulation of power and wealth. Consistent with his analysis of whiteness is the claim that distributive shares in society are regulated mainly in terms of the social reality of whiteness. According to Lipsitz:

> Despite intense and frequent disavowal that whiteness means anything at all to those so designated, recent surveys have shown repeatedly that nearly every social choice that white people make about where they live, what schools their children attend, what careers they pursue, and what policies they endorse is shaped by considerations involving race. Whiteness is invested in, like property, but it is also a means of accumulating property and keeping it from others.[30]

Investing in whiteness is not merely a matter of maximizing economic benefits in isolation but, rather, takes the form of an existential commitment. Lipsitz cites research by Mary Edsall and Thomas Byrne Edsall that establishes that "many whites structure nearly all of their decisions about housing, education, and politics in response to their aversions to black people."[31] Perhaps the area with the greatest concentration of investment in whiteness is housing. Lipsitz states that through the Federal Housing Act of 1934 and various agencies such as the Federal Housing Administration and the Department of Housing and Urban Development, as well as the lending practices of banks and local real estate agencies, housing segregation made possible all-white suburbs and gated communities, which allowed whites to live and intermarry among themselves. The economic rewards of investing in whiteness through residential segregation are not to be underestimated. Lipsitz writes:

> The appreciated value of owner-occupied homes constitutes the single greatest source of wealth for white Americans. It is the factor most responsible for the disparity between blacks and whites in respect to wealth—a disparity between two groups much greater than the differences in income. It is the basis for intergenerational transfers of wealth that enable white parents to give their children financial advantages over the children of other groups. Housing plays a crucial role in determining educational opportunities as well, because school funding based on property tax assessments in most localities gives better opportunities to white children than to children from minority communities. Opportunities for employment are affected by housing choices, especially given the location of new places of employment in suburbs and reduced funding for public transportation. In addition, housing affects health conditions, with environmental and health hazards disproportionately located in minority communities.[32]

Whiteness has value, but not intrinsic value. Its value is made possible by the various strategies designed to guarantee white privilege. Again, investing in whiteness is also a matter of the intergenerational transfer of wealth among whites.

A third example of an economic metaphor to frame whiteness is Charles Mills's idea of "the racial contract." Here, one can talk about whiteness by consensus or whiteness as contract. Mills employs the idea of the racial contract to describe the nature and dynamics of modern society. Mills's notion of Racial Contract is an extension of the idea of the social contract. The racial contract, according to him, explains the system of white supremacy that benefits whites at the expense of those considered to be nonwhite. Obviously, the racial contract is exclusionary in that it is not open to all human beings. Describing the racial contract variously as a moral, political, and epistemological compact, Mills writes:

> The Racial Contract is that set of formal or informal agreements or meta-agreements . . . between the members of one subset of humans, henceforth designated by . . . "racial" . . . criteria . . . as "white," and coextensive . . . with the class of full persons, to categorize the remaining subset of humans as "nonwhite" and of a different and inferior moral status, subpersons, so that they have a subordinated civil standing in the white or white-ruled polities the whites either already inhabit or establish or in transactions as aliens with these polities, and the moral and juridical rules normally regulating the behavior of whites in their dealings with one another either do not apply at all in dealings with nonwhites or apply only in a qualified form. . . . [B]ut in any case the general purpose of the Contract is always the differential privileging of the whites as a group with respect to the nonwhites as a group, the exploitation of their bodies, land, and resources, and the denial of equal socioeconomic opportunities to them. All whites are *beneficiaries* of the Contract, though some whites are not *signatories* to it.[33]

The metaphor of whiteness as contract or agreement reinforces the extent to which whiteness did not ontologically depend upon the biological validity of the concept of race. Rather, multiple ritual performances of enacting alleged objective principles and laws brought into being a world where those identified as white became the targets of rights and benefits denied to those identified as nonwhites, the objects of the contract and not its subjects.

PSYCHOLOGICAL METAPHORS OF WHITENESS

A third category of the metaphorical analysis of whiteness concerns psychological metaphors. One main concern of the Africana analysis of the psychological dynamic of whiteness centers on strategies of denial. Here, denial takes the form of a subject attempting to distort objective features of the social world in order to make the social world more psychologically comforting.

Kelly Oliver, although not working directly in Africana philosophy, offers useful insights into strategies of denial. Oliver introduces the notion of "false witness" within the context of the notion of reverse discrimination. She maintains that one way to conceive of subjectivity is to think of subjectivity as witness. Drawing on both the legal sense of witnessing as testifying at a trial and the sense of witnessing as testifying to something transcending the empirical realm of evidence, Oliver talks about subjectivity as the ability to address and as responsibility. She writes:

> There are false witnesses and false witnessing that attempt to close off response from others, otherness, or difference. And there are various ways to engage in false witnessing, many of them encouraged within cultures of dominance and subordination. I would argue, for example, that claims of "reverse discrimination" by white students when they are not admitted to universities is a form of false witnessing. To claim that affirmative action is a type of reverse discrimination ignores both the differential sociohistorical subject positions of whites and racial minorities and our ethical responsibility to open up rather than close off responses from others.[34]

It may seem contradictory to claim that whiteness is both affirmed and denied by whites. However, we need to distinguish the affirmation of whiteness in the sense of conjuring whiteness,—that is, of making the world white as a phenomenon of historical facticity—and affirming whiteness by pretending not to be conjuring whiteness but still succeeding in allowing the world to remain white. The world, from a historical point of view, was made white through the invention of a modern style of thinking based upon race. But once the world became white—once whiteness entitled an individual to respectable social status and to economic and political privileges—it then made rational economic sense to invest in whiteness, to keep the world white. However, unlike the original conjuring of whiteness, the investment in whiteness now takes the form of denouncing race in precisely those ways that reinforce the privileges of whiteness. Hence, when bearing false witness and rejecting affirmative action by claiming that whites are unfortunate victims of reverse racial discrimination, whites are conjuring up a world in which whiteness is a harmed ethnicity. In so viewing whiteness as victimized, that is, in democratizing oppression and placing whiteness and blackness as symmetrically disadvantaged identities, whiteness's true state of being is obscured. Hence, when bearing false witness, strategies of conjuration are employed that distort the existing asymmetry between whiteness and blackness.

The psychological dimensions of whiteness were also obvious to W.E.B. Du Bois. Du Bois describes white workers as refusing to pursue any meaningful conception of working-class solidarity with blacks. Instead, they chose to mobilize along lines of race, making clear that protecting whiteness—that is, being white and free—is better than associating with blacks. But in so choosing a white identity, white workers, according to Du Bois, settled for the "public and psychological wages" of whiteness.[35] Whiteness as a psychological wage apparently proved more valuable than the possible benefits attached to class solidarity across racial lines. Indeed, protecting the psychological worth of whiteness precluded associating with blacks, since this would have deflated the worth of whiteness.

CONCLUSION

I want to conclude this essay by briefly considering the future of whiteness. Some thinkers have called for a deconstruction of whiteness, claiming that its contingent historical status will be exposed and its reified status eradicated. Of course, revealing the arbitrary ontological and axiological status of whiteness and its relational dependence upon the other concepts does not automatically translate into an undermining of whiteness. That concepts survive attempted semantic executions is uncontested; we cannot eliminate a concept from our language simply by showing it to be the product of an economy of linguistic difference.

There is also the abolitionist position on whiteness. As is obvious, this calls for the abolition of whiteness and white identity. Abolitionists confidently call for this abolition on the grounds that whiteness is best defined negatively, that is, by what it is not. Instead of viewing whiteness as designating independent content, it is seen as designating lack and, accordingly, as fake. Because of the void at the heart of whiteness, whites fill in the blanks by devouring the Other.[36] This consuming of the Other takes place because white identity is empty, void of any content aside from its mediation as difference from nonwhiteness. As Roediger writes: "It is not simply that whiteness is oppressive and false; it is that whiteness is *nothing but* oppressive and false. . . . It is the empty and terrifying attempt to build an identity based on what one isn't and on whom one can hold back."[37] Although I agree with the critical thrust of the abolitionist program, I must express some skepticism about its ultimate impact. The idea of the abolition of whiteness requires that one clearly state the precise nature of this abolition program. Is it simply going to be a matter of the legal abolition of whiteness? Certainly, one can respond by stating that the civil rights revolution was, in part, intended to eliminate whiteness through legal strategies. Of course, what was accomplished was the promotion of a procedural formalist notion of equality that serves as a camouflage for whiteness. But with regard to the technical notion of abolition, we still need to know how the voluntary abolition of racial identity is possible beyond the courageous acts of a few isolated individuals, particularly since white identity is majoritarian and is reinforced by tremendous economic, cultural, social, legal, and political power.

From an Africana philosophical perspective, I argue for the teleological suspension of whiteness, realizing that whiteness must be transcended but not by rational argument. The point here is not to license irrationalism but, rather, to underscore the fact that rational argumentation proves blunt in the face of centuries-old social privilege. Here, the notion of the suspension of whiteness represents the third move in the historical evolution of whiteness. Let us consider a suggestive Africana appropriation of the Kierkegaardian existential dialectic. The aesthetic stage of whiteness represents the stage when whiteness and its tremendous benefits were overtly constituted. Of course, this situation generated opposition in that those excluded from the privileges of whiteness openly challenged the rightness of whiteness and exposed the immorality of white supremacy. Overt and blatant rejoicing in the privilege of whiteness could not escape challenge.

The ethical stage of whiteness is similarly dominated with a concern to do the morally right thing. This concern takes the form of bold appeals to objectivity, formal equality of opportunity, and procedural notions of justice. In this stage, there is a strong appeal to the moral worth of each individual and an equally confident emphasis on the notion of rewarding individuals strictly on merit. In conjunction with a forceful advocacy of color blindness, policies that recognize race, such as affirmative action, are considered to be immoral because they favor groups and not individuals. Consequently, race-conscious policies are denounced as flagrantly violating both moral and constitutional principles of fairness.

We are quickly approaching a situation in which appealing to formal principles of equality and opportunity and to universal principles of justice cannot effectively remedy the tremendous differential in power between blacks and whites. As this realization becomes more and more evident, there will be a need to move on to a third stage.

Unlike Kierkergaard's third stage, the religious stage made possible by an unconditional act of faith, the third stage of whiteness will more closely resemble his notion of the teleological suspension of the ethical and the inability to rationally inscribe this suspension in a universal discourse. Not being concerned with ultimate meaning or with religious affirmation, the third stage of whiteness will not be a deconstruction or abolition of whiteness but, rather, a teleological suspension of whiteness. Whiteness cannot be dismantled through rational and analytical means. Its suspension must come in the form of a continuously affirmed refusal to prolong the ontological and existential project of whiteness. The project of whiteness must be suspended for the greater good of human liberation beyond whiteness. The project of whiteness has proven too costly for human existence. The existential price is simply too costly for those who are forced to involuntarily participate in this project. Hence, teleologically suspending whiteness is a solution, a counter-project that cannot be rationally stated. It defies neutral conceptualization because there is no direct and rationally persuasive way of linguistically describing the urgency of this cause. The reason why the question of the suspension of whiteness cannot be framed in the language of our legal and political system is because our language itself is infected with the project of whiteness. After all, what would it mean to argue in favor of renouncing whiteness and its benefits by using a discourse imbued with the categories that perpetuate whiteness? To the extent that whiteness, understood as white supremacy, is a global system of white racial domination similar to patriarchy, Africana philosophers can call attention to racial bias in language in the same manner that feminist philosophers have called attention to gender bias in language. For example, the alleged neutral and universal notions of political discourse, which should function neutrally, promote racial outcomes that benefit whites.[38] Lipsitz claims that "the language of liberal individualism serves as a cover for coordinated collective group interests."[39] Robyn Wiegman, calling attention to Cheryl Harris's distinction between corrective justices, which seeks "compensation for discrete and 'finished' harm done to minority group members or their ancestors," and distributive justice, which "is the claim an individual or group would have been awarded under fair conditions,"[40] affirms Harris's claim that "the goals of affirmative action—to address the harms done to those people minoritized by racial . . . oppression—are undermined when corrective justices is the interpretative frame because not only is the harm assumed to be finished but the practices through which harm has been done are individualized, confined to the one who perpetrated it and the one who endured it. In this context, whites can claim to be innocent and therefore in need of counterlegislative protection because they have not individually perpetuated harm."[41]

Transcending whiteness, from an Africana philosophical perspective, must of necessity do more than expose the secret career of whiteness in maintaining structures of racial privilege. Such an analysis of whiteness should also serve as an opportunity to acknowledge the affirmative possibilities of conceiving alternative social modes of being. In other words, it should underscore the realization that things can be otherwise. Moving beyond whiteness requires a radically new concept of the human, a new metaphoricity of humanity.

NOTES

1. For examples, see Peter Erickson, "Seeing White," *Transition* 67 (1996): 166–85; David Stowe, "Uncolored People: The Rise of Whiteness Studies," *Lingua Franca* (September/October 1996): 68–77; Judith Levine, "The Heart of Whiteness," *Voice Literary Supplement* (September 1994): 11–16; Ruth Frankenberg, ed., *Displacing Whiteness: Essays in Social and Cultural Criticism* (Durham, NC: Duke University Press, 1997); Michelle Fine, Lois Weis, Linda Powell, and L. Mung Wong, eds., *Off White: Readings on Race, Power, and Society* (New York: Routledge, 1997); Chris Cuomo and Kim Hall, eds., *Whiteness: Critical Philosophical Reflections* (Lanham, MD: Rowman & Littlefield, 1999); Mike Mill, ed., *Whiteness: A Critical Reader* (New York: New York University Press, 1997); Virginia Domínquez, *White by Definition: Social Classification in Creole Louisiana* (New Brunswick, NJ: Rutgers University Press, 1986).

2. See Kenneth B. Clark and Mamie P. Clark, "Segregation as a Factor in the Racial Identification of Negro Pre-School Children: A Preliminary Report," *Journal of Experimental Education* (spring 1940): 101–103; and (same author) "Racial Identification and Preference in Negro Children," chapter in *Readings in Social Psychology*, 3rd edition ed. Theodore Newcomb, Eugene Hartley, (New York: Henry Holt, 1958), pp. 602–611.

3. Lucius Outlaw, *On Race and Philosophy* (New York: Routledge, 1996): p. 77.

4. Ibid., p. 76.

5. Mark Johnson, *Moral Imagination: Implications of Cognitive Science for Ethics* (Chicago: University of Chicago Press, 1993), p. 61.

6. Toni Morrison, *Playing in the Dark: Whiteness in the Literary Imagination* (Cambridge, MA: Harvard University Press, 1992).

7. Troy Duster provides another suggestive metaphorical construal of whiteness outside the context of constructionism. Duster writes:

   One side sees race as ever-changing. The other side sees enduring race privilege. Oddly, both sides are correct. Or, at least, both sides have an important handle on an elementary truth about race.

   The best way to communicate how this is possible is to employ an analogy to *water* or, more precisely, H_2O. While water is a fluid state, at certain contingent moments, under thirty-two degrees, it is transformed into a solid state—ice. This is an easy binary formulation. But things get more complicated, because when H_2O, at still another contingent moment boils, it begins to vaporize or evaporate. And now the coup de grâce of the analogy of H_2O to race: H_2O in its vapor state can condense, come back and transform into water, and then freeze and hit you in its solid state as an ice block; what you thought had evaporated into the thin air can return in a form that is decidedly and consequentially real. In short, H_2O is to serve now as more than just my analogy—and, in this context, whiteness. Race, like H_2O, can take many forms, but unlike H_2O it can transform itself in a nanosecond. It takes time for ice to boil or for vapor to condense and freeze, but race can be *simultaneously* Janus-faced and multifac(et)ed—and also produce a singularly dominant social hierarchy.

Troy Duster, "The 'Morphing' Properties of Whiteness," in *The Making and the Unmaking of Whiteness,* ed. Birgit Brander Rasmussen, Eric Kleinberg, Irene J. Nexica, and Matt Wray (Durham, NC: Duke University Press, 2001): 114–15.

8. Theophus Smith, *Conjuring Culture: Biblical Formations of Black America* (New York: Oxford University Press, 1994), p. 4.
9. Ibid., p. 5.
10. Ibid., p. 18.
11. Jean Bethke Elshtain, *Real Politics: At the Center of Everyday Life* (Baltimore: Johns Hopkins University Press, 1997), p. 93. See also Marion Young, "Is There a Women's World? Some Reflections on the Struggle for Our Bodies," in *The Second Sex—Thirty Years Later: A Commemorative Conference on Feminist Theory* (New York: Institute for the Humanities, 1979), p. 44.
12. Ian Hacking, 'Three Parables," in *Philosophy in History,* ed. Richard Rorty, J. B. Schneewind, and Quentin Skinner (Cambridge, UK: Cambridge University Press, 1984).
13. See Theodore Allen, *The Invention of Whiteness* (New York: Verso, 1994); Alexander Saxon, *Rise and Fall of the White Republic: Class Politics and Mass Culture in Nineteenth-Century America* (New York: Verso,1990); Ian Haney Lopez, *White by Law: The Legal Construction of Race* (New York: New York University Press, 1996).
14. *Critical Race Theory: The Cutting Edge,* ed. Richard Delgado (Philadelphia: Temple University Press, 1995).
15. Cheryl Harris, "Whiteness as Property," *Harvard Law Review* 106 (1993): 1715.
16. Kimerle Williams Crenshaw, "Race, Reform, and Retrenchment: Transformation and Legitimation in Antidiscrimination Law," *Harvard Law Review* 101, no. 7 (1988): pp. 1331–1387.
17. Kelly Oliver, *Witnessing: Beyond Recognition* (Minneapolis: University of Minnesota Press, 2001), p. 117.
18. Robyn Wiegman, "Whiteness Studies and the Paradox of Particularity" *Boundary 2* (fall 1999): 121.
19. Harris, 'Whiteness as Property."
20. Ibid., p. 1713.
21. Ibid.
22. Ibid., p. 1714.
23. Ibid., p. 1721.
24. Ibid.
25. Ibid.
26. Ibid.
27. Ibid., p. 1724.
28. Ibid., p. 1725.
29. Ibid.
30. George Lipsitz, *Possessive Investment in Whiteness: How White People Profit from Identity Politics* (Philadelphia: Temple University Press, 1988), p. viii.
31. Ibid., p. 19.
32. Ibid., pp. 32–33.
33. Charles Mills, *The Racial Contract* (Ithaca, NY: Cornell University Press, 1997), p. 11.
34. Oliver, *Witnessing: Beyond Recognition,* p. 19.
35. W.E.B. Du Bois, *Black Reconstruction in America, 1860–1880* (New York: Atheneum, 1969).

36. See bell hooks, "Eating the Other," in bell hooks, *Black Looks: Race and Representation* (Boston: South End Press, 1992), pp: 21–39.

37. David Roediger, *The Wages of Whiteness: Race and the Making of the American Working Class* (New York: Verso, 1991), p. 13.

38. See Alan David Freeman, "Legitimizing Racial Discrimination through Antidiscrimination Law: A Critical Review of Supreme Court Doctrine," *Minnesota Law Review* 62 (1978): pp. 1049–1119. Gertude Ezorsky also discusses the fact that neutral policies and concepts often result in negative racial impact. Gertude Ezorsky, *Racism and Justice; The Case for Affirmative Action* (Ithaca, NY: Cornell University Press, 1991).

39. Lipsitz, *Possessive Investment in Whiteness,* p. 22.

40. Harris, 'Whiteness as Property," p. 1781.

41. Wiegman, "Whiteness Studies," p. 130.

5

A FOUCAULDIAN (GENEALOGICAL) READING OF WHITENESS

The Production of the Black Body/Self and the Racial Deformation of Pecola Breedlove in Toni Morrison's The Bluest Eye

George Yancy

But what on earth is whiteness that one should so desire it? Then always, somehow, some way, silently but clearly, I am given to understand that whiteness is the ownership of the earth forever and ever, Amen!

—W.E.B. Du Bois

Until the America Negro is restored to himself aesthetically, both the Negro man and the Negro woman will be easy prey for designing members of the Caucasian type.

—Thomas N. Baker

The effort to think one's own history can free thought . . . and so enable it to think differently.

—Michel Foucault

IN THIS CHAPTER, I will explore the structure of whiteness within the framework of key Foucauldian conceptual constructions. Unfortunately, to my knowledge, there is no critical corpus of work dealing extensively with Foucault and the issue of whiteness. My sense is that Foucault has provided a helpful conceptual framework, particularly as developed in *Discipline and Punish* and the first volume of *The History of Sexuality*, for coming to terms with how whiteness, as a power/knowledge nexus, is able to produce new forms of knowledge (in this case "knowledge" about black people) that are productive of new forms of "subjects." On this reading, whiteness, as a power/knowl-edge nexus with respect to black "selves" and black bodies, produces a philosophical, epistemological, anthropological, phrenological, and political discursive field that "enables a more continuous and perva-sive control of what people do, which in turn offers further possibili-ties for more intrusive inquiry and disclosure."[1]

From a genealogical perspective, there is no deep metaphysical mystery or truth about whiteness that remains to be uncovered. As Arnold I. Davidson writes: "Genealogy, that aspect of Foucault's methodology most clearly employed in his later works, has a wider scope than archaeology. Its central area of focus is the mutual rela-tions between systems of truth and modalities of power, the way in which there is a 'political regime' of the production of truth."[2] I aim to examine whiteness as the embodiment and production of specific truth claims, claims that are inextricably linked to a (white) regime of truth and modalities of power.

Divided into two sections, this chapter first provides a genealogical reading of whiteness. This will involve a process of coming to terms with whiteness's historical "positionality." In this way, whiteness, as a presumed "universal" value code, will be shown to consist of an em-bodied set of practices fueled by a reactive value-creating power. The aim is to call into question the idea that whiteness exists *simpliciter*. What will be shown is that whiteness creates values, norms, and epis-temic frames of reference that unilaterally affirm its many modes of instantiation—political, institutional, aesthetic, and so forth.

I will also explore how whiteness attempts to hide from its historicity and particularity,[3] which I maintain is a function of how whiteness rep-resents itself as "universal." In short, whiteness masquerades as a uni-versal code of beauty, intelligence, superiority, cleanliness, and purity; it functions as a master sign. I will demonstrate how black bodies/selves are *produced* within the power/knowledge economy of whiteness, how the black body/self is disciplined and how it comes to "know" itself, that is, comes to know the "truth" of itself, as a denigrated *thing* of absence and existential insignificance. In this sense, I understand American slavery (an expression, among other things, of white *ressenti-ment* or hatred) as a form of physical and psychological subjection. The reader will note that my analysis here does not involve the elision of the primary structural profit motive involved in the enslavement of black people. To maintain that the enslavement of black people of African de-scent was a purely economic, calculative endeavor, a phenomenon re-duced to an *etic* analysis, is too conceptually and historically thin. The economic motive was there, but the formation of whiteness's *reactive* stance to blackness was a crucial and formative factor. After all, in the European imaginary, blackness signified evil. Social processes of difference and "same-other" dynamics were present in Europe, but the black body provided that which had no trace of whiteness (read: reason, divinity, subjectivity, humanity).[4] Through the existential and institutional terror of slavery, the way blacks came to relate themselves to themselves involved a technique of discipline that not only restricted and prohibited but, more significantly, *enabled* a certain destructive self-conceptualization. Blacks acquired, in stream with Foucault's analysis of sexuality, "the deep internalization of a carefully orchestrated value-laden understanding of the self."[5]

The second section will explore how Pecola Breedlove, a fictional character in Toni Morrison's *The Bluest Eye*, becomes a product of the power/knowledge nexus of whiteness. Pecola, under the disciplining regime of whiteness, comes to *know* herself as ugly, dirty, and inferior. Within the white *order of things*, Pecola's body is a site of both denigration and the normalizing disciplinary techniques of whiteness.

A *genealogical* examination of whiteness, following the lead of Foucault and Nietzsche, involves showing how whiteness is not a natural given, or has to do with an ontology that cuts at the joints of nature, but a kind of historical emergence (*Entstehung*). Upon examination, whiteness, contrary to its historical performance as a natural occurring kind, emerges as a value code deployed by a certain raciated (white) group of people that delimits and structures what it deems intelligible, valuable, normal, abnormal, superior, inferior, beautiful, ugly, and so on. As the presumed sovereign voice, treating itself as hypernormative and unmarked, whiteness conceals its status as raciated, located, and positioned. Because of its presumed ahistorical stability and ontological "givenness," whiteness is an appropriate target for genealogical examination. Commenting on the value, aim, and practical consequences of genealogy, Alexander Nehamas, with Nietzsche in mind, writes:

> Genealogy takes as its objects precisely those institutions and practices which, like morality, are usually thought to be totally exempt from change and development. It tries to show how such changes escape our notice and how it is often in the interest of these practices to mask their specific historical origins and character. As a result of this, genealogy has direct practical consequences because, by demonstrating the contingent character of the institutions that traditional history exhibits as unchanging, it creates the possibility of altering them.[6]

Nehamas's point concerning how certain practices attempt to mask themselves is key to understanding whiteness; for the hegemony of whiteness is partly contingent upon its capacity to conceal or mask its own historicity, thus representing itself as universal, decontextual, and ahistorical. With equal insight, Fred Evans writes:

> The values and practices that genealogists evaluate present themselves as "universal" or as "true" in an unqualified sense. By revealing the value-creating power that these values and practices serve and disseminate, however, genealogists show their "grounds" or basis—how it was possible for them to appear universal or true without qualification—and their limits, that is, their necessary partiality. In carrying out this critique, moreover, genealogy itself is a value-creating power, one opposed to the "life-denying" and hegemonic tendencies of practices that the genealogy attempts to critically evaluate and overcome.[7]

Under the spell of whiteness, blacks internalize a set of values and practices that create a form of *self-ressentiment.* In short, blacks become, through a process of white discipline, white indoctrination, and sheer white brute force, a reactive force toward their very own being. One wonders how many Africans fully internalized a negative will to power as they crossed the Middle Passage. As will be shown, Pecola Breedlove fully internalized the seductiveness of white beauty as a form of universal normativity. In Foucauldian terms, Pecola's socially constructed self vis-à-vis whiteness imprisons her body. Her body is trapped, as it were, within an internalized reactive value-creating force of self-denigration. All that Pecola sees is her "ugliness," a construction that is deeply historically embedded in neoclassical conceptions of beauty adopted by both Europe and America. Young Pecola is no match for the powerful aesthetic regime of whiteness. As George M. Frederickson notes: "The milky whiteness of marble and the facial features and bodily form of the Apollos and Venuses that were coming to light during the seventeenth and eighteenth centuries created a standard from which Africans were bound to deviate."[8] In short, Pecola sees herself, judges, condemns, and curses her black body as a result of the internalization of the historical norms of whiteness.

More generally, in my genealogical tracing of whiteness, I will demonstrate how whiteness, as a value code of presumed "universality," serves to create a form of self-hatred in blacks; serves to demonstrate their "natural" inferiority and ugliness; serves to demonstrate that they are bestial by "nature"; serves to demonstrate that they are *not* entitled to any rights; serves to demonstrate that they are "dirty" and "unclean"; and, indeed, serves to demonstrate that they are "subhuman." As a reactive value-creating power, whiteness, and the "architectonics of its theatre," as Luce Irigaray might say, creates a distorted black body/self through the use of theories and practices that ontologize certain distorted conceptions of the black body/self. In this way, whiteness is able to conceal the insidious economy of its hegemonic conceptual seductive practices and get blacks to believe that ugliness and inferiority constitute who they are ontologically. This process is reminiscent of what takes place in Foucault's *The History of Sexuality*, which demonstrates "how members of a society are trained to perceive themselves as having a certain sexual nature through the deployment of theories and practices that define that nature and so determine the realms of the normal and the abnormal."[9] Like the "naturally stupid" and denigrated black body/self under the regime of white racist "scientific" theorizations, sexuality is taken as given, as a thing to be found. Concerning this point, Prado argues that "what establishes the deployed theories and practices as authoritative is that, in being the object of scientific study, sexuality is taken to be something discovered and unveiled rather than constructed and imposed."[10] Whiteness not only functions as the norm for beauty, but it also functions as the norm for reason and rationality and thus as the standard by which black cognitive ability is measured and judged. The norm of whiteness constructs the "inferiority" of the black intellect as an ontological fact which occasions a form of "double consciousness," as Du Bois argues, that creates black self-doubt and lack of self-confidence.[11]

The point here is that black people were subjected to certain regimes of truth that constituted them as *objects*. Within this regime of truth, dialectically, whites constituted themselves as *subjects*. We need to come to terms with how black people made the "truths" of the discourse of whiteness their own "truths." In this regard, what Foucault says in *Discipline and Punish* about the prisoner with regard to panopticism holds true for black people: they are the objects "of information, never a subject in communication."[12] As the "unequals" of whites, blacks are spoken to, not listened to or *communicated with*. Even before the Middle Passage, black bodies/selves were disciplined to be docile. From the moment that the first black body was placed in shackles, it was being disciplined to embrace the "truth" about its "inferiority." Like the disciplined penitentiary prisoner, the black body/self is kept obedient and disciplined by the process of instilling certain beliefs and habits that produce a new subjectivity, a subjectivity which is imbued with a sense of self-surveillance, a mode of seeing blackness through white eyes. This will be demonstrated in the case of Pecola Breedlove.

In *White*, Richard Dyer argues, based upon entries in the *Oxford English Dictionary*, that the earliest example of the word "white" used to refer to a "race" of people was in 1604. He locates its emergence

within the American colonies. The historical tracing of the emergence
of the term "white" used to refer to a group of people within the context of the American colonies, particularly given the atrocious process
of Othering and "cleansing" of nonwhite Native Americans, is very
suggestive. But even prior to this date, "grafting morality through hue
on the skin of the person was already in place in paintings and literature by then, even where no developed notion of race was explicitly in
play."[13] Dyer traces the dynamics of whiteness not only to the beginning of European expansionism, but specifically to the Crusades. Although Dyer is not critical of Christianity in toto, he notes:
"Christianity brought a tradition of black:white moral dualism to bear
on an enemy [the dark Islamic powers] that could itself be perceived
as black. The Crusades were thus part of a heightening awareness of
skin colour difference which they further inflected in terms of moral
attributes."[14]

The point here is that prior to the development of an explicit conceptual apparatus of race, whiteness, as an axiological code (read: good,
religiously privileged, etc.) was already culturally operative. In short,
whiteness already had built into it the dynamic of "Otherization", a
color hierarchy that privileged whiteness and Otherized Blackness.
Commenting upon the cultural tendency of a color-coded axiological
mode of representation before the construction of race as a fixed biological taxonomy of human kinds, historian George M. Frederickson
notes:

> Artistic and literary representations of these distant and exotic peoples
> [that is, sub-Saharan Africans] ranged from the monstrous and horrifying
> to the saintly and heroic. On the one hand, devils were sometimes pic-
> tured as having dark skins and what may appear to be African features,
> and the executioners of martyrs were often portrayed as black men. The
> symbolic association of blackness with evil and death and whiteness with
> goodness and purity unquestionably had some effect in predisposing
> light-skinned people against those with darker pigmentation.[15]

So, as early as the eleventh century, a "racialized" Manichaean world
had already emerged. Whiteness had already begun to express itself in
hierarchical terms. There was not simply color-coded *difference* and
heterogeneity. The above point is important because many historians
and race theorists (Graham Richards, Ivan Hannaford, and Naomi
Zack, for example) argue that the term "racism" has no meaning prior
to the seventeenth or eighteenth centuries, for there was no "race theory" at this time.[16] On this reading, are we to believe that the enslavement of black people prior to the seventeenth and eighteenth
centuries was done without any sense of the hierarchy of whiteness

over blackness? Perhaps it is best that we speak of a kind of "proto-racism." Moreover, even in the absence of an explicit theory of race, this does not change the actions of those white enslavers of black bodies. The process of enslavement was just as brutal and dehumanizing. Lewis Gordon insightfully argues that even if the theoretical apparatus of racism came later that "the concepts were rationalizations of the deeds, but not the source of the deeds."[17] Is it possible that whiteness embodies an historically concrete form of hatred toward the Other, that is, nonwhiteness? Is it thereby parasitic upon nonwhiteness? Whiteness, on this score, then, is life-denying not only in terms of the erasure of nonwhite Others, but in terms of self-erasure. If we take the complementarity dynamic of the self-Other seriously, then the erasure of nonwhite people entails, in some form, the erasure of white people as well. Raising the issue of whiteness as *ressentiment*, Gordon maintains: "It is clear, then, in a wickedly ironic way, that perhaps the world would have been more just if their identity [whiteness] had not emerged since their identity is fundamentally conditioned by hating mine. And why should anyone continue to defend any identity that is premised upon being the primary agent of hate?"[18] Having evaluated the value code of whiteness in this way and, thereby, having revealed its partiality and concrete historicity, does this not create a space for overcoming whiteness? Genealogy, on this reading, might be said to dethrone the value code of whiteness from its presumed metaphysical status, thus revealing it as historically constructed and capable of being overcome.

The disciplinary strategies of whiteness, its aims and objectives were evident during the Middle Passage. During the voyage, Africans (Ashantis, Ibos, Fulanis, and others) were subjected to tight forms of spatialization. Although Foucault did not have black bodies in mind, I would agree where he says that "discipline proceeds from the distribution of individuals in space."[19] The Middle Passage was itself a regime of "truth," teaching the black body/self that it was chattel, bodies to be herded into suffocating spaces of confinement. This was not an issue of how many people could be comfortably accommodated, but how many *things*, owned property, can be stuffed into spaces of confinement. On the slave ship Pongas, for example, 250 women, many of whom were pregnant, were forced into a space of 16 by 18 feet. Feminist and cultural theorist bell hooks writes:

> The women who survived the initial stages of pregnancy gave birth aboard the ship with their bodies exposed to either the scorching sun or the freezing cold. The number of black women who died during childbirth or the number of stillborn children will never be known. Black

women with children on board the slave ships were ridiculed, mocked, and treated contemptuously by the slaver crew. Often the slavers brutalized children to watch the anguish of their mothers.[20]

An African slave trader tells of 108 boys and girls who were packed into a small hole: "I returned on board to aid in stowing [on the slave ship] one hundred and eight boys and girls, the eldest of whom did not exceed fifteen years. As I crawled between decks, I confess I could not imagine how this little army was to be packed or draw breath in a hold but twenty-two inches high!"[21] Molefi Asante captures the terror of the Middle Passage when he writes:

> Imagine crossing the ocean aboard a small ship made to hold 200 people but packed with 1,000 weeping and crying men, women, and children. Each African was forced to fit into a space no more than 55.9 centimeters (22 inches) high, roughly the height of a single gym locker, and 61 centimeters (24 inches) wide, scarcely an arm's length. There were no lights aboard the ships, little food, and no toilet facilities.[22]

The reader should keep in mind that the trip lasted 35 to 90 days, contingent upon the weather. Moreover, the decks where blacks were held were infested with lice, fleas, and rats. Diseased, dead, and dying black bodies were all chained together. My point here is that the sheer nondiscursive confinement of black bodies/selves within these tight spaces, filled with the putrid smell of death, sickness, blood, urine, and feces, was an exercise in the discipline. A new black body/self was in the process of being created and produced, a docile and self-hating body/self. On this score, whiteness, as a site of concentrated power, is *productive*. As Foucault maintains: "We must cease once and for all to describe the effects of power in negative terms: it 'excludes,' it 'represses,' it 'censors,' it 'abstracts,' it 'masks,' it 'conceals.' In fact, power produces; it produces reality; it produces domains of objects and rituals of truth. The individual and the knowledge that may be gained of him belong to this production."[23]

The Middle Passage was a voyage of death, bodily objectification, humiliation, dehumanization, geographical and psychological dislocation. Upon their arrival in the New World, within the economy of commodified black bodies/selves, black people were sold from auction blocks, defined as and treated like chattel. Standing naked on the auction block, witnessed by both white men and white women, the black body was gazed upon and checked and assessed liked a valued animal whose sole function is to be fit to work the land. This form of examination and the objectifying dimensions of the white gaze are part of the overall functioning of the reactive value-creating power of white people. The black body/self became a blood-and-flesh text upon which whites could project all of their fears, desires, *ressentiment*, and fantasies. The exoticizing of the black body involves its scripting as bestial and sexually promiscuous.

Whites were fascinated by the alleged large and "exotic" genitalia of black people.[24] With the help of nineteenth-century white racist biological theories, the black body/self was further discursively marked and produced. The sciences, during American and European slavery, constituted as regimes of discursivity, functioned as forms of normalizing *biopower* and *anatomo-politics* (Foucault's terms). In other words, the objective of biopower and anatomo-politics, at least in this case, was to discipline the black body/self to accept its constitution as "abnormal." Indeed, the objective here was to confirm "scientific truths" both about the ("normative") white body and ("deviant" and apelike) black body. Hence, "truths" about white and black bodies were deemed discovered, not constructed. White power networks, consisting of norms, knowledge claims, and so on, help to produce the myth of the so-called "Negro rapist." One might say that anatomo-politics and biopower are part and parcel of a power/knowledge nexus that "confirms" the rapacious nature of the black body/self.

In 1903, Dr. William Lee Howard argued that Negro males attack innocent white women because of "racial instincts that are about as amenable to ethical culture as is the inherent odor of the race."[25] The physiological basis of the problem of the "Negro rapist" had to do with the enormous size of his penis and that therefore "'the African's birthright' was 'sexual madness and excess.'"[26] Indeed, so it was maintained, the Negroes, by their very nature, are morally retrogressive, physically dirty (a trope of blackness), and morally unclean. In 1900, Charles Carroll supported the pre-Adamite beliefs of Dr. Samuel Cartwright. The Negro was described as an ape and was said to be the actual "tempter of Eve."[27]

The reader will note the lack of Foucault's direct exploration of the raciated dimensions of cleanliness and sexual control as he discusses these issues in *The History of Sexuality, Volume I*. According to Foucault, the bourgeoisie constitute themselves as a special group through their health consciousness and thereby consciousness of their sexuality. Health consciousness about their sexuality replaces the aristocratic emphasis on blood. By controlling their sexual urges, the bourgeoisie come to understand themselves as more vigorous and healthy. They use this to *distance* themselves from the lower classes. The lower classes are not encouraged to engage in these health-related sexual practices. But what would a racial, colonial reading of the health practices of the bourgeoisie suggest? The black body/self, after all, is deemed dirty (often identified with feces) and sexually lascivious, the presumed opposite of the bourgeoisie. My point here is that the discourse of the bourgeoisie is a colonial and raciated discourse, not simply one producing a "pathos of distance" from the working class. In short, constitutive of the bourgeois self is the creation and perpetuation of racial distance. The production of a white bourgeois self, with its emphasis on sexual control and cleanliness, could very well signify the extent to which the bourgeois self is *not* a black self. Anthropologist and historian Ann Stoler argues that "these discourses on self-mastery were productive of racial distinctions, of clarified notions of 'Whiteness' and what it meant to be truly European."[28] She concludes: "These discourses do more than prescribe suitable behavior; they locate how fundamentally bourgeois identity has been tied to notions of being 'European' and being 'white' and how sexual prescriptions served to secure and delineate the authentic, first-class citizens of the nation-state."[29]

The sciences of physiognomy and phrenology, with their emphasis on the prognathous jaw of Negroes, were said to clearly support the primitive nature of African people. In short, the black body/self, within the scientific discursive space of whiteness, which embodied a racist epistemology, was constructed as an object of meticulous scientific "truth." Examining the so-called Negro anatomy, the French physician Pruner-Bey observed:

> The intestinal mucus is very thick, viscid, and fatty in appearance. All the abdominal glands are of large size, especially the liver and the supra renal capsules; a venous hyperaemia seems the ordinary condition of these organs. The position of the bladder is higher than in the European. I find the seminal vesicles very large, always gorged with a turbid liquid of a slightly greyish colour, even in cases where the autopsy took place shortly after death. The penis is always of unusually large size, and I found in all bodies a small conical gland on each side at the base of the fraenum.[30]

The black body/self was also believed to be a site of disease, and, hence, a site of avoidance. William Lee Howard argued: "There is every prospect of checking and reducing these diseases in the white race, if the race is socially—in every aspect of the term—quarantined from the African."[31] Speaking to the American Social Science Association in 1899, Walter F. Willcox maintained "that the liability of an American Negro to commit crime is several times as great as the liability of the whites."[32] The criminalization of the black body/self, as should be clear, did not begin with George Bush's successful political exploitation of the image of William Horton as the black criminal par excellence. The belief that the black body/self was prone to moral and sexual retrogression was supported by those evolutionary theorists who believed that blacks were subhuman brutes and savage beasts. Dr. Paul B. Barringer drew from the Darwinian stress on heredity. According to Frederickson, Barringer argued that "the inborn characteristics of the Negro had been formed by natural selection during 'ages of degradation' in Africa and his savage traits could not have been altered in any significant way by a mere two centuries of proximity to Caucasian civilization in America."[33] The historian Joseph A. Tillinghast also theorized within the framework of Darwinian theory. For Tillinghast, Frederickson writes, "the Negro character had been formed in Africa, a region which supposedly showed an uninterrupted history of stagnation, inefficiency, ignorance, cannibalism, sexual licence, and superstition."[34]

What should be clear is the enormous impact of the biopoliticization of the black body/self, which deploys biological, phrenological, physiological, and evolutionary "truths" to regulate and stigmatize the black body/self. "The discourses of sexuality," as Stoler says, "are racialized ways of knowing that relate somatic signs to hidden truths."[35] Commenting on Foucault's discussion of the body in *Discipline and Punish*, Prado writes that "the power exercised over bodies includes the pronouncements of judges, doctors, and other experts; it includes routines imposed by prison guards and teachers; it includes the approbation and condemnation of peers."

Adding to the list of "authoritative" discourses describing the black body/self are those made by prominent European philosophers. Many European philosophers became seduced by the value code of whiteness and accepted its egregious implications for black people. This is one dimension of what I refer to as the *philosophical* performativity of whiteness. I argue that many European philosophers cannot be disentangled from an antiblack power/knowledge nexus. For example, reason, as deployed by philosophers, is also linked to power, indeed, *white* power. Joe Kincheloe and Shirley Steinberg write:

> As French philosopher Michel Foucault often argued, reason is a form of disciplinary power. Around Foucault's axiom, critical multiculturalists contend that reason can never be separated from power. Those without reason defined in the Western scientific way were excluded from power and relegated to the position of unreasonable Other. Whites, in their racial purity, understood the dictates of the "White Man's Burden" and became the beneficent teachers of the barbarians. To Western eyes the contrast between white and nonwhite culture was stark: reason as opposed to ignorance; scientific knowledge instead of indigenous knowledge; philosophies of mind versus folk psychologies; religious truth in lieu of primitive superstition; and, professional history as opposed to oral mythologies.[36]

Luce Irigaray[37] does a wonderful job of calling into question the history of Western philosophy as an expression of an androcentric discursive field, but she leaves unproblematized, to my knowledge, the power of *whiteness* and how it has structured the history of Western philosophy. Indeed, in the language of Irigaray, to what extent do the "discursive utterances" of white male philosophers conceal racial and sexual conditions under which such utterances are produced? And although Judith Butler, an insightful feminist theorist, has given some attention to white hegemony,[38] one wonders whether she sees whiteness (as she sees gender) as constituted through acts of repetition and performance. One wonders whether white *performativity* acts as the fulcrum upon which turns much of the history of Anglo-American and European philosophy. What is needed is a comprehensive work that examines how whiteness saturates philosophical performativity, how whiteness has specifically shaped the epistemology, metaphysics, ethics, aesthetics, and ontology of much of Anglo-American and European philosophy. Nothing short of a sociology of knowledge of Anglo-American and European philosophy vis-à-vis whiteness will work. After all, Hume, Kant, Locke, and Hegel (to name only a few) are notorious for their belief in the "natural inferiority" of blacks of African descent vis-à-vis white folk. Indeed, within the conceptual frameworks of Hume, Kant, and Locke, the idea of a black philosopher would be deemed a contradiction in terms. After all, philosophy is an honorific term indicative of the presence of the supreme capacity to reason. Blacks, as the racist theory goes (and still believed by many), were incapable of reason. Blacks (and women) were deemed devoid of the capacity for critical cognition. The point here is that the history of Western philosophy's presumed rational objectivity is normatively structured by a color-coded axiological scheme in which whiteness (and maleness) is the socially constructed site upon which "rational objectivity" is predicated. Hence, one might argue that much of Western philosophy's claim to universality functions as a way of *hiding* from its own surreptitious project of color-coded self-erasure, that is, where "universality," as a norm of epistemic certainty, veils the hidden political and ideological *interests* embedded in whiteness.

Despite Hume's rejection of what might be termed a *realist* theory of causality, he was quite certain that blacks were (by nature) inferior. In his essay "Of National Characters," Hume maintains:

> I am apt to suspect the negroes, and in general all other species of men (for there are four or five different kinds) to be naturally inferior to the whites. There never was a civilized nation of any other complexion than white, nor even any individual eminent either in action or speculation.

No ingenious manufactures amongst them, no arts, no sciences. In Jamaica indeed they talk of one negro as a man of learning; but 'tis likely he is admired for very slender accomplishments, like a parrot, who speaks a few words plainly.[39]

Kant appears to been awakened by Hume in some areas, but lulled back to sleep when it came to his own white racism. In his *Observations on the Feeling of the Beautiful and Sublime*, Kant writes:

Mr. Hume challenges anyone to cite a simple example in which a negro has shown talents, and asserts that among the hundreds of thousands of blacks who are transported elsewhere from their countries, although many of them have even been set free, still not a single one was ever found who presented anything great in art or science or any other praiseworthy quality, even though among the whites some continually rise aloft from the lowest rabble, and through superior gifts earn respect in the world. So fundamental is the difference between the two races of man, and it appears to be as great in regard to mental capacities as in color.[40]

Moreover, in reply to advice that a black person gave to Father Labat, Kant commented, "And it might be that there was something in this which perhaps deserved to be considered; but in short, this fellow was quite black from head to foot, a clear proof that what he said was stupid."[41]

And we must not forget Hegel, who strips Africa of any *Geist*. Can it be said that the historicological progression of Spirit is to render Africa enslaved? Emmanuel Chukwudi Eze writes:

It is clear, then, that nowhere is the *direct* conjunction/intersection of the philosophical and the political and economic interests in the European denigration and exploitation of Africans so evident and shameless as in Hegel. Since Africa, for Hegel, "is the Gold-land compressed within itself," the continent *and* its peoples become, all at once, a treasure island and a *terra nulla*, a virgin territory brimming with natural and human raw material passively waiting for Europe to exploit and turn it into mini-European territories.[42]

And concerning the issue of aesthetics, Johann Wolfgang von Goethe writes: "We venture, however, . . . to assert that the white man, that is, he whose surface varies from white to reddish, yellowish, brownish, in short, whose surface appears most neutral in hue and least inclines to any particular and positive colour, is the most beautiful."[43] Certain that there was a correlation between beauty and the power of intelligence, the German philosopher Christoph Meiners maintained that people who were light in complexion were superior and beautiful. Darker people were "deemed both 'ugly' and at best 'semi-civilized.'"[44] Charles White, who was a British surgeon, found fascinating the fact that white women are capable of blushing.[45] White (a double entendre indeed) goes on to ask, "Where, except on the bosom of the European woman, [shall we find] two such plump and snowy white hemispheres, tipt with vermilion?"[46]

It is interesting to note that both Hume and Kant presume to make a cognitively significant assertion: "Black people are inferior." The fact of the matter is that their claim is empty. This reveals just how empty the claims of whiteness are. It also reveals how whiteness's claims about black people only masquerade as cognitive claims. The truth of the matter is that such claims are grounded in emotivity, a certain attitude, a certain way of mythical world-making. For example, though the Jamaican is said to be a man of learning, Hume suggests that he is but a parrot. In other words, the Jamaican is devoid of authentic creativity; he is no better than one who mimics well without the necessary rational (white) hardware that would make him a genuine member of the community of rational and creative language users. And although initially granting that there was something of significance said by a black man, Kant concludes that the fact that he was black is itself clear proof that what he said was indeed stupid.

Clearly, Kant could not have intended the "Humanity as an End in It-self formulation"[47] of the categorical imperative to apply to blacks, given his essentialist views of blacks as an ersatz form of human being. It is interesting that Frederick Douglass used John Locke's theories to declare his self-ownership. With cutting irony, the philosopher Charles Mills notes that this was "the same John Locke who was an investor in the Atlantic slave trade and author of the Carolina Constitution, which—in seeming contradiction to his later prescriptions in the *Second Treatise*—enshrined hereditary slavery."[48] Revealing the color-coded normative assumptions of his liberalism, Locke directly benefited from the sale of black flesh.

The point here is that evidence does not seem to matter to the white racist. Blackness is sufficient evidence that someone is inferior, stupid. Again, Hume and Kant claim to provide a cognitively significant assertion about blacks: S knows that P about Y. However, the assertion is empirically empty where S continues to assert that P about Y, that is, refuses to claim *not-P* about Y, when presented with loads of countervailing evidence against the claim that P about Y. The point here is that whiteness's claims about black people are compatible with whatever happens in the world. Whatever a black does that clearly contradicts the beliefs of the white is simply denied by the white via ad hoc explanations that sustain white lies. No matter the intellectual caliber of the black, no matter how brilliant, his/her blackness occludes the possibility for intelligence. Again, the claim that "blacks are inferior and stupid" makes no real significant assertion at all. Although I will not explore the issue here, this raises the question of how one ought to approach the problem of belief change in the white racist, particularly when his/her assertions about blacks cannot be falsified. If the claims of whiteness are attitudinal, then attempting to "reason" with the claims of whiteness, to *evidentially demonstrate* the intelligence and brilliance of black people, involves a false start. Still all is not hopeless, for there are other rhetorical strategies that one might use to persuade the white racist.

The reader will note that as a reactive value-creating power, white racism (or whiteness) disciplines and shapes black bodies/selves in such a manner that they come to "discover" the "truth" that their moral and physical deformation is inherent. And it is the values and ideas of the reactive value-creating power of white people—whiteness as superior, universally normative, the paradigm of beauty—that determine the kinds of power relations that whites and blacks come to embrace as desirable or undesirable, acceptable or unacceptable.[49] For Foucault, "it is not possible for power to be exercised without knowledge [and] impossible for knowledge not to engender power."[50] In this way, the lynching, burning, beating, raping, and castrating of a black body/self, within the context of the power/knowledge nexus of whiteness, is seen as "justifiable," a logical consequence based upon what is "known" about black people.

What, for example, is the relationship between the enslavement of black bodies; the "scientific" and philosophical support of black "inferiority"; the lynching of black bodies/selves; Jim Crow laws; the Ku Klux Klan; laws requiring black passengers to sit in the back of buses; the Red Summer of 1919;[51] the killing of four young black girls in the bombing of the Sixteenth Street Baptist Church in Birmingham, Alabama, during the '60s; the killing of 14-year-old Emmett Till by white men as a result of his having allegedly whistled at a white woman; the beating of Rodney King; the story of Charles Stuart, a white man, who killed his pregnant wife and blamed it on a black man; the criminalization of the black body/self; racial discriminatory practices in Denny's restaurants; the entertainment phenomenon of blackface; D.W. Griffith's film *Birth of a Nation*; policing the black gaze through the white norm that black men were not to look white men straight in the eyes; racial profiling; and the microracist practices of a white woman clutching her purse as a black male stands with her alone in an elevator? These examples clearly involve a series of aims and objectives structured by a certain white power/knowledge nexus. What holds these examples together is not a deep racial conspiracy, but a systemic white power bloc. In short, (white) power forms a network of relations that are interlocked; indeed, a network of social, economic, and cultural relations sustain white hegemony. As Prado writes, "Power is not knowledge nor is knowledge power. Power and knowledge are the dual aspects of the comportment conditioning environment within which individuals act, and so within which subjects are formed and have their being."[52] As Foucault argues:

> This form of power applies itself to immediate everyday life which categorizes the individual, marks him by his own individuality, attaches him to his own identity, imposes a law of truth on him which he must recognize and which others have to recognize in him. It is a form of power which makes individuals subjects. There are two meanings of the word *subject*: subject to someone else by control and dependence, and tied to his own identity by a conscience or self-knowledge. Both meanings suggest a form of power which subjugates and makes subject to.[53]

The above historical context functions to inform my "textual genealogy" of the life of Pecola Breedlove. The larger historical context provides important background for understanding Pecola as "a meeting ground of investments and privations in the national treasury of [white] rhetorical wealth."[54] Following Foucault's understanding of the socially constructed emergent "self," I will, through Pecola, attempt "to expose a body totally imprinted by history."[55] Within the context of Morrison's *The Bluest Eye*, whiteness is a value code represented as constituting universal beauty. Pecola's body is negatively marked, shaped, and disciplined within a *(generative)* white normative semiotic field.

When viewed from the perspective of the recent plethora of critical work done in the field of critical whiteness studies, Toni Morrison's *The Bluest Eye*, written more than 20 years ago, is remarkably prescient and original in its attempt to locate and interrogate the semiotic spaces and the power/knowledge nexus of whiteness. Of course, it is important to note that black scholars telescoped whiteness as an object of critique long before the emergence of critical whiteness studies. It was a question of their very survival.

Although the textual foreground of *The Bluest Eye* explicitly portrays the body/self deformation of Pecola, the text "pecks away," according to Morrison, "at the [white] gaze that condemned her."[56] In short, Morrison demands that we uncover the secret of Pecola's "ugliness," her psychopathology, by turning our critical gaze toward the constituting activities, and discursive field, of whiteness.[57] But before exploring the impact of the value code of whiteness on Pecola's "lived body," I will briefly explore the larger presuppositions held by Morrison regarding the nature of the self. This excursus will help to create a framework consistent with a Foucauldian reading of the socially constructed self and, hence, help to account for Pecola's psychologically fissured identity.

The very formation of a deformed and fissured identity like Pecola Breedlove presupposes the social constructionist theorization of the self as emergent. In other words, for Morrison, it would seem, the self does not exist anterior to others; it is not a pregiven entity. The self is created and becomes *who* it is within a social matrix that presupposes Otherness. The self is not a stable entity struggling to get out of its skin, as it were, to establish a sense of relatedness. The self is always already socially linked and connected to a broader nexus of social relationships and power relations.

The view that the self is emergent rejects the notion that the self is an enclosed *thing*, a ghost in a machine, whose task it is to transverse its own "inner" space in order to make contact with others and the world. Pecola's identity, as we shall see, is dynamically constituted and shaped by an already existing racist power/knowledge nexus, one that constructs her as the wretched of the earth. Pecola, after all, is factically *thrown (Geworfenheit)* into a prenarrated, racist societal space; indeed, her formative years are spent in Lorain, Ohio, in the early 1930s. Pecola's identity emerges within a context of white racist discourse, mythopoetic constructions, and racist signs and symbols that fundamentally shape how she relates to herself as a subject of a particular kind. Foucault:

> The individual is not to be conceived as a sort of elementary nucleus on which power comes to fasten or against which it happens to strike. In fact, it is already one of the prime effects of power that certain bodies, certain gestures, certain discourses, certain desires, come to be identified and constituted as individuals. The individual is an effect of power, and at the same time it is the element of its articulation. The individual which power has constituted is at the same time its vehicle.[58]

It is Foucault's anti-individualist stance that I find of interest here, not necessarily the implied lack of liberatory discourse. The crucial point here is that the self is not a substantive entity that takes as its first existential project the task of demonstrating epistemic certainty of itself and its world. The self is always already shaped within the midst of the familiar; it is always already situated within a field of objects, signs, symbols, and power relationships. Moreover, the self is always already contextualized, historicized, temporalized, and fundamentally embodied. It is Pecola as embodied, as negatively epidermalized, that is subject to the weight of white power and the white racist gaze. It is her *dark* body, objectified and negatively configured by the normalizing white gaze, and negatively codified by scientific *racialese,* that is the indelible and indubitable mark of her existential and ontological contemptibility. Morrison insightfully characterizes the structure of the white gaze, revealing its powers of racial objectification, during a moment in the text where Pecola goes into Mr. Yacobowki's Fresh Veg. Meat and Sundries Store to buy some candy. Mr. Yacobowki's gaze, his surveillance of Pecola, is a case of gazing with knowledge, which is linked to the power to define. Morrison writes:

> She looks up at him and sees the vacuum where curiosity ought to lodge. And something more. The total absence of human recognition—the glazed separateness. She does not know what keeps his glance suspended. Perhaps because he is grown, or a man, and she a little girl. But she has seen rest, disgust, even anger in grown male eyes. Yet this vacuum is not new to her. It has an edge; somewhere in the bottom lid is the distaste. She has seen it lurking in the eyes of all white people. So. The distaste must be for her, her blackness. All things in her are flux and anticipation. But her blackness is static and dread. And it is blackness that accounts for, that creates, the vacuum edged with distaste in white eyes.[59]

Carrying the weight of internalized white racism and the white gaze, Pecola *knows* the deficits of her black "lived body" all too well. As will be shown, moving in and out of such white racist semiotic spaces, Pecola comes to *know* herself as a raciated object, limited, and somatically uglified. Focusing on the issue of *self-ressentiment* Thomas F. Slaughter argues:

> Between me and the surrounding world there exists a split of which by lopsided social contract, my body is the symbol. Blackness embodies the ostracized. Under the duress of racial domination, I undergo the now familiar two-pronged process of externally imposed inferiorization and subsequent internalization of that inferiority. It is thus probable that in my routine state, I carry White hatred of me within me as my own property.[60]

Pecola's wish for blue eyes is itself a desire to possess property (valued by the aesthetic standards of whiteness) that is fundamentally antithetical to the very being that she is to the world through her body.[61] And it is this body that is held captive, always already prefixed by the white gaze. Concerning this theme of the prefixity, overdetermination, and negative generative dimensions of the black body, Franz Fanon writes:

> I am overdetermined from outside. I am not the slave of the "idea" that others have of me but of my appearance. I move slowly in the world, accustomed now to seek no longer for upheaval. I progress by crawling.

And already I am being dissected under white eyes, the only real eyes. I am *fixed*. Having adjusted their microtomes, they objectively cut away slices of my reality. *I am laid bare. I feel, I see in those white faces that it is not a new man who has come in, but a new kind of man, a new genus. Why it's a Negro!*[62]

Unlike the idyllic (read: white) storybook family narrative that the reader encounters at the very beginning of the text, a narrative that Morrison brilliantly collapses into a maddening stream of sentences without any punctuation, Pecola Breedlove's entrance within the text of *The Bluest Eye*, narrated by Claudia, already indicates significant familial and ontological fractures and fissures: "Cholly Breedlove, then, a renting black, having put his family outdoors, had catapulted himself beyond the reaches of human consideration. He had joined the animals; was, indeed, an old dog, a snake, a ratty nigger. Mrs. Breedlove was staying with the woman she worked for; the boy, Sammy, was with some other family; and Pecola was to stay with us. Cholly was in jail."[63] Adding to an already dismal set of circumstances, Claudia adds, "She came with nothing."[64] Existentially, Pecola is just factically *there*, solitary and destitute. And like the flowers that Claudia later describes as having failed to grow, Pecola is also unyielding and barren. But what is also significant is the reality that Pecola had been put "outdoors." Within the text, being put outdoors signals a profound sense of ostracization. Indeed, it constitutes "the real terror of life."[65]

Capturing the facticity and finality of being outdoors, Claudia says, "But the concreteness of being outdoors was another matter—like the difference between the concept of death and being, in fact, dead. Dead doesn't change, and outdoors is here to stay."[66] So the sense of being outdoors is not just a spatial relationship; it also connotes an ontological stasis, a sense of nothingness. Hence, Claudia's pronouncement that Pecola came with nothing is itself rich with existential themes of dread and meaninglessness. Claudia goes on to say, "Knowing that there was such a thing as outdoors bred in us a hunger for property, for ownership."[67] In other words, in her state of "nothingness," which acts as a trope signifying both race and class, Pecola is desperate for something of value, something that she can own, a piece of property. She hungers for something that will provide her with a sense of being, belonging, and self-value. However, as Pecola fully comes to accept, being black does not confer value; indeed, Blackness is tantamount to being propertyless. On whiteness as a form of property, Cheryl Harris writes, "For the first two hundred years of the country's existence, the system of racialized privilege in both the public and private spheres carried through this linkage of rights and inequality, and rights and property. Whiteness as property was the critical core of a system that affirmed the hierarchical relations between white and Black."[68]

With descriptive clarity, indicating the degree to which blacks were subject to the greedy ways of white landlords, Morrison provides the reader with a view of the depressive physical environment within which Pecola lived. The family is described as "nestled together in the storefront. Festering together in the debris of a realtor's whim."[69] The furniture itself invokes aesthetic disgust: "In the center of the bedroom, for the even distribution of heat, stood a coal stove. Trunks, chairs, a small end table, and a cardboard "wardrobe" closet were placed around the walls. The kitchen was in the back of this apartment, a separate room. There were no bath facilities. Only a toilet bowl, inaccessible to the eye, if not the ear, of the tenants."[70] The furniture is described as having "aged without ever having become familiar."[71] On a Heideggerian reading, familiarity implies a certain quality of being-in, an indication of *lived involvement*. There is even a little artificial Christmas tree "which had been there, decorated and dust-laden, for two years."[72] The environment, like Pecola, is destitute of a positive sense of lived involvement; it is static and invokes a sense of pathos. Again, although nondiscursively, Pecola is marked; she bears the weight of this pathetic environment. But we must not divorce the reality of Pecola's physical environment from the larger context of whiteness. Having received a sofa, damaged during delivery, Cholly is depicted in conversation with one of the white movers:

> "Looka here, buddy. It was O.K. when I put it on the truck. The store can't do anything about it once it's on the truck. . . ." Listerine and Lucky Strike breath.
>
> "But I don't want no tore couch if 'n it's bought new." Pleading eyes and tightened testicles.
>
> "Tough shit, buddy. *Your* tough shit."[73]

The reader will notice the implied reference to blackness as something dirty, as feces. The point here is that Pecola's physical environment is also an important narrative feature undergirding her racial deformation. It is an environment, an unstable enclave, which is itself saturated with poverty resulting from the hegemony of whiteness. So if the physical environment is also a semiotic space of sorts, what impact does this have on identity? What is the impact of a piece of furniture, say, on the morphology and emergence of the self? With phenomenological richness, Morrison writes:

It withheld the refreshment in a sleep slept on it. It imposed a furtiveness on the loving done on it. Like a sore tooth that is not content to throb in isolation, but must diffuse its own pain to other parts of the body—making it difficult, vision limited, nerves unsettled, so a hated piece of furniture produces a fretful malaise that asserts itself through the house and limits the delight of things not related to it.[74]

Combining elements of class, race, and fundamental dimensions of internalized self-surveillance, Morrison writes: "The Breedloves did not live in a storefront because they were having temporary difficulty adjusting to the cutbacks at the plant. *They lived there because they were poor and black, and they stayed there because they believed they were ugly.*"[75]

With the exception of Cholly, the whole family—"Mrs. Breedlove, Sammy Breedlove, and Pecola Breedlove—wore their ugliness, put it on, so to speak, although it did not belong to them."[76] But what is the source of this ugliness? What has created in them the "conviction," as Morrison says, that they are ugly? If the ugliness does not belong to them, to whom does it belong? In a passage rich with figurative language, Morrison provides a glimpse into the heteronomous origins of this conviction. She captures the heart of Foucault's notion that the self is not prior to the effects of discourse. Indeed, as Prado states, "Genealogy, as the analysis of descent, painstakingly exposes the tiny influences on a body that, over time, not only produce a subject of a certain sort, a subject defined by what it takes to be knowledge about itself and its world, but a subject under the illusion that it is a substantial, autonomous unity."[77]

Morrison:

It was as though some mysterious all-knowing master had given each one a cloak of ugliness to wear, and they had each accepted it without question. The master had said, "You are ugly people." They had looked about themselves and saw nothing to contradict the statement; saw, in fact, support for it leaning at them from every billboard, every movie, every glance. "Yes," they had said. "You are right." And they took the ugliness in their hands, threw it as a mantle over them, and went about the world with it.[78]

In other words, the Breedloves are trapped within a semiotic space (or power/knowledge nexus) of white aesthetical ideals. Invoking the image of a master, Morrison is aware of the crippling impact of the institution of American slavery. She is cognizant of how deeply colonialism affects the colonized, creating a split, a doubleness, in their very souls through the construction of a semiotic space designed to "confirm" their colonized status. Morrison is clearly aware of the mutual reinforcement of power and knowledge. "You are ugly people," when applied to black people, carries an epistemic truth-value within a white discursive power/knowledge nexus that already comes replete with its own stipulated criteria for what constitutes beauty. And it is this conception of beauty which is then reified as beauty qua beauty, that is, imagined as separate from the constituting activities of white people. In this way, whites attempt to escape blame for the aesthetic violence that black bodies/selves have been made to suffer. For example, as was suggested earlier, Pecola finds her ugliness confirmed in Mr. Yacobowski's white gaze. In the language of social psychologist Charles Cooley, Mr. Yacobowski (who is said to have blue eyes) is the "looking glass" through which Pecola sees her ugliness confirmed.

The mesmerizing power of whiteness, the sheer weight of its normativity, is clear when Frieda, Claudia's older sister, brings Pecola a snack: "Frieda brought her four graham crackers on a saucer and some milk in a blue-and-white Shirley Temple cup. She was a long time with the milk, and gazed fondly at the silhouette of Shirley Temple's dimpled face. Frieda and she had a loving conversation about how cu-ute Shirley Temple was."[79] Why is Pecola so obsessed with Shirley Temple? What does she see in her? What does Pecola *not* see in herself? Indeed, why does Pecola feel a deep sense of internal vacuity when looking at Shirley Temple? On the view developed thus far, Shirley Temple represents what Pecola is not. Indeed, Pecola's difference is defined relative to Shirley Temple's whiteness. Whiteness is the standard against which difference and Otherness are constructed. As Ann duCille discloses: "This, then, is what pained me about the Shirley Temple films that filled my girlhood: her adorable perfection—her snow-whiteness— was constructed against my blackness, my racial difference made ridiculous by the stammering and shuffling of the 'little black rascals,' 'darkies,' and 'pickaninnies' who populated her films."[80] But it is not just the image of Shirley Temple that holds Pecola's attention; it is also the white substance inside the cup. It is only later in the narrative that we are told that Pecola drank three quarts of milk.

Milk is symbolic of whiteness. It is not out of greediness, as believed by Claudia's mother, that Pecola consumes so much milk; rather, it is out of her need to *become* white through the very act of consuming the milk. It is the power in the whiteness of the milk that Pecola seeks. Perhaps the whiteness in the milk will create a metamorphosis, a transubstantiation, changing her from black to white, from absent to present, from nothing to something. This theme involving the ingestion of whiteness is blatant when Pecola goes to buy some Mary Janes. Even the innocent act of buying candy becomes an opportunity for racial self-*ressentiment* and self-denigration. Something as presumably benign as a candy wrapper functions as a site of white power/knowledge and semiosis. Morrison writes: "Each pale yellow wrapper has a picture on it. A picture of little Mary Jane, for whom the candy is named. Smiling white face. Blond hair in gentle disarray, *blue eyes* looking at her out of a world of *clean comfort.* The eyes are petulant, mischievous. To Pecola they are simply *pretty.* To eat the candy is somehow *to eat the eyes, eat Mary Jane. Love Mary Jane. Be Mary Jane.*"[81] Like the whiteness of the milk, the piece of candy is believed to have the power to effect a genuine state of ontological alterity, changing Pecola from black to white, from a state of fecal dirtiness to *clean comfort.*

The process of blurring reality and fiction, and living in a profound state of bad faith, is sadly executed by Pecola's mother, Pauline. Caught within a world of filmic hyperreality, Pauline, like Pecola, hides from her blackness. She has also become a prisoner of whiteness, shaped and disciplined within its power/knowledge nexus:

> The onliest time I be happy seem like was when I was in the picture show. Every time I got, I went. I'd go early, before the show started. They'd cut off the lights, and everything be black. Then the screen would light up, and I'd move right on in them pictures. . . . Them pictures gave me a lot of pleasure, but it made coming home hard, and looking at Cholly hard. I don't know. I 'member one time I went to see Clark Gable and Jean Harlow. I fixed my hair up like I'd seen hers on a magazine. A part on the side, with one little curl on my forehead. It looked just like her. Well, almost just like.[82]

Like Pecola, shaped by regulating white discourses, Pauline has internalized the fiction that whiteness is supremely beautiful. While at the picture show, she is able to erase her blackness and imaginatively inhabit the filmic space of whiteness. She is able *to be* the luminescent Jean Harlow through a process of supplantation, substituting her blackness with those "appropriate" and "desired" identities created within the cultural space of white aesthetic ideals and epistemological assumptions. It is not only the white images themselves that hold power, but it is also the cultural uses of light, through technology, that constructs white people as hypernormative. Pauline is elevated by the medium of light used to enhance the whiteness of the characters on the screen; she partakes of the humanizing [read: white] and privileging powers of white light. Analyzing how light serves to socially construct the aesthetic value of whiteness, Richard Dyer has argued:

> It is at least arguable that white society has found it hard to see non-white people as individuals; the very notion of the individual, of the freely

> developing, autonomous human person, is only applicable to those who
> are seen to be free and autonomous, who are not slaves or subject peoples.
> Movie lighting discriminates against non-white people because it is used
> in a cinema and a culture that finds it hard to recognize them as appropri-
> ate subjects for such lighting, that is, as individuals.[83]

Dyer's point is that even the technological use of light involves the exercise of *power*. The lighting is a medium of racial structuration, a
technology of discipline that privileges white bodies/selves.

Elaborating on the powerful visual dimensions of Pauline's cine-
matic absorption of the value code of white aesthetics, Morrison is
aware of the plenitudinous character of white light where she says,
"There the black-and-white images came together, making a magnifi-
cent whole—all projected through the ray of light from above and behind."[84] Within a Platonic world, Pauline is like an artist's representation
of a sensible object, a mere copy of a copy. Gary Schwartz suggests this
interpretation when he argues: "Pauline, as the viewer and learner, has
absorbed the visions of light and darkness and becomes the engine of
their reproduction. . . . Wittingly or otherwise, Pauline not only becomes the Imitation but, in turn, imitates it. She is an imitation of an
imitation."[85]

Living her life as a copy of a copy, it is no wonder that Pauline,
when Pecola was born, said that "she looked like a black ball of hair."[86]
Pauline goes on to add, "But I knowed she was ugly. Head full of pretty
hair, but Lord she was ugly."[87] Even that pretty hair will eventually give
way to "tangled black puffs of rough wool to comb."[88] As an ideal servant of whiteness (after all, she does work as a housemaid for a white
family), Pauline plays the part impeccably, superimposing upon Pecola
her own self-hatred. Pauline perpetuates the destructive power/knowl-
edge nexus of whiteness within which Pecola has to develop. As a deli-
cate and inquisitive child, Pecola learns to "read" the negative facial,
tactile, and verbal cues exhibited by her mother, cues that she then
uses to negatively sculpture her own identity. Pecola will later sit for
long hours "trying to discover the secret of the ugliness, the ugliness
that made her ignored or despised at school, by teachers and class-
mates alike."[89] And even when she is "recognized," this further reinforces her status as Other: "She also knew that when one of the girls
at school wanted to be particularly insulting to a boy, or wanted to
get an immediate response from him, she could say, 'Bobby loves
Pecola Breedlove! Bobby loves Pecola Breedlove!' and never fail to
get peals of laughter from those in earshot, and mock anger from the
accused."[90]

As was suggested earlier, Pecola is overdetermined. Claudia relates a story in which she and Frieda found Pecola surrounded by a group of black boys hurling racial epithets her way: "Black e mo. Black e mo. Yadaddsleepsnekked. Black e mo black e mo ya dadd sleeps nekked. Black emo. . . . "[91] Again, whiteness is served. The boys, through their ritual performance of self-*ressentiment*, have demonstrated their effective capacity of negative self-surveillance. Although Claudia and Frieda helped to break the circle of this ritual of self-denial, the theme of self-hatred is subtly and symbolically reintroduced through a mulatto character named Maureen Peal. Maureen, who was only passively watching the incident with the boys unfold, suddenly puts her arm through Pecola's and walks away as if they were the best of friends:

> "I just moved here. My name's Maureen Peal. What's yours?"
>
> "Pecola."
>
> "Pecola? Wasn't that the name of the girl in *Imitation of Life*?"
>
> "I don't know. What is that?"
>
> "The picture show, you know. Where this mulatto girl hates her mother cause she is black and ugly but then cries at the funeral. It was real sad. Everybody cries in it. Claudette Colbert too."
>
> "Oh." Pecola's voice was no more than a sigh.
>
> "Anyway, her name was Pecola too. She was so pretty. When it comes back, I'm going to see it again. My mother has seen it four times."[92]

One significant point here is that the girl in *Imitation of Life* is called Peola, the "c" is absent. Schwartz suggests an interesting line of reasoning: "Pauline puts her own creative imprimatur on this child with a predestined name. The name with the 'c' has some suggestion of Latin *peccatum* (mistake, fault, error) while Peola sounds floral."[93] Through the act of giving her daughter a name that phonetically sounds like "Peola," Pauline has nominally overdetermined her. As it turns out, Pecola and Peola share the reality of internalized racial self-hatred. So although Maureen is mistaken in terms of the correct pronunciation of the name, she is right that Pecola is trapped by whiteness and would rather settle for being an imitation of whiteness than being black. One wonders whether Pauline, by naming her daughter Pecola, wished that her daughter was like Peola, pretty with "white" skin. In any case, Pauline, having been duped by white lies, enabled Pecola's self-hatred; she reinforced and cemented the belief that whiteness is a mysterious *thing* of desirability. But it is Claudia's transgressions against this *thing* of desirability that provide glimpses of the possible source of black self-hatred and perhaps, through "problematization" (Foucault's term), provide glimpses of possible ways of freeing thought *to think differently*. During a heated exchange in which Maureen reveals her own self-hatred, calling both Claudia and Frieda "ugly black emos," Claudia reflects: "And all the time we knew that Maureen Peal was not the Enemy and not worthy of such intense hatred. The *Thing* to fear was the *Thing* that made *her* beautiful, and not us."[94] It is here that Claudia demonstrates an awareness of the particularity (nonuniversality) of white beauty. This *Thing*, this signifier of purity, cleanliness and goodness, is the product of a generative context of white hegemony. This *Thing* is not an ontological notion, but something that grows out of a social nexus of power/knowledge.

The power of whiteness (this *thing*) can also be called upon in hours of need. Whiteness, on this score, is talismanic and soteriological. The theological implications (cf. earlier references to the Crusades) are quite obvious. Pecola firmly believes in the saving powers of whiteness. During a scene in which Cholly and Pauline are having one of their horrendous physical fights, fights fed by long-standing feelings of failure engineered by a society that systematically chisels away at their humanity, Pecola calls upon the omnipotence of whiteness. Claudia narrates, "If she looked different, beautiful, maybe Cholly would be different, and Mrs. Breedlove too. Maybe they'd say, 'Why, look at pretty-eyed Pecola. We mustn't do bad things in front of those pretty eyes."[95] Pecola firmly believes that she, that is, her *blackness*, is responsible for the irascible and violent behavior of her parents. However, it is the internalization of "epistemic violence" that leads her to believe this. Susan Bordo's contention that anorexia nervosa is linked to androcentric disciplinary technologies of the body is key here. For like many who suffer from this condition, Pecola is also subjected to her own "white ghosts" who speak and confirm her wretchedness and ugliness.[96] She *knows* herself as the degraded Other, she *knows* herself as a problem. This knowledge causes her to wish for her own disappearance: "Please, God," she whispers into the palm of her hand, "please let me disappear."[97] This is Pecola's way of attempting to deproblematize her identity, to escape what whiteness has told her is ugly. It is her wish not to be seen as ugly, as black, but as beautiful and desirable. In short, to be seen as *white*.

Pecola does not receive affection from her mother. Pauline's relationship with her children is evident in her requirement that they refer to her as "Mrs. Breedlove." However, the white Fisher family, who describe Pauline as "the ideal servant," are allowed to call her "Polly." Again, it is whiteness that humanizes Pauline. Whiteness also provides her with a false sense of existential meaning and emotional stability:

> Pauline kept this order, this beauty, for herself, a private world, and never introduced it into her storefront, or to her children. Them she bent toward respectability, and in so doing taught them fear: fear of being clumsy, fear of being like their father, fear of not being loved by God, fear of madness like Cholly's mother's. Into her son she beat a loud desire to run away, and into her daughter she beat a fear of growing up, fear of other people, *fear of life.*[98]

In short, similar to the power that Nietzsche says the priestly aristocrats exercised over the knightly aristocrats, Pauline taught Pecola to deny herself and to deny life. And the only time that Pauline seems close to Cholly is when her "flesh is all that be on his mind."[99] It is in these moments of bodily objectification that Pauline is made to believe that she is beautiful: "Not until he has let go of all he has, and give it to me. To me. To me. When he does, I feel a power. I be strong, I be pretty, I be young."[100] Mixed with overtones of masochism, has Pauline come to accept her self-value through her reduction to that of a "fuckee"? Pauline appears to be most happy when she is either under the control of filmic white images or being sexually objectified by Cholly. In either situation, Pauline undergoes a form of erasure.[101] Does Pauline's self-destruction and her desperate need to be recognized, though much to her psychological and physical detriment, result from living within a colonial space of whiteness?

Cholly's affections are also hermetically sealed off from his children: "Having no idea of how to raise children, and having never watched any parent raise himself, he could not even comprehend what a relationship should be."[102] Cholly spends most of his time in a drunken stupor, reflecting the pangs of anger and feelings of rejection: "Abandoned in a junk heap by his mother, rejected for a crap game by his father, there was nothing more to lose."[103] Instead of directing his anger toward the larger white social structure partly responsible for what he has become, Cholly's anger becomes implosive, affecting all those closest to him. But Cholly is known for misplacing his anger. As a young man, while attending a gathering in honor of his recently deceased aunt, Cholly and a girl named Darlene clandestinely went off to copulate. As they began, they were startled by an "invasive presence." The reader will note the overtones of white colonial expansionism: "There stood two white men. One with a spirit lamp, the other with a flashlight. There was no mistake about their being white; he could smell it. Cholly jumped, trying to kneel, stand, and get his pants up all in one motion. The men had long guns."[104] The reader should also note the reference to the effusion of light, reminiscent of Pauline's experience at the movie house. Schwartz, directing attention to the pornographic character of this scene, writes, "Flashlight and Spiritlamp, two sources of white light, looking at what looks most fascinating to them: what is not white. What is not white is obscene."[105] Clearly, Morrison captures the Foucauldian significance of the relationship between seeing and power. Forced by the voyeuristic white onlookers to continue, Cholly could only pretend: "Cholly, moving faster, looked at Darlene. He hated her. He almost wished he could do it—hard, long, and painfully, he hated her so much."[106] Was it not Frantz Fanon who reminded us of how implosive anger can become under the duress of white colonial oppression? Cholly, in other words, is reacting to a reactive value-creating force. "So it was," as Claudia sadly narrates, "on a Saturday afternoon, in the thin light of spring, he staggered home reeling drunk and saw his daughter [Pecola] in the kitchen."[107]

Reeking with self-doubt and self-hatred, feeling like a failure in the white man's world, discarded by his biological parents, and pornographically configured by the white gaze, Cholly undergoes a process of implosion that expresses itself inwardly as well as outwardly: He rapes Pecola. The reader will note that earlier in the text Pecola wonders about the meaning and feeling of love: "Into her eyes came the picture of Cholly and Mrs. Breedlove in bed. He makes sounds as though he were in pain, as though something had him by the throat and wouldn't let go. Terrible as his noises were, they were not nearly as bad as the no noise at all from her mother. *It was as though she was not even there. Maybe that was love. Choking sounds and silence.*"[108] While being raped by Cholly, did Pecola, in her silence, feel loved or was she further silenced and degraded? Was it the first time or were there other times? And like Pauline, her mother, did Pecola feel validated in her denigration? Did Pecola feel "as though she was not even there"? Hence, did she feel loved?

Having been racially Othered, rejected, uglified, put outdoors, and taught to hate herself, Pecola's rape and subsequent impregnation by Cholly decisively broke her fragile spirit, forcing a complete split in the fabric of her psyche. After seeking out a character named Soaphead, who is capable of helping the unfortunate to "overcome Spells, Bad Luck [*blackness*], and Evil Influences," Pecola successfully performs the necessary task that will grant her blue eyes.[109] When the reader encounters Pecola again she is happily engaged in a lively conversation with herself about her new blue eyes:

> Sure it is. Can you imagine? Something like that happening to a person, and nobody but nobody saying anything about it? They all try to pretend they don't see them. Isn't that funny? . . . I said, isn't that funny? *Yes.* You

are the only one who tells me how pretty they are. *Yes.* You are a real friend. I'm sorry about picking on you before. I mean, saying you are jealous and all. *That's all right.* No. Really. You are my very best friend. Why didn't I know you before. *You didn't need me before.* Didn't need you? *I mean . . . you were so unhappy before. I guess you didn't notice me before.* I guess you're right. And I was so lonely for friends. And you were right here. Right before my eyes. *No, honey. Right after your eyes.*[110]

Finally, Pecola has completely undergone a process of psychological transmogrification. Like a bird longing to fly high and envelope itself within the blueness of the sky, Pecola can be observed "beating the air, a winged but grounded bird, intent on the blue void it could not reach—could not even see—but which filled the valleys of the mind."[111] Pecola's tragedy teaches us that at the very heart of the alleged universal value code of whiteness, and the reactive value-creating power that is its source, is the reality of madness. The powerful socially constructed aesthetic allure of whiteness conceals its "ontological misplacement." Whiteness has an ontological structure, but it exists as a social, cultural, psychological, and economic network. Its power conceals its historically contingent ontological nature and cultural particularity. For Pecola, blue eyes were not enough. She was after the bluest eyes, an abstract chimera, an aesthetic and ontological feat achievable, as Morrison makes clear, at the very expense of sanity itself.

In terms of Foucault's conception of power and resistance, the only really resistant voice in *The Bluest Eye* is Claudia's. Not only does she realize that the problem has to do with what she calls this *Thing,* that is, whiteness, but she takes a resistant stance against the seductive symbolic powers of whiteness. Given a white doll one Christmas, she relates:

When I took it to bed, its hard unyielding limbs resisted my flesh—the tapered fingertips on those dimpled hands scratched. If, in sleep, I turned, the bone-cold head collided with my own. It was a most uncomfortable, patently aggressive sleeping companion. To hold it was no more rewarding. The starched gauze or lace on the cotton dress irritated any embrace. I had only one desire: to dismember it. To see of what it was made, to discover the dearness, to find the beauty, the desirability that had escaped me, but apparently only me. Adults, older girls, shops, magazines, newspapers, window signs—all the world had agreed that a blue-eyed, yellow-haired, pink-skinned doll was what every girl child treasured.[112]

Contrast Claudia's outrage and resistance toward white dolls with a story that Frantz Fanon says that he once heard:

I wish to be acknowledged not as *black* but as *white.* Now, and this is a form of recognition that Hegel had not envisaged, who but a white

> woman can do this for me? By loving me she proves that I am worthy of
> white love. I am loved like a white man. I am a white man. Her love takes
> me into the noble road that leads to total realization. . . . I marry white
> culture, white beauty, white whiteness. When my restless hands caress
> those white breasts, they grasp white civilization and dignity and make
> them mine.[113]

In many ways, the person in this story has much in common with
Pecola. Indeed, both have been dutifully disciplined and duped by the
powerful value code of whiteness.

Concerning power, Foucault writes: "Power is exercised only over
free subjects, and only insofar as they are free. By this we mean individual or collective subjects who are faced with a field of possibilities
in which several ways of behaving, several reactions and diverse comportments may be realized."[114] As with the person in Fanon's story,
Pecola does not appear to have access to a "field of possibilities." Historically, there have been many instances of black resistance (Nat
Turner, Denmark Vesey, Gabriel Prosser, Harriet Tubman, and others).
Moreover, many Africans, while crossing the Middle Passage, decided
to throw themselves to the sharks rather than settle for enslavement.

To what extent does Pecola exist within a "field of possibilities"?
Dominated by the value code of whiteness, any other actions on her
part are pretty much null and void. She does not seem to possess the
capacity to negotiate with history. Hence, Pecola appears limited to a
single actuality, the desire to be white. Foucault does admit that "without the possibility of recalcitrance, power would be equivalent to
physical determination."[115] He also writes:

> When an individual or social group succeeds in blocking a field of power
> relations, immobilizing them and preventing any reversibility of move-
> ment by economic, political, or military means, one is faced with what
> may be called a state of domination. In such a state, it is certain that prac-
> tices of freedom do not exist or exist only unilaterally or are extremely
> constrained and limited."[116]

What is problematic here is that Foucault does not seem to allow for
the possibility of *psychological* domination. Pecola is dominated by the
value code of whiteness, a code that has fissured her psychological "in-
teriority." As long as she remains a prisoner to this code, Pecola will
not be capable of "diverse comportments." Foucault does not provide
the conceptual apparatus to effectively explain Pecola's condition. We
need a phenomenology of Pecola's pain and suffering that will take us
beyond the findings of genealogy. Getting Pecola to "think her own
history" is clearly not enough. Genealogy is certainly a powerful tool
that enables us to clear space for seeing how things need *not have been*.

In Pecola's case, however, it is not radical enough. Pecola is in need of deep psychological *liberation*. Although critical of the concept of liberation, Foucault does acknowledge its importance in cases involving colonized people.[117] Again, however, he does not acknowledge the need for specific forms of *psychological* liberation. Colonization is not simply restricted to a set of actions limiting another set of actions; it tears at the very fabric of one's identity. White colonialism establishes its own ideals. Whiteness establishes its own normalizing "truths" which are designed to shape and epistemologically anchor particular ways of knowing and being. Though it is clear that Foucault would not have a formulaic solution to Pecola's situation, he does speak of new pleasures and new bodies. Perhaps by micropolitically examining Pecola's situation, that is, how she has become captivated by the ruse of whiteness, the answer lies in a "counterattack against the deployment" of whiteness.[118] This counterattack as a form of resistance, however, cannot remain at the level of resistance. Simply to resist the hegemonic regime of whiteness is to remain a prisoner to that regime. More is needed. Pecola must also engage in an act of *affirmation*.

So how do we "liberate" Pecola? There is a need to explore, through sustained psychotherapy, the intricate depths of her psychopathology. Psychotherapy, however, must work in conjunction with political resistance, and political resistance must give way to affirmation. She should be encouraged and reinforced to resist the value code of whiteness that has held her prisoner. She will need to conceptually understand how whiteness functions; she will need to see beyond the curtain of whiteness's deception. After all, when it comes to whiteness, there is no great Oz; rather, there are (white) people and their (white) practices backed by institutional and brute force. Her psychological liberation will begin with her rethinking her own individual psychohistory and the history of blacks of African descent more generally. Through the help of genealogy, perhaps she will be able to find a vocabulary to articulate the emergence of whiteness as a façade of universality. In this way, Pecola will be able to disrupt the power/knowledge nexus of whiteness on her body/self. She will come to understand the extent of destructiveness that the desired object of whiteness has had upon her. This, however, is not simply a conceptual endeavor. She will need to explore new and affirmative ways of emoting, feeling, striving, being. This will be done through the appropriation of a new narrative, a narrative of self-love and self-respect; she will come to narrate her identity within the context of a nonwhite hegemonic narrative, a narrative that accents and valorizes (in nonessentialist terms) the ever historically shifting positive modes of what it means to be black. But what specifically awaits Pecola on the other side of liberation? How will she configure her practices of freedom? Does living her body/self as black create new spaces for living aesthetically and ethically? After all, Foucault will not allow for authentic/inauthentic distinctions in terms of an onto-logically core identity. There simply is no authentic/inauthentic self.

For Foucault, once Pecola has genealogically seen through the façade of whiteness, there is no black authentic identity waiting to be discovered. After all, there is no "ontological Black self" which exists beneath the many layers of Pecola's psychopathology. My sense is that Foucault would argue that blackness, like whiteness, is a field of possi-bilities. On this score, when Pecola moves from a desire for whiteness, indeed, from her illness, she will *not* cast off one ontologically core identity for another. And, yet, Pecola does not move from wearing one false mask to wearing another false mask. There is a movement from one construction to the next. A construction, however, is not some-thing that we should understand in a facile manner. Her psychopa-thology, under the regime of whiteness, is very *real*. The white identity that was held up to her as the most glorified object is *real*. Its reality was enacted, represented, embodied, perpetuated, and sustained within a discursive and nondiscursive field that could not be denied. Indeed, it had its psychological and somatic impact. Once she comes to link her identity to a rich black narrative, this new identity, new way of self-comportment, new way of emoting, feeling, this new way of understanding how her identity can be and ought to be hermeneuti-cally mapped onto historical experiences that constitute the wealth of black people, she will come to embody another very *real* identity. Pecola will learn that blackness, though itself a field of possibilities, of-fers narratives that allow for a healthier sense of who she wants to be. Pecola, on this reading, is a relatively open text capable of acts of nar-rative regeneration. Rejecting those narratives resulting from a reactive value-creating force, Pecola will embody affirmative, ennobling narra-tive codes and symbols—*new ways of being in the flesh*—that allow her to further avoid mythopoetic codes created within narrative spaces of white *ressentiment*. She will *reinvent* her identity by inhabiting an en-abling and ennobling space of being loved for who she is/has become.

NOTES

An earlier version of this chapter, titled, "A Foucauldian (Genealogical) Reading of Whiteness: The Production of the Black Body/Self and the Racial Pathology of Pecola Breedlove in Toni Morrison's *The Bluest Eye*," appeared in *Radical Philosophy Review* 4, nos. 1–2: 1-29. I would like to thank philosopher Lewis R. Gordon for his initial praise of this piece.

1. Joseph Rouse, "Power/Knowledge," in *The Cambridge Companion to Foucault*, ed. Gary Gutting (New York: Cambridge University Press, 1994), p. 96.
2. Arnold Davidson, "Archaeology, Genealogy, Ethics," in *Foucault: A Critical Reader*, ed. David Couzens Hoy (Malden, MA: Blackwell Publishers, 1986), p. 224.
3. I would like to thank philosopher Bettina Bergo for providing the following qualification. In a personal communication, she relates: "The point about whiteness 'attempting to hide from its historicity and particularity' is extremely important. And it brings up what I call the 'racist imaginary' or 'imagination' if you prefer a less Gallic term. I think at first whiteness did not need to hide, because it could not see itself; it could not imagine that whiteness was, itself, a construction. And this is what you mean here. But writing 'whiteness attempts to hide from' suggests a degree of development of consciousness that may not have been actual among most Europeans who did not have contact with Africans."
4. Bergo, in the same personal communication, writes: "As I was reading, I thought of a missing 'link' in the European constitution of a 'whiteness,' one that is essential to any study of the operation and self-deployment of a European imaginary, predicated on the primary binary Same-Other: the Jewish Other. For the 'Jew' was white and non-white, and from everything I've studied on this, 'Jews' had 'monstrous' bodies (effeminate, where Africans and then African-Americans and African-Europeans tended to 'masculinateness' in 'monstrosity'); they 'smelled,' they 'reasoned' differently, etc."
5. C. G. Prado, *Starting with Foucault: An Introduction to Genealogy* (Boulder, CO: Westview Press, 1995), p. 52.
6. Alexander Nehamas, *Nietzsche: Life as Literature* (Cambridge, MA: Harvard University Press, 1985), p. 112.
7. Fred Evans, *Psychology and Nihilism: A Genealogical Critique of the Computer Model of Mind* (Albany: State University of New York Press, 1993), p. 14.
8. George M. Fredrickson, *Racism: A Short History* (Princeton, NJ: Princeton University Press, 2002), pp. 59–60.
9. Prado, *Starting with Foucault* short title, p. 97.
10. Ibid.
11. I would like to thank philosopher Clarence S. Johnson for stressing the importance of the connection between white racist denial of black intelligence and how this leads to the phenomenon of double consciousness.
12. Michel Foucault, *Discipline and Punish*, trans. Alan Sheridan (New York: Pantheon, 1995), p. 200.
13. Richard Dyer, *White* (New York, NY: Routledge, 1997), p. 66.
14. Ibid., p. 67.
15. Frederickson, *Racism*, p. 26.
16. Naomi Zack, "Interview with Naomi Zack," in *African-American Philosophers, 17 Conversations*, ed. George Yancy (New York: Routledge, 1998). Actually, Graham Richards is reluctant to use the term "racism" prior to 1850. See his *"Race," Racism and Psychology: Towards A Reflexive History.* (New York: Routledge, 1997), p. 5.
17. Lewis R. Gordon, *Existentia Africana: Understanding Africana Existential Thought* (New York: Routledge, 2000), p. 116.
18. Ibid., p. 117.
19. Foucault, *Discipline and Punish*, p. 141.
20. hooks, bell, *Ain't I a Woman: Black Women and Feminism* (Boston: South End Press, 1981), pp. 18–19.
21. Molefi K. Asante, *African American History: A Journey of Liberation* (Maywood, NJ: Peoples Publishing Group, 1995), p. 61.
22. Ibid., p. 59.
23. Foucault, *Discipline and Punish,* p. 194.

24. Bergo writes: "Black 'genitalia' get doubled by the 'castrated' Jew. The European, or German, imagination called the clitoris 'der jud,' so that masturbation was called 'playing with the Jew,' in a deliberate reference to a truncated penis. In short, the binarism is at play, even if at times in a sort of inversion relative to Black bodies and 'souls.'"

25. Quoted in George M. Frederickson, *The Black Image in the White Mind: The Debate on Afro-American Character and Destiny, 1817–1914* (Hanover, NH: Wesleyan University Press, 1971), p. 279.

26. Ibid.

27. Ibid., p. 277.

28. Ann L. Stoler, *Race and the Education of Desire: Foucault's History of Sexuality and the Colonial Order of Things* (Durham, NC: Duke University Press, 1996), p. 8.

29. Ibid., p. 11.

30. Graham Richards, *"Race," Racism and Psychology: Towards A Reflexive History.* (New York: Routledge, 1997), p. 16.

31. Quoted in Frederickson, *Black Image*, p. 268.

32. Ibid., p. 281.

33. Ibid., p. 253.

34. Ibid.

35. Stoler, *Education of Desire*, p. 204.

36. Joe L. Kincheloe and Shirley R. Steinberg, "Addressing the Crisis of Whiteness: Reconfiguring White Identity in a Pedagogy of Whiteness," in *White Reign: Deploying Whiteness in America*, ed. Joe L. Kincheloe, Shirley R. Steinberg, Nelson M. Rodriguez, and Ronald E. Chennault (New York: St. Martin's Press, 1998), pp. 6–7.

37. For an examination of Luce Irigaray's and Jean-Francois Lyotard's critique of metanarrativity and how this might relate to whiteness, see my article "Lyotard and Irigaray: Challenging the (White) Male Philosophical Metanarrative Voice," in *Journal of Social Philosophy* 33, no. 4 (winter 2002): 563–80.

38. See Judith Butler's *Bodies That Matter* (New York: Routledge, 1993), p. 182.

39. David Hume, "Of National Characters" in *The Philosophical Works of David Hume*, ed. by T. H. Grose (London 1882), vol. III, p. 252n.

40. Immanuel Kant, *Observations on the Feeling of the Beautiful and Sublime*, trans. John T. Goldthwait (Berkeley: University of California Press 1965), pp. 110–11.

41. Ibid., p. 113.

42. Emmanuel C. Eze (ed.), Introduction to *Postcolonial African Philosophy: A Critical Reader* (Cambridge, MA: Blackwell Publishers, 1997), pp. 9–10.

43. Dyer, *White*, p. 70.

44. Frederickson, *Racism*, p. 59.

45. Ibid.

46. Ibid.

47. See Mark Timmons's *Moral Theory: An Introduction* (Lanham, MD: Rowman & Littlefield, 2002), p. 157.

48. Charles Mills, *Blackness Visible: Essays on Philosophy and Race* (Ithaca, NY: Cornell University Press, 1998), p. 199.

49. Gail Bederman, *Manliness and Civilization: A Cultural History of Gender and Race in the United States, 1880–1917* (Chicago: University of Chicago Press, 1995), p. 24.

50. Prado, *Starting with Foucault*, p. 71.

51. As Molefi Asante notes: "The summer of 1919 was called *Red Summer* because there was so much blood shed in violent acts. There were 25 race riots in 1919 alone. The most violent occurred in Chicago, which lasted 13 days. Twenty-three African Americans and 15 whites were killed. More than 300 African Americans and 178 whites were injured. Red Summer was the opening act for the turbulence that was coming in the 1950s and 1960s" (*African American History*, p. 295).

52. Ibid.
53. Michel Foucault, "The Subject and Power," in *Michel Foucault: Beyond Structuralism and Hermeneutics*, ed. Hubert L. Dreyfus and Paul Rabinow (Chicago: University of Chicago Press, 1983), p. 212.
54. Hortense J. Spillers, "Mama's Baby, Papa's Maybe: An American Grammar Book," in *Feminisms: An Anthology of Literary Theory and Criticism*, ed. Robyn R. Warhol and Diane Price Herndl (New York: Routledge, 1997), p. 384.
55. Prado, *Starting with Foucault*, p. 56.
56. Toni Morrison, *The Bluest Eye* (New York: Plume, 1970), p. 210.
57. Toni Morrison, *Playing in the Dark: Whiteness and the Literary Imagination* (Cambridge, MA: Harvard University Press, 1992), p. 90.
58. C. G. Prado, *Descartes and Foucault: A Contrastive Introduction to Philosophy* (Ottawa, Canada: University of Ottawa Press, 1992), p. 159.
59. Morrison, *Bluest Eye*, pp. 48–49.
60. Thomas F. Slaughter, Jr., "Epidermalizing the World: A Basic Mode of Being Black," in *Philosophy Born of Struggle: Afro-American Philosophy from 1917*, ed. Leonard Harris (Dubuque, IA: Kendall/Hunt, 1983), p. 284. 60.
61. Ibid., 284.
62. Frantz Fanon, *Black Skin, White Masks*, trans. Charles Lam Markmann (New York: Grove Press, 1967), p. 116. My emphasis.
63. Morrison, *Bluest Eye*, p. 18.
64. Ibid.
65. Ibid., p. 17.
66. Ibid., pp. 17–18.
67. Ibid., p. 17.
68. Cheryl Harris, "Whiteness as Property," in *Black on White: Black Writers on What It Means to Be White*, ed. David R. Roediger (New York: Schocken Books, 1998), p.18.
69. Morrison, *Bluest Eye*, p. 34.
70. Ibid., p. 35.
71. Ibid.
72. Ibid.
73. Ibid., p. 36.
74. Ibid., pp. 36–37.
75. Ibid., p. 38. My emphasis.
76. Ibid.
77. Prado, *Starting with Foucault,* p. 36.
78. *Bluest Eye.* p. 39.
79. Ibid., p. 19.
80. Ann duCille, "The Shirley Temple of My Familiar," *Transition* 73, no. 1 (1998): 21.
81. Morrison, *Bluest Eye*, p. 50. My emphasis.
82. Ibid, p. 123.
83. Dyer, *White*, p. 102.
84. Morrison, *Bluest Eye*, p. 122.
85. Gary Schwartz, "Toni Morrison at the Movies: Theorizing Race through *Imitation of Life*," in *Existence in Black: An Anthology of Black Existential Philosophy*, ed. Lewis R. Gordon (New York: Routledge, 1997), p. 123.
86. Ibid.
87. Morrison, *Bluest Eye*, p. 126.
88. Ibid., p. 127.
89. Ibid., p. 45.
90. Ibid., p. 46.
91. Ibid., p. 65.
92. Ibid., pp. 67–68.

93. Schwartz, "Toni Morrison," p. 123.
94. Morrison, *Bluest Eye*, p. 74.
95. Ibid., p. 46.
96. Jana Sawicki, "Foucault, Feminism, and Questions of Identity," in *The Cambridge Companion to Foucault*, ed. Gary Gutting (Cambridge, UK: Cambridge University Press, 1999), p. 292.
97. Morrison, *Bluest Eye*, p. 45.
98. Ibid., p. 128. My emphasis.
99. Ibid., p. 130.
100. Ibid.
101. I would like to thank philosopher Linda Alcoff for a counter reading of Pauline's relationship with Cholly. In a personal communication, she writes, "In the description of Pauline's sex with Cholly, I wonder if you read this too negatively. She is getting attention, after all, and a kind of positive valuation in his desire for her. Being sexually objectified is not equivalent to rape. Here is where Sartre's characterization of sexual activity lacks complexity."
102. Morrison, *Bluest Eye*, p. 160.
103. Ibid.
104. Ibid., p. 147.
105. Schwartz, "Toni Morrison," pp. 124–25.
106. Morrison, *Bluest Eye*, p. 148.
107. Ibid., p. 161.
108. Ibid., p. 57. My emphasis.
109. Ibid., p. 173.
110. Ibid., p. 196.
111. Ibid., p. 204.
112. Ibid., p. 20.
113. Frantz Fanon, *Black Skin, White Masks*, p. 63.
114. Foucault, "Subject and Power," p. 221.
115. Ibid.
116. Michel Foucault, "The Ethics of the Concern of the Self as a Practice of Freedom," in *Ethics, Subjectivity and Truth*, ed. by Paul Rabinow (New York, NY: The New Press, 1997), p. 97.
117. Ibid., pp. 282–83.
118. Michel Foucault, *The History of Sexuality, Volume I,* trans. Robert Hurley (New York: Vintage, 1980), p. 175.

6

WHITENESS VISIBLE

Enlightenment Racism and the Structure
of Racialized Consciousness

Arnold Farr

THE CHALLENGE OF RACE

SEVERAL YEARS AGO A colleague approached me and asked: "What do people mean when they say that there are two Americas, one white and the other black?" I tried to explain to my colleague that there is a color line separating whites from blacks in America. This separation is not merely physical or geographical, but is manifest in terms of the distribution of social and economic resources, cultural capital, respect, and opportunities for self-development. My colleague refused to believe that there is such a color line producing radically different experiences of American society. On another occasion the same colleague inquired about my schedule on that day. I explained that I was busy hosting Professor Charles Mills, who was visiting our institution to give a talk on race. My colleague was not familiar with philosophy of race or Africana philosophy. After I explained to him in more detail what philosophy of race was, he proceeded to warn me that we should be careful because "this sounds like what the Nazis were doing." Needless to say, I was quite puzzled by this comment. My colleague's comment was the result of his assumption that because race is a myth, any attempt to explore racial difference could only lead to further conflict between the races. As I tried to explain further that what we are doing is in no way similar to Nazi racist science it became clear that he was simply not hearing me. As I listened to him state his case he became an object of study for me, much like (as I later realized) I had been for him. It became clear to me that this colleague had a thoroughly white way of seeing the world. This colleague was not a mean-spirited racist, but just a white male whose entire epistemic grid for deciphering social data was *too white* to empathize with and comprehend the African-American experience. By "too white" I mean that my colleague's experience of the world as a white male produced a barrier between himself and those who experience the world in black bodies. Such a person tends to speak to and not hear from those whose different bodies have forced them to experience the world differently.

Unfortunately, this kind of anecdote is not an anomaly in academic circles. Those of us who attempt to focus our analytical skills on issues of race, gender, sexual orientation, oppression, and other such issues are often marginalized by unsympathetic or unempathetic colleagues. In this chapter I will focus on the problem of race in academic circles, particularly philosophy. The title of this chapter is partially inspired by Charles Mills's book *Blackness Visible: Essays on Philosophy and Race*. Mills challenges the idea that philosophy is color-blind. I will continue the argument begun by Mills, but from a different angle. Mills's task was to make blackness visible in philosophy. My task is to make whiteness visible.[1] Until recently, whiteness was almost completely absent as a category for study. White identity and all of its parochial concerns were able to hide behind a façade of neutrality or normalcy. As a result of systematic attempts to make blackness and whiteness invisible in philosophy, philosophy has been instrumental not in overcoming the color line in Western societies but in perpetuating this color line and all of the social consequences that come with it. It is strange that a discipline such as philosophy, which concerns itself with wisdom, morality, and the human condition, can exclude the role that race plays in the constitution of consciousness and social order. In this chapter I will lay the foundation for a systematic interrogation of whiteness and the role that it plays in perpetuating the problem of race. My attempt to make whiteness visible will be developed through what I call *racialized consciousness*. This term, as used in this chapter, will replace racism as the traditional operative term in discourses on race. The concept of racialized consciousness will help us examine the ways in which consciousness is shaped in terms of racist social structures. I will avoid the term *racism* because it tends to imply that one has a conscious commitment to race-based discrimination and acts of hate.[2] "Racialized consciousness" is a term that will help us understand why even the

well-intentioned white liberal who has participated in ⸍
against racism may perpetuate a form of racism unintentic

My approach is to begin by examining a case of obviou⸗ ⸍⸗
consciousness in philosophy. Recent literature on racism in philosophy has excavated the hidden racism in the works of some of our most
important philosophers. There is a growing literature on the racism of
such thinkers as Hume, Locke, Kant, Hegel, and others. I will focus on
Hegel since his philosophy represents the culmination of the Enlightenment project and is one of the most systematic philosophies in the
history of Western philosophy. First, however, we must examine the
notion of color blindness in philosophy.

THE MYTH OF COLOR-BLIND PHILOSOPHICAL INQUIRY

Philosophers of African descent have challenged the idea that philosophy, with its alleged ability to construct the view from nowhere, is
capable of a color-blind inquiry into the human condition. Any cursory glance at the history of philosophy would seem to indicate that
race has no place in philosophy. Indeed, philosophy attempts to transcend physical, empirical boundaries for the purpose of discovering
and disclosing some universal Truth that cannot be determined by
material conditions such as race, class, gender, and sexuality. The
human person about whom philosophy speaks is viewed as a brain in
a vat or the thinking stuff in Descartes's skeptical closet, or pure rationality under Rawls's veil of ignorance.

Philosophy's own self-understanding is very problematic for many
of us of African descent who enter the field of philosophy. Philosophy's universal claims about the human condition systemically, systematically, and persistently omit the experience of oppressed social
groups, especially those of African descent. There is no end to the texts
in philosophy that attempt to explain rationality or the development
of human consciousness without considering the ways consciousness
develops in the oppressed. There is an assumption that race has no
place in philosophy. As Lucius Outlaw writes:

> But why bring such a dangerous and seemingly discredited notion as
> "race" into philosophy to be legitimized, even if not "properly" justified,
> in support of a possibly misguided quest to "conserve" racial and ethnic
> groups? For should not philosophizing, as has been claimed for centuries,
> be devoted to setting out principles and norms of reason to guide human
> beings in fashioning their lives through which they can become fully,
> flourishingly *human*? Various philosophers have long argued that if such
> principles and norms—of truthfulness and justice, for example—are to

be binding on all, they must not rest on the valorization and privileging of the norms and life-agendas of any particular groups, races, or ethnicities.[3]

Philosophy's goal of universality forces it to dismiss the particulars of one's existence. The possibility of introducing "perspective" into philosophy undermines philosophy's claim to the privileged view from nowhere. It is feared that once the perspectives of various social groups are introduced, philosophy will find itself struggling to make coherent sense of incommensurate truth-claims. However, as Outlaw goes on to point out, we are biological creatures who are affected by our biological and geographical situations.

One of the tragedies in Western philosophy is the idea that we can somehow approach philosophical inquiry in a disinterested manner. A second problem is the assumption that insofar as we may not achieve a disinterested disposition our interests are still universal. The philosopher tends to assume that his/her interests are universal without carefully examining the biological, geographical, racial, cultural, and class basis for that interest. The view from nowhere is an impossibility because this view is initiated by an interest that has its foundation in the material world of the philosopher. As Charles Mills has pointed out, we are members of various epistemic communities. These epistemic communities influence our interest, and they also determine what questions are important for us. Our epistemic communities also provide us with a basis for evaluating what lies outside of our community.[4]

The idea that our philosophical inquiry begins within the confines of a particular epistemic community, is legitimated by that community, and develops by employing the theoretical tools of that community is an idea that has not yet been well received by philosophers. The idea that philosophical principles are universal and that philosophy itself is color-blind allows the whiteness of traditional Western philosophy to make itself invisible. The task of this chapter is to make the whiteness of philosophy visible. There are many ways this may be accomplished, though it is not possible in the confines of this chapter to discuss or apply all of them. Hence, I will confine myself to the case study of Hegel and the whiteness of *Geist*.

THE WHITENESS OF *GEIST*

Hegel's philosophy is in some ways the culmination of the Enlightenment project. The Enlightenment project is best defined by Kant in his 1784 essay "An Answer to the Question: What Is Enlightenment?" Kant claims that "Enlightenment is man's emergence from his self-imposed immaturity. Immaturity is the inability to use one's understanding without guidance from another. This immaturity is self-imposed when its cause lies not in lack of understanding, but in lack of resolve and courage to use it without guidance from another."[5] There are two features of the above passage that we must keep in mind as we examine Enlightenment racism: the notion of immaturity and the idea of self-imposed immaturity. The first simply refers to a state or condition in which humanity finds itself. This condition could be the result of misfortune. The second idea contains a normative judgment. It implies that some people are immature as a result of choice, moral weakness, or laziness.

In his most racist writings such as the *Anthropology* and the *Observations*, Kant implies that some races are more inclined to laziness than others; indeed, some races are more immature than others. In his 1763 essay *Observations on the Feeling of the Beautiful and Sublime*, Kant writes:

> The Negroes of Africa have by nature no feeling that rises above the trifling. Mr. Hume challenges anyone to cite a single example in which a Negro has shown talents, and asserts that among the hundreds of thousands of blacks who are transported elsewhere from their countries, although many of them have even been set free, still not a single one was ever found who presented anything great in art or science or any other praiseworthy quality, even though among the whites some continually rise aloft from the lowest rabble, and through superior gifts earn respect in the world. So fundamental is the difference between these two races of man, and it appears to be as great in regard to mental capacities as in color. The religion of fetishes so wide spread among them is perhaps a sort of idolatry that sinks as deeply into the trifling as appears to be possible to human nature. A bird feather, a cow's horn, a conch shell, or any other common object, as soon as it becomes consecrated by a few words, is an object of veneration and invocation in swearing oaths. The Blacks are very vain but in the Negro's way, and so talkative that they must be driven apart from each other with thrashing.[6]

Hegel will echo these sentiments in his discussion of Africa in his *Philosophy of History*. This points to two important features of the Enlightenment, the idea of progress and race.

It is no secret that one of the fundamental driving forces behind the Enlightenment was the idea of progress. Kant's notion of maturity implies a progressive development of the human species. Hegel develops the idea of progress in a more systematic manner than anyone else in the eighteenth and nineteenth centuries. The historian Robert Nisbet writes: "In no philosopher or scientist of the nineteenth century did the idea of progress or of unfolding advance through successive stages marked by great civilizations of the past have greater weight than in Hegel's thought."[7] Further, it was Hegel who most successfully merged the concept of race with a universal philosophy of history.[8]

Hegel's philosophy is a developmental one wherein there are two distinct lines of development. The first line of development occurs in the context of metaphysics and epistemology. Here epistemology itself eventually meets its demise as Hegel takes the reader through shapes of theoretical consciousness to a higher level of practical consciousness. This is the movement of the *Phenomenology of Spirit*. This line of development is not of interest here. Our concern is with the second line of development wherein history undergoes stages of development. In human history, *Geist* (Spirit) or world historical essence actualizes itself.

It is the place that certain groups of people or races occupy in this drama of the unfolding of *Geist* that is problematic. In his *Lectures on the Philosophy of History*, Hegel claims that human history begins in Asia and ends in Europe. In light of some of his comments about America it is legitimate to include the United States in this end of history. Of interest here is who gets excluded from history—and why. Hegel's text is a detailed account of the unfolding of *Geist* in different epochs among different peoples or races. It is not possible to present Hegel's entire argument in the scope of this chapter.[9] Here I will focus on the place of Africa in Hegel's scheme.

The place of Africa in Hegel's drama is that Africa has no place at all. Hegel mentions Africa and its peoples only to show why (according to his taxonomy) it has no place in history. What are the conditions for such an exclusion? Hegel attempts to show that because of certain geographical features and group traits, the unfolding of *Geist* has not occurred in that region. Of course, the unfolding of *Geist* is the unfolding of rationality. It is human beings becoming fully human by overcoming nature. Spirit must perpetually gain control over nature. Human history is this struggle between nature and Spirit.[10] In the *Lectures* Hegel's principle of exclusion is the overrepresentation of nature in non-European races.

It is often claimed by defenders of Hegel that his negative, racist comments about Africa must not taint one's view of his general philosophical system. It is very common for students of Hegel and Kant to argue that their negative attitudes toward Africa are personal prejudices that have no implications for the truth of their philosophies. I will address some of the attempts to defend Hegel in more detail later, but there is one issue that must be addressed here. It is a bit disingenuous to claim that the attitudes of Kant and Hegel toward Africa have no relation to their philosophies. Indeed, it is a claim that Kant and Hegel would disagree with. Indeed, Hegel's principle of exclusion is directly derived from his interpretation of the movement of *Geist*, his view of universality, consciousness, and other Eurocentric values.

As Hegel delivers his lectures on the philosophy of history, he applies evaluative, normative concepts and categories, developed elsewhere in his system, to the progress of the species. These concepts and categories have their basis in Greek and European philosophy and are the criteria by which other cultures and peoples are evaluated and excluded from history. In the introduction to the *Lectures*, Hegel writes:

> The peculiarly African character is difficult to comprehend, for the very reason that in reference to it, we must quite give up the principle which naturally accompanies all *our* ideas—the category of Universality. In Negro life the characteristic point is the fact that consciousness has not yet attained to the realization of any substantial objective existence,—as for example, God, or Law,—in which the interest of man's volition is involved and in which he realizes his own being. This distinction between himself as an individual and the universality of his essential being, the African in the uniform, undeveloped oneness of his existence has not yet attained; so that the Knowledge of an absolute Being, an Other and a Higher than his individual self, is entirely wanting. The Negro, as already observed, exhibits the natural man in his completely *wild and untamed* state. We must lay aside all thought of reverence and morality—all that we call feeling—if we would rightly comprehend him; there is nothing harmonious with humanity to be found in this type of character.[11]

Hegel's characterization of African people echoes the widespread sentiment of many thinkers of his time.[12] The negative views of Africa among European thinkers during the seventeenth through the early nineteenth centuries were based on travelogues and the reports of missionaries, both of which are questionable sources. Many of the details discussed in these reports have since been refuted. However, the accuracy of Hegel's sources and his use of them is not at issue here. It is enough that Africa and its descendants are depicted as subhuman.

Hegel's criticism of Africa develops through his comparison of Africa with what is valued in European society, particularly in his philosophy. Of course, this is not in itself a bad thing. The point here is that philosophical discourse is always situated. The principle by which Hegel excludes Africa from world history is the apparent absence of the principle of universality. However, universality is itself a value, a perspective that is questionable. Further, Hegel's view is simply not true about all Africans. Even the most "disturbing" practices of the Africans had some meaning that was not grasped by Europeans. In his discussion of the African "worship of the dead" Hegel writes:

> But from the fact that man is regarded as the Highest, it follows that he has no respect for himself; for only with the consciousness of a Higher Being does he reach a point of view which inspires him with real reverence. For if arbitrary choice is the absolute, the only substantial objectivity that is realized, the mind cannot in such be conscious of any Universality. The Negroes indulge, therefore, that perfect *contempt* for humanity, which in its bearing on Justice and Morality is the fundamental characteristic of the race. They have moreover no knowledge of the immortality of the soul, although specters are supposed to appear. The undervaluing of humanity among them reaches an incredible degree of intensity.[13]

The above passage seems to be a criticism of religious practices in Africa. In the pages where this passage is found, Hegel writes about African cannibalism and other disturbing/non-European practices. Indeed, although some of the practices mentioned by Hegel would appall any "civilized" person, many of them had religious significance. While one may disagree with these practices, one cannot deduce from them contempt for humanity. Further, on what rational grounds can one argue, given their sheer brutality, that the slave trade and the institution of slavery are morally superior to cannibalism? On what grounds can one argue that those Europeans involved in the slave trade did not harbor a barbaric, perfect *contempt* for humanity? Hegel continues:

> Another characteristic fact in reference to the Negroes is Slavery. Negroes are enslaved by Europeans and sold to America. Bad as this may be, their lot in their own land is even worse, since there a slavery quite absolute exists; for it is the essential principle of slavery, that man has not yet attained a consciousness of his freedom, and consequently sinks down to a mere Thing—an object of no value. Among the Negroes moral sentiments are quite weak, or more strictly speaking, non-existent. Parents sell their children, and conversely children their parents, as either has the opportunity.[14]

Hegel's reasoning here is puzzling. One wonders who is worse, the Africans who "cannot help" their lack of moral sentiments or the Europeans who made money off of that lack.

GEIST AND RACIALIZED CONSCIOUSNESS

We see from the previous section that Hegel's attitude toward Africa was very problematic. However, is Hegel's critique of Africa enough to label him racist? Yes and no. With respect to the alleged superiority of Europeans it seems clear that Hegel was a racist. However, he does argue that slavery is wrong in the whole scheme of things and that Africans sold into slavery should eventually be liberated. One might suggest that because Hegel does not argue that Africans are inherently and eternally inferior, he is off the hook. Such a move would be hasty, and unsympathetic to the victims of the long-term effects of racism.

One of the major contributors to the false belief that we are now citizens of a color-blind society—with only a few racists—is the idea that since overt acts of racial discrimination are illegal and frowned upon by the majority of society, racism no longer exists. There is ample evidence that racism still exists in our society. However, the existence of overt racism is not the point of this chapter. The purpose of this chapter is to use Hegel as a case study for the sake of excavating the invisible, tacit form of racism that is racialized consciousness. In this final section I will address some of the attempts to defend Hegel against the charges of racism, and I will develop more fully the concept of racialized consciousness.

Well-meaning interpreters of Hegel are often inclined to defend Hegel against the charge of racism. The problem with this is that these interpreters fail to do justice to the real problem of race in Western philosophy. In his *Hegel on History*, Joseph McCarney writes:

> There is no suggestion in Hegel's account that Africans, or Laplanders are of inferior stock. It is rather that any people would be overwhelmed in their situation: climatic forces are simply "too powerful for human beings". A final point to note at this stage of the discussion is that racist assumptions are not merely otiose in Hegel's argument and lacking in textual warrant. They would also directly contradict the universalism of his philosophy of spirit with its central themes of freedom as the birthright of all human beings as bearers of spirit and of history as the process by which it is won for them. It is true, and only to be expected, that different peoples will at different times exhibit differences in the degree to which they embody and advance these themes. There is, however, no room in Hegel's vision for such radical and elemental divisions between human groups as racists characteristically propose. Indeed, a firmer theoretical basis for the fundamental equality of human beings than Hegelian spirit provides can scarcely be conceived.[15]

The above passage is a classic example of some of the theoretical maneuvers employed by philosophers to rescue Hegel from the charge of racism. Interestingly, Hegel is depicted as a champion of equality. In a sense, McCarney and other defenders of Hegel are right. Hegel's comments may not necessarily be acts of overt racism. In the whole scheme of things, Africans who have been enslaved are supposed to be liberated eventually. Overall, slavery is wrong according to Hegel.

However, while these attempts to rescue Hegel are based on a reasonably accurate understanding of Hegel's intentions, they are misguided and overly simplistic with respect to the ways in which the idea of race is internalized by many white male philosophers and in the social and historical reality of the victims of racism. Further, it is not entirely clear that Hegel was not a racist in the old-fashioned sense of a commitment to the doctrine of Caucasian superiority. One move made in defending Hegel is to emphasize that he is not committed to any notion of biological racial superiority, but that his claims about Africa reflect the effects of geography on the development of Spirit or reason. There is some textual evidence for this view. In his *Philosophy of Subjective Spirit*, Hegel writes: "The difference between the human races is still a natural difference in that it relates initially to the natural soul. As such it is connected with the geographical differences between those environments in which people are gathered together in great masses."[16] This defense is too simplistic and does not get Hegel off the hook; it is geography instead of skin color that shapes the human soul. However, this dichotomy is not so easily achieved. In their notes to these lectures, Kehler and Griesheim write:

> The races are connected with and dependent upon localities, so that no conclusion can be reached with regard to there being an original difference between them. The question of racial variety bears upon the rights one ought to accord to people; when there are various races, one will be nobler and the other has to serve it. The relationship between people determines itself in accordance with their reason. People are what they are in that they are rational, and it is on account of this that they have their rights, further variety being relevant to subordinate relationships. Particular variety makes itself evident everywhere, but such superiority confines itself solely to particular relationships, not to what constitutes the truth and dignity of man. Enquiry into it is therefore of no import or intrinsic interest. Blackness is the immediate outcome of the climate, the descendants of the Portuguese being as black as the native Negroes, although also on account of mixing. No color has superiority, it being simply a matter of being used to it, although one can speak of the objective superiority of the color of the Caucasian race as against that of the Negro.[17]

Here, race (at least as it is related to certain physical features) is the product of geography and climate. Nevertheless, Hegel still uses this to construct a hierarchy between races. It is very clear throughout all of Hegel's writings on race that there is a connection between geography, the formation of race, and the hierarchy of races wherein *Geist* is more manifest in the "superior races."

There is much more that can be said about the place of race in Hegel's system. The problem is very complex and, again, it is not possible to treat in detail in the scope of this chapter. My point here is that we cannot gloss over the fact that Hegel excludes Africa from world history and sees the culmination of history in Europe. As the place where *Geist* has chosen to manifest itself, Europe is the true bearer of the humanity to come. All other peoples must submit themselves to Europe, its values, will, and reason if they are to enter human history proper. Robert Bernasconi writes: "So far as Hegel was concerned Africans did not contribute to history, but they could be integrated into world history by the so-called more civilized peoples using whatever means they judged necessary."[18]

Bernasconi's interpretation is borne out in the following passage from Hegel:

> The same determination entitles civilized nations [*Nationen*] to regard and treat as barbarians other nations which are less advanced than they are in the substantial moments of the state (as with pastoralists in relation to hunters, and agriculturalists in relation to both of these), in the consciousness that the rights of these other nations are not equal to theirs and that their independence is merely formal.[19]

The above passage is a striking testimony to Hegel's commitment to the superiority of one race over another. Hegel legitimates the mistreatment of so-called less advanced peoples. Advanced nations—which happen to be European with the exception of America—by right of their superior status may enslave others. In the *Philosophy of Right* the state is the manifestation of *Geist* or God on earth.

Hegel's philosophy of history makes clear that *Geist* has actualized itself among the Caucasian peoples. As the bearers of *Geist*, white people of European descent are fully human and are entrusted with the task of humanizing the rest of the world. It is strange that this humanizing of the rest of the world may occur through dehumanizing means such as slavery. However, such a view was not uncommon among thinkers like Kant and Hegel. There are several problems that I would like to point out. First, the defenders of Hegel never question his assumptions about rationality, history, or culture. Hegel's view of world history begins with problematic assumptions and is guided by questionable European values. As Bernasconi points out, Hegel's view was not the only possible alternative. Indeed, the overtly racist views of both Hegel and Kant were challenged by some of their contemporaries. Second, the defenders of Hegel never make the connection between Hegel's way of thinking about race and Africa and the unthinkable experiences of Africans who were victims of the transatlantic slave trade. They never take seriously the dehumanizing effects of slavery and racial discrimination. They never consider the long-term effects of racism and racist social structures.

In their zeal to defend Hegel, his interpreters attempt to hide the effect of their whiteness on their approach to philosophy. Their goal (conscious or unconscious) is to make whiteness invisible. That is, in philosophy there is no white perspective but only the universal, impartial, disinterested view from nowhere. However, for those who have been and are victims of racism and its long-term effects, the whiteness of these interpreters is quite visible. Whiteness becomes visible in the very absence of a serious consideration of the problem of race in philosophy.

CONCLUSION: WHITENESS VISIBLE AS RACIALIZED CONSCIOUSNESS

Although philosophers pride themselves on the alleged color blindness of philosophy, such a view is misguided and is indicative of a failure of self-reflection. The whiteness of philosophy is visible in two ways. First, the discipline itself has been dominated by white males. This is clear from any cursory glance at a philosophy text book or any history of philosophy. However, this is not the most problematic feature. The second way in which whiteness is visible in philosophy is in terms of philosophy's attempt to ignore the fact that we are racialized beings. In this sense whiteness is visible as privilege. That is, the ability to ignore race and the impact that it has had on the formation of social consciousness in the West is a sign of white privilege. The so-called view from nowhere in philosophy is the view of privilege. Even the kinds of questions raised by the philosopher are indicative of the degree of social comfort that the philosopher enjoys. In his discussion of Ralph Ellison's *Invisible Man* in his *Blackness Visible*, Charles Mills writes:

> What are the problems that this individual faces? Is the problem global doubt? Not at all; such a doubt would never be possible, because the whole point of subordinate black experience, or the general experience of oppressed groups, is that the subordinated are in no position to doubt the existence of the world and other people, especially that of their oppressors. It could be said that only those most solidly attached to the world have the luxury of doubting its reality, whereas those whose attachment is more precarious, whose existence is dependent on the goodwill or ill temper of others, are those compelled to recognize that it exists. The first is a function of power, the second of subjection. If your daily existence is largely defined by oppression, by *forced* intercourse with world, it is not going to occur that doubt about your oppressor's existence could in any

way be a serious or pressing philosophical problem; this idea will simply seem frivolous, a perk of social privilege.[20]

Mills's point is that one's position in life determines what kinds of questions are important. The kinds of questions that philosophers generally raise reflect a certain degree of social comfort and absence of the immediate threat of dehumanization. Mills, as well as many feminists, argues that we are born into certain epistemic communities. That is, the cultural and social context into which we are born is already constituted by a background of experiences, a particular self-understanding, a web of meaning, expectations, interests, and concerns. This context provides us with a certain trajectory of inquiry that is legitimated by our community.

The assumption that philosophers can engage in a color-blind investigation of the human condition can be made intelligible only by ignoring the human condition. The inquiring gaze of the philosopher must turn upon the philosopher and examine the ways in which our questions are driven by our social location. This social location affects the process whereby we include certain questions in our philosophical inquiry, while excluding others. By and large, white philosophers have failed to subject themselves to the inquiring gaze they have turned on others. This failure to examine the position from which one speaks and the ways in which that position is related to others does not make whiteness invisible, but it does reveal the blindness of the philosopher.

The experience of African-Americans as victims of the color line puts us in a social place different from that of white philosophers. The white philosopher has the luxury of experiencing himself as a human being and not as a raced being or race category. The white philosopher is not reminded of his racial identity on a daily basis. The white philosopher is not forced to question his humanity because of his race. Such luxury allows the white philosopher to think that his questions and concerns are not related to his position as a raced being. We have stumbled into a circle here. The luxury of being able to establish oneself as a human being and not as a raced being is from the beginning the product of racialization. To the extent that the human condition in America is such that black philosophers are not allowed this luxury, the whiteness of philosophy becomes visible. It becomes clear that there is a certain feature of the human condition that traditional philosophy has omitted.

The desire to make universal claims about the human condition has produced and supported racialized consciousness in two ways. First, philosophers of European descent have been too quick to reduce all humanity to their theoretical framework without first seriously challenging this framework. These philosophers develop their "universal" principle in conversation with themselves and then assume that such principles or values are adequate to describe the experience of non-European peoples. As in the case of Hegel, the degree to which non-European peoples do not reflect back to Europeans European values and ways of being is the degree to which they are considered subhuman. Second, contemporary philosophers of European descent continue to labor in a theoretical framework that has never been seriously tested by non-European philosophers.

The difference between historical figures like Kant and Hegel and contemporary philosophers of European descent is that Kant and Hegel attempted to include race in their philosophical systems by constructing a hierarchy of races that placed Africans and their descendants at the bottom. Contemporary Euro/Anglo philosophers attempt to exclude race from their philosophical systems, arguing that race is not relevant. However, the problem is that hundreds of years of white male conquest of non-European peoples has produced a situation that has created significant inequalities among whites and Africana people. This social reality does affect the life prospects of the disadvantaged social group. The task of Africana philosophy is to challenge the premature closure of Euro/Anglo philosophical systems. The theoretical framework of Euro/Anglo philosophy has benefited whites while ignoring the struggles of people of African descent. Hence, philosophy embodies a certain degree of whiteness which must be interrogated. European Enlightenment thinkers defined themselves and their place in history against the backdrop of blackness, an Africanist presence. The construction of whiteness was an unconscious result of the construction of blackness and its alleged negative qualities.

A critique of whiteness and the whiteness of philosophy does not imply that the questions raised by white philosophers are not legitimate or important. It would be a huge mistake for Africana philosophers to attempt to sideline traditional philosophy. The questions raised by Plato, Aristotle, Kant, Hegel, Descartes, Quine, and others are very important questions. However, if the object of study for the philosopher is the human condition, such study must acknowledge that we are constituted as raced beings and that race membership does affect one's opportunities and the ways in which self-consciousness develops. The task before us is to make philosophical theories truly universal and comprehensive by recognizing the ways in which we are situated as philosophers. The discourse that we call philosophy must not be reduced to any one locality but expanded so as to account for all localities.

NOTES

1. In her book *Playing in the Dark: Whiteness and the Literary Imagination* (New York: Vintage Books, 1992), Toni Morrison examines the ways in which white identity is constructed in the American novel against the backdrop of an invisible Africanist presence. Blackness is made invisible for the purpose of making the white hero of the novel visible. However, the white hero does not identify himself as white but as human. The triumph of the white hero is the triumph of humanity. Hence, whiteness is also invisible. Morrison and Mills uncover the black backdrop whereby white identity is constructed. My claim is that as blackness becomes visible it discloses the white identity that was constructed on its back.

2. My attempt to construct a way of talking about racism while avoiding the pitfalls of the term "racism" is inspired by Joel Kovel and Iris M. Young. In her *Justice and the Politics of Difference* (Princeton University Press, 1990), Young examines the role of the body in the formation of social groups and their victimization and oppression. She applies Kovel's three forms of racism to the problem of race. In his *White Racism: A Psychohistory,* (New York: Columbia University Press, 1984), Kovel argues that there are three forms of racism. Dominative racism involves direct domination. Here the victim is not even in possession or control of his or her own body. Aversive racism is manifest in avoidance of the hated race. Metaracism is an unconscious form of racism. The metaracist is no longer committed to the view that his or her race is superior to others. However, the metaracist is unaware of the ways in which structural racism affects his or her decisions and interactions on a daily basis. For example, many well-meaning whites are unaware of the ways in which they benefit from their whiteness. They are quick to claim that since dominative and aversive forms of racism are illegal or have been greatly minimized, we are now in a color-blind society.

3. Lucius Outlaw, *On Race and Philosophy* (New York: Routledge, 1996), p. 9.

4. One may also view white male Western philosophy as a sort of narrative about Truth, reason, humanity, and so forth that assimilates all persons without a serious conversation with the various social groups represented. Human beings are defined by a master narrative that situates persons according to the master's view of rationality. In her *Maternal Ethics and Other Slave Moralities* (New York: Routledge, 1995), Cynthia Willett writes: "A primary target of postmodern critique is what Lyotard terms the master narratives of the Enlightenment and nineteenth-century European philosophy. Behind these narratives lies the narcissistic presumption that one's own standards for the 'progress of mankind' are adequate for the interpretation of alternative cultures. Such a position leads to the perception of non-Europeans as children and/ or subhuman brutes lacking the requisite rationality or moral development to count as mature persons in their own right"(p. 97).

5. Immanuel Kant, "An Answer to the Question: What Is Enlightenment?" in *Perpetual Peace and Other Essays*, trans. Ted Humphrey (Indianapolis: Hackett Publishing Company, 1988), p. 33.

6. Immanuel Kant, *Observations on the Feeling of the Beautiful and Sublime*, trans. John T. Goldthwait (Berkeley: University of California Press, 1960), pp. 110–11.

7. Robert Nisbet, *History of the Idea of Progress* (New York: Basic Books, 1980), p. 276.

8. Robert Bernasconi and Tommy Lott, *The Idea of Race* (Indianapolis: Hackett Publishing Company, 2000), p. ix.

9. In several articles Robert Bernasconi examines in great detail Hegel's placement of different peoples in the history of human development. I am indebted to Professor Bernasconi for providing me with these articles. See Bernasconi, "Hegel at the Court of the Ashanti," in *Hegel after Derrida*, ed. Stuart Barnett (London: Routledge, 1998) pp. 41–63; "With What Must the Philosophy of World History Begin? On the Racial Basis of Hegel's Eurocentrism," *Nineteenth-Century Contexts: An Interdisciplinary Journal* 22: 171–201; "With What Must the History of Philosophy Begin? Hegel's Role in the Debate on the Place of India within the History of Philosophy," in *Hegel's History of Philosophy: New Interpretations*, ed. David A. Duquette (New York: State University of New York Press, 2003), pp. 35–49; and "Krimskrams: Hegel and the Current Controversy about the Beginnings of Philosophy," in *Interrogating the Tradition: Hermeneutics and the History of Philosophy*, ed. Charles E. Scott and John Sallis (New York: State University of New York Press, 2000), pp. 191–208.

10. The struggle between spirit or reason and nature is from the beginning a problematic white male construct that has been used to justify racism and sexism. See Cynthia Willett's *Maternal Ethics and Other Slave Moralities*.

11. G.W.F. Hegel, *Hegel's Philosophy of History*, trans. J. Sibree (London: George Bell and Sons, 1890), p. 97. My emphasis in penultimate sentence.

12. The fact that Hegel's views are consistent with the widespread sentiment of his time by no means constitutes an argument that Hegel should be let off the hook because he is a product of that time. There were also opponents of Hegel's racist views. Hegel's chief opponent was Alexander von Humbolt. Kant's chief opponent was his former student Johann Gottfried von Herder. One will also note that Hume's racism was challenged by his interlocuter James Beatte.

13. Hegel, *Hegel's Philosophy of History*, p. 99.

14. Ibid., p. 100.

15. Joseph McCarney, *Hegel on History* (London: Routledge, 2000), p. 144–45. For similar strategies invoking the use of cultural difference see chapter 1 of Stephen Houlgate's *Freedom, Truth, and History: An Introduction to Hegel's Philosophy* (London: Routledge, 1991). See also W. H. Walsh's "Principle and Prejudice in Hegel's Philosophy of History," in *Hegel's Political Philosophy: Problems and Perspectives*, ed. Z. A. Pelczynski (Cambridge, UK: Cambridge University Press, 1971), pp. 181–98.

16. G.W.F. Hegel, *Hegel's Philosophy of Subjective Spirit*, Vol. 2, ed. and trans. M. J. Petry (Dordrecht: D. Reidel Publishing Company, 1978), pp. 47–48.

17. Ibid., p. 47.

18. Bernasconi, "With What Must the Philosophy of World History Begin?" p. 189.

19. G.W.F. Hegel, *Elements of the Philosophy of Right*, ed. Allen Wood, trans. H. B. Nisbet (Cambridge, UK: Cambridge University Press, 1991), p. 376.

20. Charles Mills, *Blackness Visible: Essays on Philosophy and Race* (Ithaca, NY: Cornell University Press, 1998), p. 8.

7

REHABILITATE RACIAL *WHITENESS?*

Lucius T. Outlaw, Jr.

THE UNITED STATES OF AMERICA, forged out of settler colonies, was established as a nation-state by and for persons who were thought of, and who valued themselves, as being characterized fundamentally by *racial* characteristics symbolized and summarized by the color code *white*. Nation building and efforts to identify, to form and maintain, a U.S. American "white" *race* were co-constitutive processes, so much so that nationality and racialized white supremacy became all but one and the same venture. Consequently, "[f]or over 80% of U.S. history, its laws declared most of the world's population to be ineligible for full American citizenship solely because of their race, original nationality, or gender. For at least two-thirds of American history, the majority of the domestic adult population was also ineligible for full citizenship for the same reasons."[1] The most recent 20 percent or one-third of U.S. history has been conditioned very substantially by efforts large and small scale, including the transformative Civil Rights, Black Power, anti–Vietnam War, and second-wave Women's Rights movements, to restructure the nation-state's social, political, and economic orders so as to realize greater social justice and the benefits and responsibilities of democracy for those long denied them.

Such efforts continue, among them very recent efforts on the part of a significant number of "white" folks, especially—though others, too, are involved—to come to terms with all that is connoted and denoted by the color code white: all that has been, and still is, intended, made possible, enabled, sustained, and ordered by notions of white.

White is a covering notion routinely taken to refer to a variety of characteristics that are thought to have in common the defining property, character, and valorizations of *whiteness*, the base ordering notion being a color term for the visually prominent characteristic of color tone of the skin, though the term was always meant to gather together a number of additional heritable characteristics, physical (hair texture and colors, skull shape and brain size and capacity, facial shape and body builds) and charactological (i.e., moral, mental, intellectual, emotional, developmental, etc.), that were believed to be clustered together and definitive of raciality.

"The Making and Unmaking of Whiteness" conference at the University of California at Berkeley in April 1997 was in many respects a watershed occasion in academic institutions for giving focal, deconstructively critical attention to matters of whiteness *by white folks.* (Nonwhite, "colored" folks have long *had* to give studied attention to figuring out what made white folks tick and to developing strategies for contending with them. Two, among many, especially poignant efforts by intellectuals of African descent are W.E.B. Du Bois's searing 1920s "The Souls of White Folk"[2] and Toni Morrison's deeply probing, possibly retasking effort in critical literary studies *Playing in the Dark: Whiteness and the Literary Imagination).*[3] The publication of essays from that conference[4] is but one of a rapidly growing number of works conveying the articulate considerations, and spurring the efforts, that are now regarded by many as constituting the not quite new academic venture of "whiteness studies" or, as one of the leading participants in and contributors to this venture, David R. Roediger, prefers to refer to the venture, "critical studies of whiteness."[5]

A welcome and long-overdue development. I suspect a great many folks of color agree with me that "it's 'bout time!" For the truth of the matter is that there can and will be no substantial renovative work on notions, instantiations, practices, and institutionalizations of, and "investments" of all kinds in, whiteness without the willing embracing of such ongoing work and of its progress-spurring consequences by those identified and living as white folks.[6] At issue are questions that must be answered by those for whom focal notions of racial whiteness have salience as defining factors of self-and natal reference-group identification and social ordering: namely, whether, for such persons, the phrase "racial whiteness" has viable referents; and, if so, whether it can and should be reworked and rehabilitated and continue to have salience, on what terms, and to what ends; and, at any rate, questions of what we are to make of, how we are to deal with, ongoing invocations of notions of whiteness and of references to "white" folks.

These are not questions for which I, a U.S. citizen of African descent, can provide definitive answers that must be taken up and lived by folks who identify as "white." I do not presume to set the terms and valorizations of white folks' self-identifications; nor am I concerned here to engage in condemnations of folks for being white. We have had more than enough of such color-oriented disrespect, and much worse, in this country. I would have us be done with such business. Rather, I wish to join in and, I hope, make a positive contribution to critical studies of whiteness by exploring questions of prospects for, and possible gains from, reworking and rehabilitating notions of racial whiteness that might aid all concerned in our efforts to realize and sustain in the United States of America more democratically just and stable social, political, economic, and cultural orders that are increasingly more complicated and enriched by a dynamic multiplicity of persons and peoples of various biocultural—that is, racial and ethnic—groupings. For as is generally known, we are living through one of the most profound demographic transformations in our nation-state's history, such that in fewer than 25 years, if present immigration and birth-and-death-rate trends continue, most inhabitants will neither be from, nor trace their ancestry to, continental Europe, the supposed origin of white folks. Soon, gone will be what had been for centuries the demographic base that prompted and facilitated the rationalizations and legitimations of programmatic efforts to achieve and secure white supremacy: the predominance of supposed Anglo-Saxons and of other folks from Europe whose privileged and privileging raciality was signed and symbolized by the color term "white."[7]

Many of the folks involved in critical studies of whiteness do so because they are convinced that reworking notions of whiteness is a necessary requirement if the work of supplanting white supremacy is to continue with ever more success in achieving and sustaining a democratically just racially and ethnically pluralist nation-state. Not all, however, are convinced that notions of whiteness should, or even can, be rehabilitated instead of being abolished.[8] I, on the other hand, am firmly convinced that it is, indeed, possible to rework and rehabilitate notions of whiteness such that they become additional important tools that can be used to "make sense of and effectively intervene in the reimagining of a heterogeneous nation" and to engage in this "reimagining" work as a countereffort to those who continue to imagine the U.S. American nation-state as "an ethnically [and racially] homogeneous group that has been overwhelmed by peoples of different culture . . . a kind of public history that has been repeatedly told from the top down."[9]

The source of my confidence? The success, both psychologically deep and sociologically wide, of efforts to effect what Carolyn F. Gerald termed the "reversal of symbolism" that was the heart and soul project of the Black Consciousness Movements of the '60s and '70s in the United States and elsewhere in the African diaspora: namely, the transformation of the color code black from the vehicle for debased, "zero" images and conceptions of folks of African descent into a unifying, mobilizing vehicle for positive images, conceptions, projections, and political and cultural work of black folks' own best makings:

> Even the word *black* is a translation from the Portuguese slave term *negro*, gone into the English language as Negro. But black is also the generalized term which we use to symbolize unity of origin, whether we are called Anglophone, Francophone, coloured, mulatto, West Indian or American Negro by the white image-makers. *Black* is the highly imagistic term we use to do away with all such divisionary euphemisms. It is the term we use to destroy the myth based on the complex of images which polarize black and white. These images must be mythically torn down, ritually destroyed. . . . Our work at this stage is clearly to destroy the zero and the negative image-myths of ourselves by turning them inside out. To do this, we reverse the symbolism, and we use that reverse symbolism as the tool for projecting our own image upon the universe.[10]

Symbol-reversal work on notions of whiteness, then, I take to be the socially necessary complement to the reversal work on notions of blackness, work that has as many possibilities for success as has been true for the work on blackness.

But why advocate the rehabilitation of whiteness rather than its abolition? Because, I believe, abolition is unlikely and unnecessary. Unlikely because of the social-anthropological significance of the *ordering* forcefulness invested in notions of whiteness and their deployment. That is, one of the most important anthropological needs pursued through the construction and use of such notions as whiteness (and blackness, too) is that of identifying, by way of some salient and shared characteristic(s), all those thought to be and desired as being sufficiently similar and appropriately related (ideally by "blood") as to constitute a social grouping whose members' relations are ordered by priorities of intimacies and obligations so compelling as to define, to substantial degrees, who each person in the group is, who the group is relative to other groupings, and the grouping's raisons d'être for its being and place(s) in the world, thereby defining important aspects of the meanings (past and present) and agenda (future) for the group and its members.

Such notions, strategies, and agendas, are indeed "social constructions," but they are altogether *real* and anthropologically necessary,
though the particularity of the constructions, in response to the historical and circumstantial particularities of the needs, are contingent
and variable. Such efforts are all about social and self-definitions in
meaning making by way of which human social individuals are compelled to forge relations with others in order to reproduce biocultur-
ally and through which they endeavor to endure and flourish *as all too
social beings.* However, since it is clear, I trust, that a drive for racial or
ethnic supremacy is not a genetically encoded and thus ineliminable
aspect of our species being—and with the compelling example of the
enormous transformative work of reversal black folks have achieved
against all the odds—we should be sanguine regarding the possibilities
for rehabilitating whiteness, for, that is, the possibilities for new social
constructions of whiteness that will be of service to the "slow and tortuous progress toward a truly pluralist society."[11]

For unless the new abolitionists of whiteness—of all construals of
notions of raciality—are preparing to engage in full-scale racial
cleansing or equally full-scale enforced "cross-racial breeding" as programs of tyrannical social engineering intended to eliminate distinguishing characteristics heretofore mobilized into projects of racial
formation, we should expect that human beings will continue to draw
resources from racialized and ethnicized biocultural storehouses of
meanings though often in new ways and while making novel additions
to these same reservoirs, resources needed to fashion identities and
strategies for living and enduring in increasingly anthropologically
and dynamically complex social worlds. Successive generations of
folks in the United States will continue to be white, we should expect,
but in ways and on terms often quite different from previous generations of white folks.

This process is already well under way, according to researcher
Charles Gallagher, especially for young white folks who, "born around
1975, grew up with a brand of racial politics and media exposure that
are unique. This generation is the first to witness the full social, political, and cultural effects of identity politics."[12] For this generation, and
for some in older generations, "Whiteness is in a state of change. . . .
The meaning of whiteness is not to be found in any single . . . description . . . of how whites imagine themselves or come to understand their
racial identity. The contemporary meaning is an amalgamation of . . .
white narratives."[13] What I find worthy of note, though, is that these
young folks are not giving up *entirely* on notions of being white, but

are reworking the notions, sometimes to rather great lengths as in the case of "wiggers," that is white kids who act like and "wannabe" black and are derided for this by white (and black) peers, and "wiggahs" or those young white folks who conduct themselves verbally and behaviorally with enough accomplishment—one might even say with enough authenticity—as to be accepted by some black folks as honorary "niggahs" or sho 'nuf intimate insiders.

Well short of this extreme, however, what Gallagher terms a "fundamental transformation" of whiteness is well under way: "The majority of whites in this study have come to understand themselves and their interests as white. Many of my respondents now think about themselves as whites, not as ethnics; they see themselves as individuals who are members of a racial category with its own particular set of interests. They have attached new meanings to being white and have used those meanings as the basis for forging an identity centered around race."[14] Contrary to the "rise of the unmeltable ethnics" of the 1960s and '70s chronicled by Michael Novak,[15] for these young people racial whiteness has supplanted ethnicity as a basis of identification: "The markers of ethnic identity have all but disappeared. A 'subjective belief in common descent' did not exist for the majority of my respondents."[16] And it is Gallagher's judgment that this development has been conditioned substantially by these young people's having been racialized (that is, socialized into notions of raciality) during a historical period in this country conditioned by "the decline of ethnicity, the rise of identity politics, the perception that whiteness is a social and economic liability, and the precepts of neoconservative racial politics."[17]

Notions of whiteness, then, continue to be fashioned and construed in service to projects of social ordering: identity formation for purposes of individual orientation and associative living in concert with others thought to be "like" oneself on important terms. All the more so in a social order that is increasingly diverse racially and ethnically (the decline of ethnic consciousness among white folks notwithstanding) combined with and substantially affecting distributions of power and access to resources among all of these groups.

Under such conditions, I would not expect the new abolitionists to make much headway beyond a small cadre of hypercosmopolite academics. Hence my concern for the work of rehabilitating notions of whiteness in service to reimagining the U.S. American nation-state as a racially and ethnically heterogeneous democracy. And I would have this rehabilitative work proceed on terms and according to an agenda substantially different from those pursued by many who are generally characterized as on the political right: that is, those white folks who are fighting to preserve white racial hegemony in the absence of white supremacy. Persuading a good many white folks to give up this fight will require more than convincing them, as Roediger wishes to do, that they should give up the illusion that being identified as white will produce happiness.[18] In addition, rehabilitative efforts will have to dislodge two other deep-seated sentiments and long cultivated passions as constitutive aspects of lived notions of whiteness: greed and fear—the one giving rise to racialized imperialism in all its manifestations, the other to defensive mobilizations of identities and related meaning configurations that are then put to work making war on other peoples, supposedly in defense though the best form of defense has long been said to be offense.

After the Union victory in the Civil War of the nineteenth century and the successes of the Second Reconstruction of the twentieth, the United States of America is no longer a nation-state explicitly organized as a venture devoted to White Supremacy. I do believe, however, a good many white folks would prefer white racial hegemony, though they are not prepared to argue for it openly. Why this preference, if I am even close to being right? *Fear.* Fear of being "overwhelmed" by racially cultured others. This fear was one of the most deeply felt and widely shared sentiments experienced by the settler colonists from Europe who survived the voyages and resettlement and, especially, by those engaged in the transgenerational enslavement of African peoples: fear of being both similar to (as male, female; adults, children) and profoundly different from the supposed inferior peoples encountered in the New World and mistakenly identified as "Indians" (by European explorers who thought they had found their way to India), and from those encountered in Africa and brought to the New World as slaves; different in terms of physiological characteristics and life-worlds (spoken and written languages, sociopolitical and cultural convictions, behaviors, practices, traditions, etc.).

And what was feared? *Contamination*, genealogically and culturally, by these more or less radically different, presumed inferior non-European Others; fear of *being overwhelmed* demographically; fear of *prospects of diminished socioeconomic existence* if the exploitative dominance and enslavement of the so-called "Indians" and Negroes/Africans were ended; fear of a civilizational *catastrophe* if the presumed superior Anglo-Saxon white race were to "mix" with inferior colored red and black races—*especially* mixing by way of sexual intercourse between males of color and white females, and mixing via social intercourse generally. Strategies of separation were devised and institutionalized, with elaborate supporting rationalizations and legitimations, to prevent such mixings *and* to allow the hyperexploitation of enslaved Africans and their descendants and the genocidal programs perpetrated against native peoples. The elaborations of notions of racial whiteness were devoted to the organization and perpetuation of this apartheid social ordering and exploitation and to the perpetuation of racialized groupings across spaces and times.

Though White Supremacy is no longer the reigning public philosophy, nor an explicit agenda for any except certain extremist white nationalist groups, a great deal of whiteness-racialized sociocultural and political-economic inertia continues to play out in notable patterns and agendas—in civic and social, political, and economic institutions and organizations; in the ebb and flow of neighborhood life; in the forging of relationships with significant others, especially those that give rise to the production of succeeding generations—that are a direct consequence, a legacy, of centuries of racialized White Supremacy as a nation-state project. And because this inertial racialism of white predominance is no longer legitimated by a public philosophy conveyed by key figures in roles crucial to the definition and maintenance of orderings of social realities, it is especially insidious; the lack of public legitimacy has simply thrust it deeper, to be insinuated in life-world convictions and practices while largely unacknowledged, masked, and even denied in the face of a now predominant public philosophy of antiracism and fair equality of opportunity (and of unequal outcomes—acceptable as long as these outcomes are to the advantage of white folks; hence the opposition on the part of a majority of white folks to affirmative action endeavors).

Here, then, is the rub: the inertia of white racialism and white racial predominance while our nation-state is being transformed demographically into one in which predominance by number belongs to persons of color, a great many of whom understand themselves to be, and value themselves as, constituents of distinct peoples. Should we not expect that, as a very likely consequence, a great many white folks will once again react out of fearful concerns for their demographic situation and that the consequent judgments they come to regarding the implications and possibilities for their well-being will involve efforts to reinvigorate notions of racial whiteness?

They shall, and are, if the research by Gallagher noted earlier is a definite indication. The conservation of racial whiteness has not ceased to be a driving concern for many white folks, nor, by my lights, does it seem something that is about to be given up by them, the injunctions of abolitionists of racialism to the contrary notwithstanding. Indeed, articulations and embracings of white racial identity have become serious quests for many young nonethnic white folks. In this they are motivated, I think, by those previously mentioned anthropological needs (social needs deriving from our species being, as it were) driving social life-world *ordering* efforts (though the needs do not necessitate any particular meaning configuration for the ordering projects). These needs have become more pronounced in the contemporary postapartheid United States as prevailing demographic and political complexities and dynamics have shifted. I am speaking of the anthropologically necessary, socially mediated needs for place and person-securing identity-with-similar-others in a historical circumstance conditioned substantially by an intense "politics of identity and recognition" and by subsequent felt needs for transgenerational, transhistorical, transgeographic sociality of the kinds sought and gained, more or less, in collectives and associations characterized as races and ethnie, tribes, clans, poli, peoples, and nation-cum-nation-states.[19]

Such needs, I believe, help to explain the inertial persistence of racial/ethnic groupings, the heterogeneity of the designated populations notwithstanding, though in such heterogeneity the groupings are now characterized by historic degrees of "mixing."[20] Servicing such felt and cultivated needs is what gave rise to and sustained the dynamic (changing), complex racial and ethnic patternings of social life in the United States of America, among white folks in particular (patterns of schooling, housing/neighborhood choices, partner selection, etc.), racialized and ethnic patternings (though also conditioned by other variables such as realities and aspirations regarding education, income levels, social class, religion, etc.) that set determinate but leaky limits on flexibility regarding, and willingness to endure challenges to, the predominance—or the loss—of the complex, dynamic repertoires of identity-defining and sustaining characteristics constitutive of racial/ethnic biocultural whiteness. In the new, more diversity-complex demographic situation, notions of whiteness are available, certainly, though circumstances will not permit a return to White Supremacy.

What, then, is to be done, should be done? Continuing the work of critical studies of racial whiteness, intensified and broadened to include many more folks who are or would be white (and to include nonwhite folks, as well, who join in the work as supportive critics and critical supporters), but with the clear commitment to exploring and adopting the real prospects and possibilities for renovative reconceptualizations and revalorizations of racial whiteness as an identity-setting aid to group formation and culture making *without aspirations for White Racial Supremacy or hegemony*. Matters of the particular positive, constructive race-formational aspects of whiteness, what the forms and instantiations of transformed, rehabilitated notions of whiteness must be, I must entrust to my white consociates. I offer, however, encouragement and support and the lessons from the continuing work of reversals of symbols and of lived experiences of black folks engaged in rescuing and rehabilitating ourselves and our peoples on behalf of a world made more humane and just.

More and more folks are joining in the critical work on whiteness. Roediger, for example, believes that in this work "the first and most critical contribution lies in 'marking' whiteness as a particular—even peculiar—identity, rather than as the presumed norm."[21] Well, yeah. But it was not just a *presumption* that whiteness was normative,—it was indeed the case legally, even constitutionally, and was reconfirmed and sustained *for centuries* through instantiation in the specification and regulation, formal (i.e., legal) and informal, of all of the relations definitive of social life, from the most formal to the most mundane. These specifications and regulations became what social scientists would come to characterize as the etiquette of race relations in conditions of racialized white supremacy.

Indeed, "marking" the whiteness at play in the myriad structurings of social life is important work of critique as prelude to either abolition or rehabilitative transformation. Such critical marking is ongoing, several manifestations of which are the discussions of the "transparency" and "invisibility" of whiteness to many white folks that allow them to enjoy the privileges of whiteness without a concomitant sense of responsitility, as well as discussions of the "historically located, malleable, and contingent" nature of whiteness.[22] Ideas of "transparency" and "invisibility" have come to have significant prominence these days as characterizations of experiences of whiteness. Perhaps this prominence is justified; I must leave this to white folks to confirm or disconfirm. However, if confirmed, such modes of experience must be understood in strict keeping with a guiding notion of critiques of whiteness: that the latter is, indeed, historically contingent and malleable. For experiences of whiteness as transparent and invisible are likely to be much more characteristic in postapartheid conditions in this country than in earlier conditions: that is, after substantial dismantling of the formal institutions and explicitly racialized and regulated practices of segregated race relations governed by agendas of White Supremacy; after the "White" "White Only" and "Colored" or "Negro," "Colored/Negro Only" signs have come down.

For during the long period of postslavery formal apartheid, white folks marshaled and invoked their whiteness in myriad ways as the powerful identification card that it was. Visibility and recognition as *white*, consciousness of the ability—the *power*—to marshal and invoke *whiteness*, and to require that it be recognized and deferred to as supreme, were normal routines and assumptions structuring daily life. Invisibility and transparency are conditions of significantly different historical, social, political conditions. Thus, the workers in whiteness studies should not take postapartheid modes of experiencing whiteness as constituting its very essence, their salutes to notions of contingency, malleability, and social construction notwithstanding. Perhaps talk of privileged experiences of invisibility and transparency is by those white folks who are themselves the privileged offspring, later descendants, or raced inheritors of the social order of those who constructed and maintained projects of racialized White Supremacy, efforts that required constant vigilance and self-consciousness while constructing and sustaining lifeworlds in which subsequent generations of folks made white could, indeed, take their whiteness for granted because normalized?

I am thoroughly convinced that while notions of *race* do change, and have changed substantially even during my lifetime, and notions of racial whiteness are being subjected to substantial reconsideration, there is no real prospect—let alone a viable possibility—that ordering schemes of meanings and practices, of consciousness and behavior, of racial whiteness will soon be things of the past.[23] Rather, I expect that the demographic changes under way will generate fearful concerns for many white folks which will be experienced as needs for increased racial solidarity and the consolidation of power and resources in order to protect themselves from feared domination by peoples of color when they (colored folks) predominate demographically. For out of such predominance may well come, over time and with appropriate consciousness-raising, organization, and mobilization, including coalition building, the political predominance of peoples of color—unless the terms of political representation and voting have been changed to support proportional representation of racial/ethnic groups. (Stay tuned: Lani Guinier may well become white folks' most sought-after consultant.) The sociocultural and economic changes as a consequence of this political predominance will likely be quite stupendous. As most white folks are still recognizably white folks, though there have been substantial progressive changes in recent decades to conceptions of whiteness that must be duly noted, and appreciated by all, I think it unwise, even foolish, to expect that such folks will not be recognized as "white" over the next several decades of U.S. history. Moreover, I think it disrespectful, even antihuman, to advocate, let alone demand, that white folks repudiate *all* claims on and embracings of identities and legacies defined, more or less, in terms of racial/ethnic whiteness when they do so while repudiating the very idea of white supremacy. Racial whiteness without white racial supremacy or hegemony in a just and democratic, racially and ethnically heterogeneous nation-state would constitute successful rehabilitation, indeed! And with that, what possibilities for our nation-state?

NOTES

1. Rogers M. Smith, "Beyond Tocqueville, Myrdal, and Hartz: The Multiple Traditions in America," *American Political Science Review* 87, no. 3 (September 1993): 549.
2. W.E.B. Du Bois, "The Souls of White Folk," in *W.E.B. Du Bois: Writings*, ed. Nathan Huggins (New York: Library of America, 1986), 923–38.
3. Toni Morrison, *Playing in the Dark: Whiteness and the Literary Imagination* (Cambridge, MA: Harvard University Press, 1992).
4. Birgit Brander Rasmussen, Eric Klinenberg, Irene J. Nexica, and Matt Wray, eds., *The Making and Unmaking of Whiteness* (Durham, NC: Duke University Press, 2001).
5. David R. Roediger, *Colored White: Transcending the Racial Past* (Berkeley: University of California Press, 2002), p. 15. In the section "Nonwhiteness, History, and the Critical Study of Whiteness" in the book's first chapter, "All about Eve, Critical White Studies, and Getting Over Whiteness," Roediger provides a very helpful "brief account of the way studying white identity has come into vogue in the recent past and of the far longer and more important tradition of such study by intellectuals of color," an account especially rich in annotated briefs of a substantial number of published essays and books devoted to critical explorations of matters of whiteness.
6. For an especially insightful and informative discussion of investments in whiteness, see George Lipsitz, *The Possessive Investment in Whiteness: How White People Profit from Identity Politics* (Philadelphia: Temple University Press, 1998).
7. For a sobering critical historical reconstruction of projects devoted to the formation and legitimation of "Anglo-Saxon" white racial supremacy in the United States—and throughout the world, as some involved proposed—see Reginald Horsman, *Race and Manifest Destiny: The Origins of American Racial Anglo-Saxonism* (Cambridge, MA: Harvard University Press, 1981).
8. David Roediger has been one of the most persistent and prominent among the "new abolitionists." In this regard, see, especially, his *Toward the Abolition of Whiteness: Race and the Making of the American Working Class* (New York: Verso, 1994).
9. Vron Ware, "Perfidious Albion: Whiteness and the International Imagination," in *The Making and Unmaking of Whiteness*, ed. Birgit Brander Rasmussen et al. (Durham, NC: Duke University Press, 2001), p. 208.
10. Carolyn F. Gerald, "The Black Writer and His Role," in *The Black Aesthetic*, ed. Addison Gayle Jr. (Garden City, NY: Doubleday, 1971), pp. 375–76.
11. Ware, "Perfidious Albion," p. 211.
12. Charles A. Gallagher, "White Racial Formation: Into the Twenty-First Century," in *Critical White Studies: Looking behind the Mirror*, ed. Richard Delgado and Jean Stefancic (Philadelphia: Temple University Press, 1997), p. 9.
13. Ibid., p. 6.
14. Ibid., p. 7.

15. Michael Novak, *Unmeltable Ethnics: Politics and Culture in American Life*, 2nd ed. (New Brunswick, NJ: Transactions, 1996), and *The Rise of the Unmeltable Ethnics: Politics and Culture in the Seventies* (New York: Macmillan, 1972).
16. Gallagher, "White Racial Formation," p. 8.
17. Ibid., p. 7.
18. "What I propose . . . is to think . . . about how the *nation* can become something other than white and how these people who are tempted to identity as white can be, as Franklin Rosemont puts it, 'disillusioned' regarding that identity and its alleged ability to produce happiness." Roediger, *Colored White*, p. 17.
19. For an interesting discussion of the "politics of identity and recognition" see the lead essay on the subject by Charles Taylor and essay responses by a number of accomplished thinkers in Amy Gutman, ed., *Multiculturalism and "The Politics of Recognition": An Essay by Charles Taylor* (Princeton, NJ: Princeton University Press, 1992).
20. "One of the results of the 2000 census is that it became clear that America is far more of a melting pot than it may have imagined. . . . Coupled with changing social attitudes towards race, people today are far more likely than their ancestors to have children of mixed ethnic backgrounds. While this is certainly a good thing socially, leading to the breakdown of racial stereotypes, it does mean that our genetic identities are becoming ever more closely entwined. Admixture is destroying the old, regional patterns of genetic diversity, replacing them with cosmopolitan melting pots of markers. . . . The patchwork quilt of diversity that has distinguished us since human populations started to diverge around 50,000 years ago is now re-assorting itself, blending together in combinations that would never have been possible before." Spencer Wells, *The Journey of Man: A Genetic Odyssey* (Princeton, NJ: Princeton University Press, 2002), 193–94.
21. Roediger, *Colored White*, p. 21.
22. Martha R. Mahoney, "The Social Construction of Whiteness," in *Critical White Studies*, ed. Richard Delgado and Jean Stefancic (Philadelphia: Temple University Press, 1997), p. 330.
23. "Whiteness has functioned both as a category . . . and as a consciousness" (Roediger, *Colored White*, p. 22).

8

CRITICAL REFLECTIONS ON THREE POPULAR TROPES IN THE STUDY OF WHITENESS

Lewis R. Gordon

MY AIM IN THIS CHAPTER IS to explore three dominating themes of whiteness studies: (1) the notion of "white privilege," (2) the notion of victimization as a characteristic of the relationship between whites and communities of color, and (3) the academically popular notion that the concept of race, divorced from the illuminating ascription of social constructivity, leads to consequences both epistemologically false and ethically misguided. More, this collection of tropes stimulates political responses that are contradictory to its goals in that whites are expected to respond to a situation for which they are claimed responsible while facing structural arguments that militate against the agency required for such responsibility. The result in such an aim-inhibiting situation is one, as Du Bois observed little more than half a century ago in his reflections on black petit-bourgeois consciousness, of standing still in many forms—a condition wrought, inevitably, with guilt.[1]

THE NOTION OF WHITE "PRIVILEGE"

The notion of white privilege depends on the argument that white supremacy is a structural feature of contemporary global politics, and more specifically, the cultural reality of North American, European, and Australian societies. The impact of this politics is the institutionalization of white supremacy in the governments and societies on those continents. White supremacy entails a radical inequality between whites and other groups in every aspect of social life, from the distribution of wealth to the evaluative force and significance of the self. The accumulation of such endowments is an economy of possibilities wedded to power of skin, an epidermal reality constitutive of a social role and identity the lived reality of which requires a bevy of invisible, suffering souls amid penumbrae.[2]

Must it be the case, however, that a structural reality that places a particular group at an advantage over another group constitutes a "privilege"? The term itself has an intriguing etymology. From the Latin *privus*, meaning "one's own," conjoined with *lex*, meaning "law," it means to exempt oneself from laws applied to others. The moral significance should be obvious here in that from a deontological or Kantian point of view it is a blatant violation of the second formulation of the categorical imperative. Recall that the categorical imperative is the moral law, and in Kant's use of "law," this means having no exceptions. In the second formulation, a kingdom of ends or rational beings would be compromised if any member were to make him or herself an exception since that would subordinate others into a means to his or her end.[3] From a Kantian point of view, a privilege as a rule of society can be advanced as a political practice, but it would be a severely limited one in that it would fall seriously short of normative legitimacy or moral soundness. Ironically, the notion of privilege could also fail from a utilitarian and virtue perspective as well. From a utilitarian point of view, the *rule* or principle of utility could have the consequence of one *having* a privilege (say, for the welfare of the community), but the conditions that make that privilege emerge are not one's own. In other words, its rationalizations are by definition beyond one's own law, which could mean the odd consequence of an individual or group being the recipients of an unwanted privilege. (I will leave aside here the problem of whether a privilege is *in itself* and *by itself* patently against a community's interest, which would mean that it could never be grounded as a principle *of utility*, since it is already demonstrated here that in either case, it cannot be grounded as a rational principle by the recipient alone without paradox.) With regard to virtue ethics, a similar problem arises: To cultivate oneself as an exception requires appealing to a rule that transcends one's exception to that rule.

Although these remarks on the performance of a privilege as a law of morality or a principle of social welfare pertain to their logical viability, they tap, as well, into a problem faced by people who find themselves in advantageous circumstances into which they have been born. They have an ascription that they could not, and indeed did not, *will*. This is not to say that a form of agreement with it, perhaps even enjoyment of it, could not occur and constitute a form of *willing* by virtue of approbation. Such a case would be an act with its own moral significance. But the one I am interested in is the case in which the individual does not want the privilege, is disgusted by the privilege, and may find him- or herself in a struggle against it. Such an individual sees himself or herself living a mundane life in which notions of privilege fall sway to notions of human fragility. What he or she looks for in life are things that it would seem unimaginable for other people to reject: safety; food, clothing, and shelter; education through which each generation can achieve its potential; positive aesthetic imagery to transform spaces into places, dwellings into homes; a positive sense of self; and meeting another human being with whom to build and share these features that mark the transformation of a human world into a humane one.[4] Yet this is the problem with the notion of white privilege, for it is to the achievement and reception of these features of contemporary societal life that the charge is made. But these features are not just *any* features of contemporary social life; they are features the absence of which can lead to claims of human rights violations by whoever limits them. These goods are, in other words, *human rights*, and as such, the term "privilege" runs counter to their normative import since such rights are by definition imperatives that apply to and for *all human beings*. In effect, the constitution of these goods as privileges would mark a serious problem in society itself, and most critics of whiteness who advance this notion argue just that—there is a serious problem in, say, American society of that sort.

There is, however, another dimension of the problem of privilege, but it is not of the kind that one might immediately expect. The immediate expectation is that it is a problem of their availability to a particular class or group—namely, whites—instead of to all humankind, and there the argument would pertain to dignity: the making of others "lower" than whites constitutes a harm against their dignity. Another problem to consider is that of making a human right a privilege in the first place. To do that would mean to diminish the value not only of other human beings, but also of the notion of rights. It would require eliminating rights/privilege for the sake of a leveled playing field (the absence of privilege) that awaits *below*. But that would mean to lower the standard of rights, which would defeat the purpose of rights, for rights are, after all, advanced in an effort to *raise* the standards of the human world. Ortega y Gasset identified this problem well in *Revolt of the Masses* when he argued that the purpose of ruling is to set standards by which human beings should live.[5] The problem with white *supremacy* is that it would be by definition a standard that only a certain group of human beings could possess, but even worse, they could do so without *performance* but simply by birth. Internal to white supremacy, then, is a form of white leveling in which a form of massism appears since distinction as a function of performance would have been eliminated between whites and other groups; "any" white would function as the equivalent of "all whites" *as superior*, however underachieving that white may be. To put it differently, white supremacy is by definition not meritocratic. It is a lowering of standards—at least standards of performance.[6]

Consider the familiar conflict over the expectations of, say, a college education versus that of an Ivy League education or one at a first-tier school. Although a convincing argument can be made that all members of contemporary society need to have a college level of education, the opposite is the case for, say, having a degree from the college of one's *choice*. It may be disappointing to have got into Princeton but not Harvard, but how, in the scheme of things, is Harvard a "right"? One could see, immediately, another difference between privilege and right. A privilege is something that not everyone needs, but a right is the opposite. Given this distinction, an insidious dimension of the white-privilege argument emerges. It requires condemning whites for possessing, in the concrete, features of contemporary life that should be available to all, and if this is correct, how can whites be expected to give up such things? Yes, there is the case of the reality of whites being the majority population in all the sites of actual privilege from prestigious universities to golf clubs and board of directors for most high-powered corporations. But even *among whites* as a group, how many whites have *those* opportunities?

The white-privilege argument creates an imaginary ideal whiteness as the norm for all whites, and this ideal stands in opposition to things black in a similar, closed way. Whites become all things that blacks are not and vice versa. Thus, the larger populations of whites find themselves structured as a reality that has nothing to do with their lived experience. Harvard and Yale and the social pedigree they offer, as in Cambridge and Oxford in the United Kingdom, or Queens and McGill in Canada for that matter, only work as a function of excluding most of the population. The availability of excellence in education does not, however, rely on those institutions, and that there are fields in which the best institutions that offer their study are also those more egalitarian in their practice and promise serves to substantiate the point of those institutions standing more like icing on the proverbial cake or excess than need. To make *those* institutions the true mark of whiteness introduces the performance question of getting into them (raising the standards), but there are whites who don't care about getting into first-tier institutions and are instead concerned with their daily, means-to-means subsistence. For such whites, nothing they have acquired is a privilege but a right. And in fact, they often harbor resentment against those other, genuinely privileged whites because, in the end, those whites often have the privilege of mediocrity—which is always a privilege since it would be odd to exempt oneself, at least in Socrates's view, from virtue or excellence—insofar as they are able to rely more on their institutions and pedigree than their performance. For everyday white people, the logical response should not be to eliminate or make them feel guilty for what they have but to transform the mechanisms of access so such things—rights—are really available to all.

VICTIMIZATION AS A CONDITION OF OPPRESSION—A CRITIQUE

Just as the notion of privilege obscures the discussion of racism by making it impossible to do anything about it—how, after all, could one give up a privilege that is literally in one's skin?—the equating of oppression with victimization limits the options available to oppressed people. In other words, the notion itself exemplifies a form of oppression.

Returning to etymology, the word "victim" emerges from the Latin word *victima*, which means "beast for sacrifice." Here, one could readily see the tragic dimensions of victimization by virtue of the etymology of "tragedy," which is from the Greek *tragōidia*, literally the conjunction of *tragos* (goat) and *ōidē* (song). The links between victim and scapegoat reveals the tragedy in all tragedies—namely, the suffering of the innocent. This conclusion is, however, the problem with victimization as a model of oppression. For what should be done with cases in which the suffering individual is not an innocent one?[7] Is it analytically the case that suffering is a constitutive feature of all innocence? Would it then be the case that he or she who does not suffer cannot be oppressed? Or even more enigmatic, could there be a form of oppression that exists in spite of the absence of *experienced* suffering?

Many of these questions are a function of the advancement of suffering, which is an experiential term. It is from the Old French word *sofrir*, which is derived from the Latin *sub* (underneath) and *ferre* (to bear). The familiar connections with the scapegoat or sacrificial beast becomes clear, as well as the string of connotations in the Greek version marked by their word for suffering—namely, *pathos*. For the ancient Greeks, compassion for another's suffering elicits sympathy (*synpathos*, suffering with another), but by the time we get to the Romans, there is the Latin *pietas* (dutiful conduct), from which we get the contemporary word, saturated with patronizing connotations—*pity*. Is pity what oppressed people want?

A noticeable feature of the terms of this etymological exercise is the peculiar absence of a familiar feature of oppression: its peculiarly institutional form. Within such institutions, certain individuals may take advantage of the imbalance of power afforded by their social roles and wreak havoc on another individual, the consequence of which is suffering. But this is not always so. There are individuals who could live as a member of an oppressed group within an oppressive system and never experience an instance of suffering by the direct deed of an individual from the oppressing group. We could call this the anonymity of oppression. In such an instance, the oppressed and the oppressor are estranged from each other. The problem, then, with the model of victimization is that it means that in order to be identified as oppressed, one must both be suffering and innocent and have a victimizer. That would, however, create a circumstance in which guilt of any sort of the oppressed would render their claims of oppression void. In such instances, the demand of innocence would have the consequence of a red herring by putting the claimant on a form of trial instead of examining the status of the claims made. This creates an untenable situation, at least with adult populations, for how is it possible to have an entire adult population of innocents? Although it is true that the various European empires and their American offspring have brought trails of death in their rise and decline, it is also true, as Hannah Arendt has shown, that such processes have unfolded in a world of complicity even among their victims.[8]

Yet oppressed groups do make a special kind of claim. All oppressed groups lay claim to possessing something that nonoppressed groups (usually oppressors) claim to have exclusively, and that is their humanity. Implicit in all oppression is a special kind of inequality; it is inequality over the conditions by which everyday life can be lived. They are demanding their right to an everyday mode of existence. To illustrate, think of the distinction between options and choices. *Options* are those objective features of our environment, whether material or social, that are available to us. Although I say "material" and "social," the impact of options is such that they could become one, for a social world with limited options is as material as a brick wall in its effect. *Choices* are what we make in relation to the options available. When there are many options, our choices appear isomorphic with them to the point of its appearing inconsequential to distinguish between options and choices. For a god, for instance, all options are choices since the mere making of a choice creates a reality. For a human being, however, options are exhausted by our finitude, and we eventually find ourselves making choices that exceed our options. When directed out at the world in which we are socially impotent, such choices become fantasy, hope, or wishes. Eventually, we discover that we have a set of choices that are also inward-directed; at least, we think, we can affect ourselves. Those choices begin to constitute a world of the self. They convey who we are by virtue of *how* we respond to our situation of limited options. These choices lead to a phenomenon that I have coined elsewhere as "implosivity."[9] It is the all-too-intense inward-directed exploration of the self that is a function of social impotence.

There is no reason for inequality in itself to be a problem. There are simply many things that some individuals can do better than others. Where difficulties emerge is when a shift emerges in which (1) limitations are imposed on the options available to one group over another, (2) what is *ordinarily* expected exceeds the options available to the group on which the limitations are imposed, and (3) the existence of imposed limitations are denied. In the first instance, members of the imposed-upon group find themselves exhausting their outward-directed effectiveness quickly and soon begin an exploration of inward-directed choices. For the second, the ordinary becomes an *extraordinary achievement* because it requires achieving an equal effect with fewer options.[10] Third, if we deny that there are limitations imposed upon some members of a group versus others, then we are compelled to conclude that it is they, not their circumstance, that limits them.[11] In effect, we would have created a theodicy of our system or economy of distributing options. Although a theological term, theodicy (from the Greek *theos* [god] and *diké* [justice]), meaning *God's justice*, asserts itself as the grammar of modern rationalizations of justice where the societal system becomes the substitute for God. Under such instance, it is not simply that the system is just and right, but that it *must be so*. If that's the case, then evil, injustice, and suffering must be outside of the system. Put differently, since the system cannot be at fault, responsibility for the limitations imposed upon oppressed peoples must lie with themselves.

The problem for the oppressed subject, however, is that he or she lives the contradiction of the theodicean thesis every day. The implosivity of oppressive life is such that individuals blame themselves with inward-directed choices all the time in the face of the limitations encountered in outward-directed choices/actions. It is no accident that oppressed people tend to treat their bodies as whole canvasses on which to express their creativity. Their bodies—themselves—exemplify the scope of their power, which, from the standpoint of a social world that mediates power relations as far as the entire globe, means that they are without power. They become their own prisons, which makes their efforts to reach out to the social world constantly jeopardized by the appearance of force instead of power. What's the difference between the two? Force requires the physical reach of one's own body. Power transcends that reach because of its ability to affect the mechanisms of the social world. A powerful person can, for example, make a decision in one part of the globe that affects many people at another part. This is why, try as we might, none of us are as powerful as government executives (presidents, prime ministers, commissars, kings, and queens), and although celebrity may occasion a listening ear everywhere, the rituals and processes of command at the disposal of an executive have more severe consequences of life and death.

Oppressed people usually lack power, and when they have power at all, its reach is not very far. Michel Foucault's observation in *Discipline and Punish* that power has been dispersed in the modern world into micro regions provides insight into how many of us inhabit the social world; without any power, our reach and consequence disappear.[12] Individuals who suffer that fate find themselves in a circumstance aptly described by Kevin Bales as being "disposable people."[13] Although individuals within an oppressed group can at times acquire a great deal of power—for example, Disraeli in Victorian England or Colin Powell in the contemporary United States—that power rarely translates into the group, for that individual stands as an exception instead of the rule. Because of this exceptionalism, the *group* remains limited in an insidious way: the exception stands as further rationalization of the supposed absence of limits. This is a tortuous situation to be in, for *not succeeding* is hardly a rational imperative to place on individuals who may emerge as exceptions, but the point, at least from the perspective of the oppressed, is that the exception should count for something other than the viability of the system—and that is as evidence of the potentials of the group; in other words, within his or her group the exception is not necessarily so exceptional, but outside of the group, such a narrative is needed to maintain an oppressive order.

Another consideration. The link between victimization and innocence leads to a narrative that befits children, for who exemplify innocence more than they? Oppression, however, is a circumstance that affects adults. It is not that children do not suffer or are not exploited, and it is not that they are never agents with moral responsibility. The reality of guardianship, however, still lays the trail of responsibility for the welfare of children to adults. Adulthood for oppressed groups is, however, an achievement challenged by an oppressive society. As Frantz Fanon famously observed in the sixth chapter of *Black Skin, White Masks*, an antiblack society has no coherent notion of a normal black adult.[14] With adulthood comes absolute instead of limited responsibility for one's actions, and with such responsibility comes the loss of innocence.

NORMALITY AND NORMATIVITY

Our discussion of victimization and innocence raises the question of normality and normativity. The attack on white privilege and the reality of oppression connect in the concept of white normativity. White normativity is the schema in which whites serve as the exemplification of the human being and the presumption of what it means to be human. Consider, for example, the use of supposedly race-neutral terms such as "woman," "man," "girl," "boy," "child," and "one." The impact of white normativity is readily apparent in that these terms, with very few exceptions, stand for white exemplars wherever there is the absence of an adjective designating color. There is, in other words, a parenthetical "white" before each of these terms—that is, (white) woman, (white) man, (white) girl, (white) boy, (white) child, and the anonymous (white) one. How often is "the reader" in literature expected to be, if not white, at least a white perspective? This is not to say that it is impossible for these terms to designate a multiracial and multiethnic community of agents, but where normativity is the factor, it is unlikely.

Normativity is a perversion of normality. In Fanon's reflections, the goal is not to get rid of normality.[15] If that were the case, notions of therapy and liberation would lose meaning since abnormality would reign, and since communities of color are already derailed by white normativity, they would simply have been "cured" and "liberated" by virtue of being considered abnormal by the dominant group. One would, in other words, have normalized abnormality. Normality, however, stands as the healthy functioning of a subject. It does not signify the "ideal," which implies a subject who functions perfectly. It simply stands as a general theme of good functioning with aims or "purpose" that are not inhibited or thwarted. We see here the connections with rights to an everyday existence in our preceding discussion of privilege and our critique of innocence. Normality does not require perfection;

it requires, simply, good functioning or what can reasonably be expected of every member of a species. It is from that basis that we are able to determine concepts like the extraordinary and underachievement. Normativity is a perversion of this process because it eliminates performance or actions from the subject and collapses the concept of normality into the subject itself. What this means is that there becomes no criterion under which that subject can become abnormal except by becoming another subject. And the same applies to those outside of the sphere of normativity; they can become normal only by becoming other than they are. The result is thus as follows: Blacks could become normal only by becoming white; and whites can become abnormal only by becoming black. The problem, in other words, is that there is nothing one can *do* under such a schema that is not an affirmation of two Manichean poles.

SOCIAL CONSTRUCTION OF RACE—A CRITIQUE

A difficulty in analyzing notions of normality is that the "normal" is not an intrinsic feature of the natural world.[16] In the natural world, things simply are, and for a time they continue to be by virtue of either their own life span or their ability to reproduce (if they are living). If we ascribe values to such phenomena and their processes, we collapse into what C. W. Cassineli has described as "Hitler's logic."[17] Such a logic ascribes superiority to what is and inferiority to what either cannot be or has passed out of being. Values are linked to meaning, and meaning is a function of signs and symbols and their grammar or rules of usage that make them communicable. Without such systems, they are merely pragmatic with a tinge of hedonism: we enjoy what works out, and we suffer from and learn to avoid what does not ("Eat this, but make sure not to eat *that*"; "Stay off the moors at night!"). But the irony of our ability to enjoy things that are not good for us, and even those things that might make us suffer, brings the force of meaning to the fore. What is meaningful for us is already constitutive of my use of the object pronoun "us." Meaning and the language in which it is embedded are functions of a social world. The social world is, however, a fragile world premised upon the intersubjective web of intentions and their intended features. This means, as Alfred Schutz so aptly observed, that the social world, like normality, is an *achievement*, and although we are all born into this achievement, the achievement of its continuity and adaptation is a function of our participation in this world, a world of selves and others.[18] Whiteness, then, as a system of meaning and identity is an achievement.

It is constructed by the societies in which we live, or as it is often put in contemporary academic parlance, it is a social construction.

The portrait I have just given is not, however, the way in which whiteness is often discussed and criticized in whiteness studies and critical race theory, and this is because of the prevailing way in which race is generally treated in at least the North American academy. A simple experiment illustrates this point, and I encourage readers who are academics to try it. Whenever I speak to students on the subject of race, I usually begin by asking them what race is. With few exceptions, students simply respond, "Race is a social construction." The expression has acquired recitational force; simply recite it and the good student will be left alone. But what happens if we do not leave such students alone? What if many of us, as I have, then ask the students two questions: (1) What does it mean to say that race is a social construction? and (2) Do you believe it? The answer I often get for the first question is that race does not exist. But the second question usually jolts them. After some discussion, I have found it rarely the case that students answer "yes," which entails the following conclusion: Many academics are teaching students to advance a position that most students do not believe. What is the point of such an exercise?

We could advance the Aristotelian strategy of achieving virtuous actions and dispositions through habit.[19] In other words, even if the students don't initially believe in the fictionality and constructivity of race, their continued appeal to such conclusions will eventually lead to their believing such because that's all they have come to know. Such a position is, at least from a philosophical perspective, hardly desirable, however, because it lacks a crucial element in a philosophical treatment of the subject—namely, a critical reflection on the subject.[20] The mere recitation of this trope of social constructivity is, in other words, a kind of authority pressuring instead of a genuinely critical position. A genuinely critical position occasions a response to the query, "Is that *true*?"

Here are some reflections that have come from students (and I suspect most nonacademics) when provided a genuine opportunity to speak their mind on the subject of racial constructivity.

1. If race is a social construction, why is it that when members of the same designated race pair with each other, they don't produce children of or who look like the other designated race?
2. If scientists believe that race is a social construction, why is it that medical doctors, who are practitioners of modern

medical science, respond to race as matters of life and death? For example, there are treatments that could literally kill a patient if the medication isn't adjusted along racial lines.[21]

3. If race is a social construction, why do we "see" races and can identify them sufficiently to create systems that don't have wider margins of error?

All three of these objections are a function of a tendency to ontologize the social to the point of solipsism in much contemporary race theory. This making of the social world into *all there is* leads to a form of disciplinary decadence in which all knowledge claims from disciplinary perspectives outside of the social sciences are rendered illegitimate by virtue of not being social scientific.[22] For such theorists, saying that race is a social construction is equivalent to saying that race is *only* a social construction. Although there are philosophical critics of race who appeal to some of the life sciences—biology, for example—some of them do so through an isolation of that science from the conjunction of interdisciplinary considerations that would make much sense of such a complex as race. Could one imagine contemporary genetics, for instance, if its methods remained exclusively in biology or philosophical treatments of biology through old Darwinism?[23] New Darwinism or evolutionary theory incorporates analyses of sequences and the complexity of computer programing; think, for example, of how contemporary geneticists see genes as chemical programs. And even there, contemporary geneticists take seriously, as do physicists with the study of actual things in motion, that one should consider such intervening forces as climate, radioactivity, ecological sustainability, and other factors. In short, research in genetics takes seriously the intervening forces of reality.

What haunts contemporary discussions of whiteness is an insight from the story of human evolution, and that insight is that the emergence of whites and many people of color in between white and black is a very different story than the emergence of blacks. To say that blacks are a function of white modernity is to chart the course of European expansion and the story of the forms of difference articulated by its efforts at self-understanding.[24] Blackness and whiteness, in other words, are not ascriptions by which people on the African continent regarded each other prior to the advent of the Arabic, transatlantic, and East Indian Ocean slave trades and colonization by Europeans. Whiteness, on the other hand, is not an ascription imposed from without but one developed from *within* European civilizations. So here we have two social constructions—one imposed from the outside, the other developed from within. Limits to these narratives emerge, however, when we conclude that their being constructed means that there is no material, historical difference prior to those constructions. If this were so, then earlier generations of groups of human beings should be indistinguishable, and the history of the morphological appearance of those groups should lack any causal explanation. One should be able, if it were possible to do so, to go in a time machine and look at human beings in different periods of the first 70,000 years of our species' existence and "see" the same range of morphological differences that we see today. Or, if we were to pluck members of various communities of human beings from that period and plop them on a street in the contemporary world, we should expect the identity imposed upon those human beings to be any one of the basic ones we use today—that is, black, white, brown, or "mongoloid" versions of those three. As we explore this hypothesis, however, something crucial for the study of whiteness immediately emerges: For a substantial period of the life our species—namely, at least 190,000 years (90,000 as an earlier protohuman community and the other 100,000 as "modern" human beings)—there were no people whom we would today upon observation consider to be "white" people. Such people are relative newcomers on the scene.

The reason for this conclusion rests in understanding evolution and the human body. Today we have a tendency to talk about people as though people are not of flesh and bone, of consciousness as though it could live disembodied in the social world. Edmund Husserl and Maurice Merleau-Ponty have pointed out many of the limitations of such a point of view—that disembodiment lacks a perspective (a body, which is a somewhere), which would consign consciousness to being nowhere and having no point of view.[25] The problem with disembodiment as a model is that it eliminates the basic "here" and "there" through which knowledge emerges as a process of distinction. It is, as Jean-Paul Sartre aptly points out with his theory of nihilation, the basis of negation. Knowledge could never emerge if we could not distinguish ourselves from other things, and other things from each other.[26] Alfred Schutz builds on the insight of embodied consciousness in his phenomenological treatment of social reality as something achieved; it is precisely because there are "Others" (other embodied consciousnesses) that the world is constituted through a process of reaching them but doing so in a constantly limited way by virtue of the ongoing processes of their actions or choices. The body is not, however, simply a perspective. It is a *living* one in an environment that is part of a planet that, too, is part of a solar system that is part of a galaxy that is part of the universe. The planet is subject to forces of gravity and radiation from the sun, so any living thing on the earth must function within such conditions. This means that its "mechanics," if we will, must be able to do things like regulate heat, and acquire and process energy.[27] We know that human beings (*Homo sapiens sapiens*) evolved from a one-million-year-old *Homo erectus* (with some versions arguing for the 600,000-year transition of *Homo heidelbergensis*) on the continent of Africa roughly 220,000 years ago and then, in some paleoanthropologists' view, went through a transition into "modern" human beings about 100,000 years ago. A distinct advantage of this new species was the capabilities of its brain, results of which include development of language and culture. Now at this point in the story, the imagination of most readers and many writers has unfortunately been affected by white normativity, for in many portraits, these early prototypical human beings are depicted as very hairy and dirty white people.[28] The problem with this portrait is that if they had been so, they would have died out long ago, and there would be no "us." Some critics of this criticism think the point of this argument rests on a form of fallacious geographicism.[29] The point is, however, not about geography but about the challenges posed by a variety of factors in different parts of the world at different moments in time. We see this in the difference of other animals such as foxes and bears, where members of the same species look different in accordance with hot and cold climate zones. Our species evolved in a hot place with wide-open savannas. Its members faced a merciless sun, and although their intelligence eventually made them the most feared species in that region, which enabled them to develop such abilities as REM sleep, they did not yet have the resources for protecting themselves against the climate beyond the resources of modest shelter and their own skin. In short, those early human beings were dark-skinned because they had to be so. Otherwise, melanoma would have been an immediate peril of their existence (especially so for the occasional albino child who did not achieve sexual maturation and proliferate there because of cancer). So, in spite of white normativity's depiction, the reality is that early human beings were very dark beings with tightly curled hair and all the other features necessary to protect them from the sun's radiation and enable the release of heat. (The danger of an overheated brain is well known today: heat stroke.) As the story unfolds of the mechanics of the human organism, it becomes clear that what *we* would see if we were to look at them would be the people today we call black people. Those people managed to spread to parts of the Southern Hemisphere by taking to the seas at least 50,000 or 40,000 years ago, evidenced by recent discoveries that people inhabited such regions as

Australia, the South Pacific islands, and South America by those early periods.[30] (Another presumption of white normativity is the notion that human beings have an irresistible urge to move "up" or "northward." It strikes me that it may be more logical for early people to have followed the movements of the sun, which would mean eastward or westward.) Since climactic conditions do not remain constant, neither do such resources as food, and if we add to this equation another dimension of the human brain—namely, *curiosity*—the global spread of our species was inevitable.

As the story goes, another species had evolved from our common *Homo erectus* ancestors a little earlier than us during those primordial periods, and they had done so in Ice Age Europe and Western Asia. They were *Homo neanderthalensis*. This species used to be presented in popular culture as rather stupid cave dwellers, but their depiction was radically "humanized" upon the discovery that they had to have been "white" in the sense of light complexioned and straight-haired. They were physiologically different from our species in many ways that contradict popular portraits. Instead of huge male oafs with clubs over their shoulders dragging the female members of their species along the ground by their hair, they turn out to have been short, stocky creatures with long biceps and short forearms, a skull governed by a very large face and a larger brain than *Homo sapiens sapiens*, very dense bones, and a variety of adaptations to retain heat, such as compactness, a very large nose, and white or very pale skin. They made tools and survived in Europe and Asia till about 20,000 or 30,000 years ago. Some of our ancestors entered Europe and Western Asia about 40,000 years ago, which meant that for a time they lived alongside the Neanderthals, but the latter species soon died out, and debate rages today on whether they were absorbed by those early *Homo sapiens sapiens* into a new species ("us") or were rendered extinct under pressures of environment or conflicts with our ancestors.[31] Much evidence, the most compelling of which is the absence of neanderthal DNA in our species, suggests the latter.[32] With regard to the continued story of members of our species who went into Europe and Asia, their migration stimulated a morphological change in their descendants. It was not only the severe cold that posed a threat to those bands of human beings who settled in such challenging regions, but also the effects of environments governed by limited sunlight. Melanin, which was great protection from the sun, becomes a liability in the North, where it would inhibit reception of vitamin D, which comes from the sun. By contrast, living along the equator posed a different problem: enough vitamin D but *too much* sun. In the north, absence of enough vitamin D led to rickets in those who had too much melanin. Lighter skin, which was a liability in the southern regions, became an asset in the North, and those individuals began to thrive.[33]

The upshot of this story, which is the prevailing story of human evolution and subsequent morphological differentiation, is that the physical features that we have come to associate with whiteness were not always apparent in our species. Such features, and consequently the people we associate with them, have only been around for probably 20,000 years or less. What this means is that the operative conditions of identity in historic inquiry that have dominated our studies of human beings should be radically changed, for those are built upon the question, "How did black people come about?" when in fact they should pose the opposite question: "How did white and other light-skinned peoples come about?"

We are already seeing some of the ideological responses to this realization through new efforts to reassert white normativity, as witnessed by the popularity of such racist books as *Guns, Germs, and Steel* and *The Bell Curve*, the first of which garnered the Pulitzer prize.[34] These books accept the evidence of the movement of human beings, but they add to the equation the notion that morphological changes in the North over the past 20,000 years were *evolutionary* changes that stimulated the great achievements of human civilization. They are, in other words, white Manifest Destiny updated. In a nutshell, they argue that the pressures of Africa stimulated the development of a species with limited intelligence, but the unique conditions of Europe and Asia stimulated greater intelligence and cultural development. We see here the return of Hitler's logic. What is missing from these narratives is the fact that human beings have never stood still. It is not that they went north and did not return till times of Greek and Roman expansion. There has always been a back-and-forth and sideward set of movements in which "outside" genes entered communities. But more, the development of human culture led to something that brought to a halt the pressure to evolve, and that is our achievement of homeostasis. Human beings, in other words, no longer have to adapt to environments because we carry our environment with us. Wherever human beings are today, they manage to manipulate their immediate environment to a range of roughly 50 to 70 degrees Fahrenheit. There is, in other words, an environmental normativity that most human communities live by these days, and that is roughly those along the Mediterranean latitudes.

What we have today externally, then, is our species as we have looked since about 20,000 years ago, but internally we are the same as we were, with very minor mutations, 200,000 years ago or so. Given human movement and the achievement of homoeostasis, genetic advantages and disadvantages are constantly mixing, so what with complete isolation and no homeostatic response would have been the continued creation of new species of hominids has come to a halt, and we remain a single species, evidenced by our ability to produce fertile offsprings from what has become known as racial mixture.[35] What is more, globalism—begun thousands of years ago as human beings migrated, got lost in various regions, and then kept finding each other and initiating trade and marriages across communities living in different climactic zones—has brought such a spread of genes that, as Winthrop Jordan pointed out recently, whatever viability the notion of races may have once had has been lost, and the reality of the future is that there will be only one race, marked by a maximum presence of diverse genes.[36] In an odd way, our future is becoming our past.

CONCLUSION

My aim in this chapter has been to outline some of the limitations I have encountered in whiteness studies. The account I give is not meant to apply to every researcher on whiteness but only to those tropes that have become both popular and dominant. What is needed is a concerted struggle against the subtextual reintroduction of notions of white Manifest Destiny that undergird scholarship saturated with white normativity. The reason for fighting against this is a matter of getting the story—the true story—right on the human past so as to understand the human present and make sensible decisions for our future. It is clear, for example, that getting the story wrong has led to rationalizations that make our notions of difference that govern our understanding of who and what we are appear more radical than they in fact are. And more, failure to understand the complex mechanisms by which we have been able to survive for so short a period on our home planet are such that we could imagine the absurdity of policies that demand no less than a lighter-skinned future for humankind. Whiteness, in other words, is a very costly venture for our species. Its hegemony functions much like the folly of the continued effort to make European pastures out of deserts. In the words of Gregory Stock:

> If you wanted to build a superior human, you would probably choose black skin, at least if the person was going to spend much time in the sun. A comparison of an elderly black person's skin with the wrinkled, damaged hide of an elderly white or Asian sun worshiper shows this clearly.

Moreover, the genetic controls of melanin production are probably not complex, since a mere three to five genes seem to determine skin color. But don't hold your breath waiting for such engineering. A genetic module for black skin is unlikely to be in big demand anytime soon. Blacks certainly don't need it, and few nonblacks will want it. Race and parentage carry so much cultural baggage that few parents would use their children as political billboards when sunscreens, clothing, or even drugs and lotions that stimulate melanin production to create natural-looking tans, can protect their skin.[37]

In the end, a key reminder in whiteness studies should also be bringing out the humanity of white people. It is absurd for us to expect people to argue against the value of their own survival. But with such critical engagements should also, always, be an understanding that our liberating pleas for common ground bring along with them an underlying optimism not only of what is to be done, but also what *can* be done.

NOTES

1. See W.E.B. Du Bois's poignant reflections on his Atlanta years in *The Autobiography of W.E.B. Du Bois: A Soliloquy on Viewing My Life from the Last Decade of Its First Century* (New York: International Publishers, 1968), especially pp. 222 and 228.

2. The most influential discussion of white privilege is Peggy McKintosh's "White Privilege: Unpacking the Invisible Knapsack," *Independent School* (winter 1990): 31–36. For an excellent recent summary of some of these views with some philosophical reflections, see Cynthia Kaufman, "A User's Guide to White Privilege," *Radical Philosophy Review* 4, nos. 1 and 2 (2002): 30–38. See also Frances V. Rains, "Is the Benign Really Harmless?" Deconstructing Some 'Benign' Manifestations of Operationalized White Privilege," in *White Reign: Deploying Whiteness in America*, ed. Joe L. Kincheloe, Shirley R. Steinberg, Nelson M. Rodriguez, and Ronald E. Chennault (New York: St. Martin's Press, 1998), pp. 77–102.

3. See Immanuel Kant, *Foundations of the Metaphysics of Morals,* trans. Lewis White Beck (Indianapolis: Bobbs-Merrill, 1959), pp. 54–55 [*Prussian Academy,* pp. 436–37].

4. On this point, cf. Cynthia Kaufman, "User's Guide," pp. 31–32.

5. See José Ortega y Gasset, *Revolt of the Masses* (New York: W. W. Norton, 1932), chapter 14, "Who Rules the World?," especially p. 134.

6. Many whites use the term "merit" in bad faith. They appeal to it only when the decks are stacked in their favor. Many institutions function pretty well with mere average performance. The effort to include people of color usually leads to a response on the part of homogenous institutions in the form of attempting to justify their past exclusions and continued exclusionary practices. Under the latter circumstance, many whites depend on the absence of merit while advancing it as a rationalization. That is why it is a form of bad faith. While depending on whiteness as a trump card, they advance merit under the presumption of black mediocrity, while blacks in such situations find themselves facing a nihilistic situation wherein no amount of achievement ever becomes relevant. I have seen this phenomenon time and again in many of America's first-tier educational institutions, where there are two extremes—either inflated standards on black candidates or deflated standards for "less threatening" black candidates. The most threatening blacks are consistently those who are the

highest ranked people at what they do. Many such institutions could, in other words, use a healthy dose of genuine meritocracy. For discussion of how bad faith configures in this discussion, see Lewis R. Gordon, *Bad Faith and Antiblack Racism* (Amherst, NY: Humanity Books, 1995), *passim*, but especially part 3. For a discussion of the "mass" dimension of American meritocracy, which is the model of whiteness here, see also Ortega, *Revolt of the Masses*, especially pp. 25–26.

7. For an analysis of this question, see Marilyn Nissim-Sabat, "Victims No More," *Radical Philosophy Review* 1, no. 1 (1998): 17–34.

8. See Hannah Arendt's discussion of anti-Semitism in *The Origins of Totalitarianism*, new edition with added prefaces (San Diego: Harcourt Brace & Company, 1979), part 1: "Antisemitism." See also Mark Sanders, *Complicities: The Intellectual and Apartheid* (Durham, NC: Duke University Press, 2002).

9. See, for example, Lewis R. Gordon, *Fanon and the Crisis of European Man: An Essay on Philosophy and the Human Sciences* (New York: Routledge, 1995), chapter 3, and Lewis R. Gordon, *Existentia Africana: Understanding Africana Existential Thought* (New York: Routledge, 2000), chapter 4.

10. For a more detailed discussion of this phenomenon, see Gordon, *Fanon and the Crisis of European Man*, chapter 3.

11. For development of this argument, see Gordon, *Existentia Africana*, chapter 4.

12. Michel Foucault, *Discipline and Punish: The Birth of the Prison*, trans. Alan Sheridan (New York: Vintage, 1979). Foucault's point addressed the modern sociological situation of a near symbiotic relationship between power and knowledge, where the presence of one carries the association of the other, a circumstance that he describes as "power/knowledge."

13. Kevin Bales, *Disposable People: New Slavery in the Global Economy* (Berkeley: University of California Press, 1999). Bales argues against fixed models of vulnerability and advances a theory of shifting vulnerability. An individual could find him- or herself powerful at one moment and radically vulnerable at another to the point of being enslaved. In those moments, his or her knowledge of others is irrelevant because he or she is not considered a point of view—that knowledge, contra Foucault, does encounter itself as power. But the enslaver "knows" the slave as a function of power over the slave. We thus find a unilateral structure of disciplinary inculcation where, in defense of Foucault, the practice of disciplining the slave is a disciplinary practice of its own of the master. But Bales's point would be that it is not the *slave*'s doing.

14. See Frantz Fanon, *Black Skin, White Masks*, trans. Charles Lam Markmann (New York: Grove Press, 1967), chapter 6.

15. Ibid.

16. For discussion, see Gordon, *Bad Faith and Antiblack Racism*, chapter 6. See also Gorden, *Existentia Africana*, pp. 114–15.

17. C. W. Cassineli, *Total Revolution: A Comparative Study of Germany under Hitler, the Soviet Union under Stalin, and China under Mao* (Santa Barbara, CA: Clio Books, 1976), pp. 21–27.

18. See Alfred Schutz, *The Collected Papers*, Vol. 1, *The Problem of Social Reality*, ed. with an intro. by Maurice Natanson; preface by H. L. Van Breda (The Hague: Martinus Nijhoff, 1962), part 2. See also Gordon, *Fanon and the Crisis of European Man*, pp. 20–22 and 50–56; and *Existentia Africana*, 72–80.

19. See, for example, Aristotle's *Nichomachean Ethics*, trans., historical intro., and commentary by Christopher Rowe and philosophical intro. and commentary by Sarah Broadie (Oxford: Oxford University Press, 2002), 1103a14–1104b3.

20. As a political strategy, it functions like the imposition of a new religion; subsequent generations will simply believe such since that is what they have always been told. In this case, the strategy is not for the present generation but subsequent ones.

21. The varieties of race-identified genetic diseases such as sickle cell anemia and Alpha (Mongoloid/Northeast Asian) and Beta (Semitic/Middle Eastern) Thalassemia are examples, the presence of which indicate recent ancestors from particular racial groups from particular regions. The paths certain diseases might take—such as that of Pityriasis Rosea—differs for blacks than other groups (for discussion, see C. Finch). Medications show different patterns as well. Here is an example: A black colleague of mine suffers from Myasthenia. On one occasion of relapse, he was suffering from severely high blood pressure. His physician prescribed hydrochlorot to reduce his blood pressure. His condition was worsened, however, by his treatment. Fortunately, there was a Ghanaian physician on staff who was the senior supervisor for the day. He quickly prescribed Zestril, and my colleague's blood pressure immediately began to lower. Here is what that physician told my colleague: "Many white physicians do not understand that some medications have adverse side effects upon black bodies." He informed the general physician, and that physician agreed to prescribe Zestril. Although the human gene pool has sequences permeating across racial lines, the reality is that there is a greater diversity of genes among blacks than any other population group. Thus, medication developed through presumptions of white normativity will encounter nonwhites, and especially blacks, as "abnormal." The probability is greater of finding a normal sample by moving from the greatest diversity of sequences to those of less diversity. See, e.g., Gregory Stock, *Redesigning Humans: Our Inevitable Genetic Future* (Boston: Houghton Mifflin, 2002), pp. 114–15.

22. For discussion of disciplinary decadence, see Lewis R. Gordon, "The Human Condition in an Age of Disciplinary Decadence: Thoughts on Knowing and Learning," *Philosophical Studies in Education* 34(2003): 105–123.

23. For a succinct discussion of old Darwinism and its limits, see Benjamin Farrington, *What Darwin Really Said: An Introduction to His Life and Theory of Evolution*, foreword by Stephen Jay Gould (New York: Schocken Books, 1966).

24. For a wonderful, influential portrait, see V. Y. Mudimbe's *The Invention of Africa: Gnosis, Philosophy, and the Order of Knowledge* (Bloomington: Indiana University Press, 1988).

25. See Edmund Husserl, *Cartesian Meditations: An Introduction to Phenomenology*, trans. Dorion Cairns (Dordrecht: Martinus Nijhoff, 1960), and Maurice Merleau-Ponty, *Phenomenology of Perception*, trans. Colin Smith (New York: Routledge, 1962).

26. See Jean-Paul Sartre's essay "Intentionality: A Fundamental Idea of Husserl's Phenomenology," *Journal of the British Society for Phenomenology* 1, no. 2 (1970): 4–5; and his discussion of nihilation in *Being and Nothingness: A Phenomenological Essay on Ontology*, trans. Hazel Barnes (New York: Washington Square Press, 1956), introduction and part 1.

27. The discussion that follows draws much from Dr. Charles Finch III's "Race and Human Origins," in his *Echoes of the Old Darkland: Themes from the American Eden* (Decatur, GA: Khenti, 1991), pp. 1–57. See also Donald Johanson and Blake Edgar, *From Lucy to Language* (New York: Simon & Schuster, 1996). Johanson has also put together a website summary: *http://www.becominghuman.org/*.

28. This is rampant. Even the Johanson website documentary depicts, for example, the first Australian Aboriginals who left finger paintings in the Koonalda cave some 40,000 years ago as very hairy naked white men, complete with straight red hair! We need simply wonder why, then, the European settlers some 39,700 years later encountered only very dark-skinned Aboriginals.

29. See, for example, Naomi Zack's *Philosophy of Science and Race* (New York: Routledge, 2002), pp. 36–37.

30. For research on early migrations through East Asia, Australia, and to South America, see the groundbreaking work of Walter A. Neves and Hector Pucciarelli, "The Zhoukoudian Upper Cave Skull 101 as seen from the Americas," *Journal of Human Evolution* 34, no. 2 (February 1998): 219–22; and Walter A. Neves, André Prous, Rolando González-José, Renato Kipnis, Joseph Powell, "Early Holocene Human Skeletal Remains from Santana do Riacho, Brazil: Implications for the Settlement of the New World," *Journal of Human Evolution* 45, no. 1 (July 2003): 19–42.

31. See, for example, C. J. Mauricio, P. B. Pettitt, P. Souto, E. Trinkaus, H. van der Plicht et al., "The early upper Paleolithic Human Skeleton from the Abrigo do Lagar Velho (Portugal) and Modern Human Emergence in Iberia," *Proceedings of the National Academy of Sciences of the USA* 96 (1999): 7,604–609, and the rebuttal by I. Tattersall and J. H. Schwartz, "Hominids and Hybrids: The Place of Neanderthals in Human Evolution," *Proceedings of the National Academy of Sciences of the USA* 96 (1999): 7,117–19. See also the website: *http://www.talkorigins.org/faqs/ homs/ lagarvelho.html.*

32. This argument is made by Tattersall and Schwartz in "Hominids and Hybrids."

33. See Finch, "Race and Human Origins," pp. 34–37. We may wonder about individuals who went north but coastal. The cold may have stimulated a change in their hair, since long, straight hair is better protection under the cold, but not necessarily a change in their skin since they would have access to another source of vitamin D—namely, deep-sea fish. Research on indigenous peoples along such northern islands as those in Japan may reveal, for instance, a story of dark-skinned straight or at least more loose curly haired peoples. We may wonder if a similar story might not have been the case for those along what is today known as the British islands or the coasts of Scandinavia.

34. Jared M. Diamond, *Guns, Germs, and Steel: The Fates of Human Societies* (New York: W. W. Norton, 1997), and Richard J. Herrnstein and Charles Murray, *The Bell Curve: Intelligence and Class Structure in American Life* (New York: Free Press, 1994). A feature of these books is their posing of the question of white dominance as though that were an inevitable path of history. But we should bear in mind that white domination is very new on the scene, and the rate of consumption that such domination has entailed does not make it a sustainable condition for our planet. Who knows what the future will bring?

35. Consider the implications of a term from old racial ideology: *mulatto.* This term emerged from comparing an offspring of a white and a black to that of a horse and a donkey the result of which is a mule. In this view, race is akin to species. An ontopolitical jolt emerges, then, at every moment such an offspring either becomes pregnant or impregnates another human being.

36. Winthrop Jordan, "The Uniqueness of the One-Drop Rule," presented at the conference *Race, Globalization and the New Ethnic Studies,* The Center for the Study of Race and Ethnicity in America, Brown University, March 6–9, 2003, the proceedings of which are forthcoming.

37. Gregory Stock, *Redesigning Humans: Our Inevitable Genetic Future* (Boston: Houghton Mifflin, 2002), pp. 114–15.

9

WHITENESS AND AFRICANA PHENOMENOLOGY

Paget Henry

INTRODUCTION

THE COLONIAL SOCIETIES OF the New World, such as the United States, Brazil, and the Caribbean, were and still are immigrant societies. This influx of people from different regions of the globe made these societies multicultural in nature. Hence, in both their colonial and postcolonial periods, they were confronted with the problem of transforming immigrant populations, whose identities were inscribed in autonomous or national cultures, into subnational races or ethnicities. In contrast, the national cultures of the imperial societies of old Europe were undergoing processes of transnational expansion that would make them appear universal in nature. It is between these two processes of subnational ethnogenesis in the colonies and transnational universalization in imperial Europe that I want to situate the problem of whiteness and Africana phenomenology. In particular, I will link these two processes to Hegel's phenomenological account of the nature of the modern European self and to the responses of a number of Africana phenomenologists to the supremacist needs of this self. My analysis suggests that these needs are in a resurgent phase that is casting a very disquieting shadow over black identities in the post–affirmative action era.

NEW WORLD RACE/ETHNIC ORDERS

Given the New World pattern of ethnogenic nation building, it is now well recognized that these societies developed very clearly defined

race/ethnic orders. These orders were and still are discursively legitimated hierarchical formations that function like social machines for
producing races and ethnicities out of national or autonomous cultures. As discursively legitimated formations, race/ethnic orders have
deep roots in the national imaginary of a people, as well as in the institutional structures established for their long-term preservation.

By the national imaginary, I am referring to those specific spaces in
the creative imaginations of citizens where self-construction and national construction have become inseparable. In these imaginary
spaces, we find the continuous reproduction of narratives of individual
and collective origin that affirm and legitimate the order and growth
of the nation. In colonial societies, the simultaneous existence of a
national identity and a number of subnational races and ethnicities
was often a result of the imposition of the origin narratives of the
imperial group on the others. Thus, in the case of the United States, its
first origin narrative was an Anglo-American one that made America
an extension of sixteenth-century England, which in turn derived
from ancient Germanic tribes—the Anglos and Saxons.

By the institutional structures of a race/ethnic order, I am referring
to the specific set of legal and normative arrangements that have been
established to ensure that this order is observed by members of the
society. In the cases of the United States and the Caribbean, these
structures can be described as a race/ethnic ritual that requires all
immigrants to undergo a period of "social death." The latter is a
liminal state in which immigrants are no longer what they were before
arrival, but not yet American or Caribbean. During this period, the
immigrant group must show gratitude and loyalty to its new host,
allow itself to be stereotyped, racialized, ethnicized, and reduced to
cheap labor. Further, it has to agree to a process of extensive cultural
surgery that will give it an Anglo-American or Anglo-Caribbean
facelift. As a result of this surgery, its language, religion, style of dress,
family patterns, and attitudes toward other race/ethnic groups in the
society will have to reflect those of the established order. At the end of
this ethnogenic ritual, the immigrant group should emerge from its
period of social death, reborn as an "acceptable" ethnic with a distinct
place in the hierarchy, and its members full citizens. However, thepas-
sages through these rituals have been very different for different cultural groups. In both of these societies, it has been easiest for English
and other European immigrants and most difficult for Africans.

If we take this notion of a race/ethnic order as a discursively legitimated hierarchical formation, then it should be clear that these are

structures that have changed over time. Legitimating origin narratives change as well as the elements and legal framework of the race/ethnic ritual. Thus in the United States, it is possible to distinguish at least four phases in the history of its race/ethnic order. Second to the Anglo-American phase of this order (1607–1865) was the Euro-American phase, which produced acceptable American ethnics out of a number of European groups (1870–1956). Third was the multicultural phase, which failed for the most part to produce acceptable ethnics out of non-European immigrants (1965–88). The greatest success occurred in the case of Asian Americans and the least in the case of African Americans. Fourth, and finally, is the contemporary (1980–present) color-blind phase in which American society has declared that it no longer sees color.

The failure of these changing race/ethnic orders to assimilate non-Europeans and African Americans, in particular, raises the question of the exclusionary criteria that barred these groups from completing the ritual. Between the first and second of these race/ethnic orders, the criteria of Anglo-Saxon origin and Protestant Christianity were removed, making it possible for non–Anglo-Saxon Europeans to become Americans. However, these changes left a number of exclusionary criteria in place, including the requirement of being white. The importance of whiteness as a criterion of the American ethnogenic ritual emerges as soon as we look at its third and fourth phases. With the former coming immediately after the African-American civil rights movement, whiteness was formally removed for the first time as a criterion for completing the ritual. However, the failure of the multicultural phase pointed to the normative and informal persistence of whiteness as just such a criterion. With the high levels of denial and premature claims informing the color-blind phase, it is very unlikely that it will succeed where the multicultural phase did not.

Given these antiblack outcomes, Africana thought must of necessity raise the question of whiteness and its dehumanizing impact on peoples of African descent. Consequently, many Africana scholars have addressed this question—from Quobna Cugoano, Frederick Douglass, and W.E.B. Du Bois right down to Toni Morrison, Sylvia Wynter, Lewis Gordon, Cornel West, and Charles Mills. In his now-classic definition of whiteness, Du Bois declared: "I am given to understand that whiteness is the ownership of the earth forever and ever, Amen!"[1] What is striking about this definition of whiteness is that it does not explicitly thematize color, but puts the accent on the power and imperial might of a racial capitalism. Given this fact, we need to understand how whiteness became a trope for power, ownership of the earth, and the appropriation of the labor of those whose land had been taken. It is here that we need the help of the African presence and of philosophy—particularly, phenomenological philosophy.

As noted earlier, race/ethnic orders are rooted in the national imaginaries of societies. It is in these creative spaces that they get their initial thematizing and subsequent revising after being institutionalized. The imaginary is our founding or world-constituting faculty. It provides humans everywhere with the originary classifications and other semiotic foundations upon which we construct our knowledge of both self and world. We have been able to examine and elaborate these elementary classifications and semiotic formations through self-reflective discourses such as literature and phenomenological philosophy. Consequently, philosophy has consistently played a crucial role in the elaborating and explicit thematizing of the contents of the national imaginary. It is precisely in this regard that Hegel's phenomenology of the European mind can help us to understand the rise of its imperial self that was brought into such clear focus by Du Bois's definition of whiteness. Further, as we examine the role of the African in the production of whiteness as a trope for this imperial self, we will open chapters in Africana phenomenology that are closely connected to the race/ethnic orders of American and other new world societies.

HEGEL AND THE IMPERIAL SELF OF WHITENESS

Crucial to the stability of any race/ethnic order is the defining and evaluating of the identities of the groups that make up the order. In the ethnogenic rituals of New World societies, we saw this evaluative process in the actions of the self-defining, hegemonic Anglo-Saxon groups as they redefined and evaluated the identities of various subordinated groups. Hegel's philosophical elaboration of this hegemonic self and its relations to others is extremely helpful here.

In the years before writing *The Phenomenology of Spirit*, Hegel made several attempts to grasp the distinct nature of the modern European subject that had emerged around him and within his own person. He caught glimpses of it in Descartes, Rousseau, Kant, Fichte, and Schelling. Each had wrestled with the distinctive "I" that was grounding and helping to shape European modernity. Kant had captured the drives for rationality, autonomy, and universality that marked this self by defining it as the unity of the transcendental ego grasping itself through cognitive acts of self-reflection. However, Hegel remained unconvinced by the apparent circularity, transparency, and autonomy of this new subject. He was skeptical because it came at the price of losing contact with the sociohistorical world and the role of the latter in shaping the very reflecting consciousness with which this subject was attempting to grasp itself. Consequently, Hegel needed a definition of the modern European self that would retain the Kantian features of autonomy and rationality but also take into account its sociohistorical formation through work, language, and social interaction with others. The result was Hegel's famous "master" self that comes into being through a dialectic of recognition in a master/slave relationship.

The essence or core of the Hegelian master self is free self-consciousness. Like the Kantian self, Hegel's master self strives to be self-determining and self-grounding through circular attempts at grasping its own tail. However, in Hegel, the circuit of selfhood cannot be closed self-reflectively, but only by going through another. This need for self-realization to pass through an other leads to what Hegel calls "the duplication of self-consciousness within its unity."[2] The first moment of this duplication is indeed the abstract unity and autonomy of the Kantian self, while the second is its intersubjective and other-determined aspect. As a result of these two opposing tendencies, the European master self can grasp and know itself as freedom only by negating the freedom and power of all others who are capable of determining it from without. In other words, "self-consciousness *is* primarily simple existence for self, self-identity by exclusion of every other from itself."[3] In the second moment of its duplication, the master self has to acknowledge its dependence on recognition from another self-consciousness. In other words, "self-consciousness *is* only by being acknowledged or 'recognized.'"[4] It is the distinct manner in which this second moment contributes to the formation of the master self that separates Hegel from Kant. For Hegel, this second moment has its own double significance. First, it points to the loss of the unity of the first moment as it must find itself in the other. Second, it points to a sublating of the other as "it does not regard the other as essentially real, but sees its own self in the other."[5] In the language of Wilson Harris, this is "the dead seeing eye" of master self.[6]

This sublating of the other is no friendly affair. On the contrary, it is a life-and death-struggle that turns the other into a slave whose defeat and submission confirms the freedom and self-consciousness of the master. Without this defeat of the other, the modern European master self cannot come to know itself as self-consciousness. As Kojeve puts it: "to speak of the 'origin' of self-consciousness is necessarily to speak of a fight to the death for 'recognition.'"[7] This is Hegel's phenomeno-logical description of the inner and outer dramas that define the nature of the modern Western subject. The latter is a subject who must strive to approximate the autonomy of reason by self-reflectively grasping its own tail while gaining confirmation of this autonomy through negating the freedom and power of all others to determine it from without. Hegel's description is a philosophical formulation of the imperial self that we encountered in our earlier examination of the ethnic orders of American and Caribbean societies, and most definitely a referent of Du Bois's revealing definition of whiteness.

THE WHITENESS OF THE MASTER SELF

Hegel does not explicitly thematize the whiteness of the master self in *The Phenomenology of Mind*. Here skin color is not a major trope of this self, which finds its symbolic reflection in images such as freedom, rationality, autonomy, and self-consciousness. Indeed, the rise of the master self and its problems of conscious realization all take place largely without reference to skin color. This should make clear that the slave of Hegel's master/slave dialectic is a European Other and not necessarily the African slaves on the plantations of the New World. This sharing of skin color between European master and slave led to its irrelevance in their life-and-death struggle for recognition, and to the special importance of labor. In *The Philosophy of History*, these dynamics change very sharply as Hegel examines the growth of self-consciousness in both Europeans and non-Europeans. Here, the tropes of color, race, ethnicity, and geography compete with self-consciousness, rationality, and autonomy to represent the selves of both masters and slaves. Further, it is in negating the non-European other, particularly the African, that the Hegelian master self discovers its whiteness.

Our examination of the changing American race/ethnic orders revealed a persistent and long-term inability to recognize the humanity of people of African descent. They were among the most dehumanized victims of dead seeing eyes. This stark failure pushed many Africana philosophers to question whether the African functioned as a genuine other within the dialectic of the master/slave relationship. For example, this concern has been raised by Frantz Fanon, Ato Sekyi-Otu, Lewis Gordon, Lou Turner, and Nelson Maldonado-Torres,[8] who have all been great contributors to the distinctive tradition of Africana phenomenology. The question is also there implicitly in Du Bois's reworking of Hegel in *The Souls of Black Folk*. But before getting any deeper into this Africana phenomenology, we must return to what Hegel had to say on the subject of why Africans do not constitute a genuine other.

In *The Philosophy of History*, Hegel makes absolutely clear that Africans cannot play the role of a genuine other in the master/slave relationship because "the Negro" is without self-consciousness. The consciousness of the African remained mired in nature and was without any capability for exit and subsequent development into self-consciousness.[9] Consequently, the master self would be able to get from the African only the recognition it gets from nature rather than the recognition it would get from another self-consciousness. The nature-centered recognition offered by Hegel's African clearly does not meet the requirements of the second moment of the duplication in the unity of the master self. This intersubjective moment requires a battle with an other who possesses self-consciousness. As the African is precisely this lack of self-consciousness he/she does not meet Hegel's criteria for playing the role of a slave capable of confirming the humanity of the master. Here the African is what Lewis Gordon has called "a barred other,"[10] or what Nelson Maldonado-Torres has called "a sub-other."[11] Both are unable to play the Hegelian game of recognition with the master because they are one with nature and unaware of themselves as freedom and autonomy. Because of this double displacement, the African can be an Other to the Hegelian slave. The former is on the same level as the tools, animals, land, and other natural media in which the Hegelian slave labors, and through which he/she comes to self-consciousness. This is precisely the judgment that Prospero had already made after his experimental casting of Caliban in the role of a self-conscious other.

In short, looked at through Hegel's dead seeing eye, the African is the furthest removed from the European as self-consciousness. He/she stands behind the Indians, the Chinese, and the Egyptians (whom Hegel linked to Europe). Africans were outside of history, the domain in which consciousness is transformed into self-consciousness. This perception of Africans as doubly displaced was the basis for Fanon's suggestion that the master laughs at the consciousness of the African and demands from him not recognition but work.[12]

AFRICANA PHENOMENOLOGY AND WHITENESS

To the extent that African peoples have internalized this image of subalterity coming from the dead seeing eye of the Western master self, the dialectic of recognition that will bring Africana subjectivity to self-consciousness must of necessity be different from that between the master and the European slave. Indeed, the primary concern of Africana phenomenology has been coming to terms with the intersubjective impact of this barred status, its changing modes of discursive elaboration, and its concretization in race/ethnic orders.

In its exchanges with the African, the Western master self has struck with the negating power of a racial gaze. As we've seen, this racially negated African cannot return looks of recognition that confirm the self-consciousness and autonomy of the master self. Rather, this racialized intersubjective exchange can only return to the master confirmation of something natural—his whiteness. Consequently, it is in negating the African as a black that the master secures a mirror for his whiteness. Here the dialectic of recognition becomes epidermal. Whiteness becomes the surface, the public mask of the master self. As its skin, whiteness becomes one of its natural endowments that this autonomous self has chosen to affirm rather than negate. As the African's essence is nature, he is very capable of intersubjectively confirming this natural feature. Consequently, we have a dialectic of recognition that moves solely on the surface of the skin, not affecting in any substantial way the two moments in the unity of the master self. Epidermal in its movements, the dead eye of this dialectic constitutes the African as a dark creature of nature whose negation provides a mirror in which the master self can see its whiteness. This is all that the natural subalterity of the African can do for the identity of this self.

AFRICANA PHENOMENOLOGY AND BLACK SUBALTERITY

If white racialization was the primary outcome for the master of the epidermal dialectic with the black, then we must now consider what its inherent positions of subalterity did for the African. To begin, we must recall that the master self does not really see the other but its own self in the other. In other words, its dead seeing eye is a blind seeing eye. Consequently, when it looks at the African it sees only what it means to be not white. African racialization within the framework of this dialectic is the internalization of blackness as that appearance which whiteness must negate in order to know itself. This negating of blackness produces a freezing of the identity of Africans that bars them from participating in dialectics of recognition that generate self-consciousness. This phenomenon of black racialization has been the primary outcome of the epidermal dialectic on the African side. Because its subalterity has so radically separated the black from self-consciousness, many Africana philosophers have been forced to raise the question of the path that African people must take in order to recover their humanity and to find confirmation of self. Clearly, it cannot just be the path of labor that Hegel held out to the European slave. Not surprisingly, this phenomenon of black racialization has been much more important to Africana phenomenologists than white racialization has been to Western phenomenologists.

Among the first phenomenological explorations of black racialization by Africana thinkers were those of Du Bois. In his analyses, Du Bois begins with the response of African people to their racial barring from human dialectics of recognition that produce self-consciousness and autonomy. This negation produced a definite fissure or division within the psyche and consciousness of Africans. As blacks, Africans could not be white. But to be white is also to be, say, German, American, French, self-conscious, rational, and autonomous. Consequently, Africans could be none of these in the master's eyes, discourses or race/ethnic orders, no matter how much they were in fact self-conscious, rational, and autonomous in their own eyes, discourses, and self-constituting acts. Hence, the difficulty of being a black and an American, "the two warring ideals," the "double consciousness" about which Du Bois wrote so eloquently.[13]

However, this double consciousness is different from Hegel's duplication within the unity of the self. In the latter, we saw that the first moment was one of being for self, while the second was being for others. It is in its second or intersubjective moment that the African self has been shattered by its racialization within the epidermal dialectic. In its mode of being for others, it can find no confirmation from the master of its capacity for self-conscious existence. Rather, the African gets only confirmation of his/her blackness, which at best becomes a trope for his/her animality. For Du Bois, the healing of this division in the second or intersubjective moment of the African self will require the mobilizing of a variety of intentional and cultural resources. The most important of these are the self-constituting resources of the first moment in Hegel's theory of the self, and the cultural images of self that predated the African's forced incorporation into the epidermal dialectic of recognition with the Western master self. These are the resources that Du Bois draws upon in his efforts to grasp the new pattern of doubling produced by black racialization.

Du Bois describes for us in a very self-revealing manner his own redeploying of the intentional resources of the first moment of being for self. First, he uses the symbol of the veil to represent the wall that arises between blacks and whites as a result of black exclusion from the dialectics of recognition that produce self-consciousness.[14] This veil is in part a black creation as white exclusion has elicited intentional acts of rejection from blacks. Second, Du Bois describes elevating himself to the top of a tower from which, as a writer, he would survey and look down upon the world.[15] Veil and tower are intentional moves that draw upon the self-constituting resources of the first moment in Hegel's theory of the self to heal the division in the second moment produced by black racialization. In short, double consciousness arises when the self-constituting claims of the first moment of being for self are not confirmed in the second or intersubjective moment by the racial/epidermal gaze from the dead seeing eyes of dominant others. It is a gap between the self-defined and the other-defined moments of black existence, where the racial identity of the dominant other requires the negation of blackness. Double consciousness is the price that African Americans have paid for being the barred racial other who has confirmed the whiteness rather than the self-consciousness of the Euro-American master self.

Du Bois's analyses found confirmation and extension in Fanon's probing phenomenological analyses. The focus of these analyses moves in two directions. The first is toward detailed and pointed phenomenological descriptions of the unusual destructive power of the dead seeing eye of the master self. It is an eye that sees with light of negation, erasure, racial genocide, and death. Hence, Fanon's disturbing declaration: "When I search for Man in the techniques and style of Europe, I see only a succession of negations of man, and an avalanche of murders."[16] Fanon's second focus is on some of the more problematic and self-contradictory responses that Africans have made to their racialization. The most disturbing of these has been the tendency to cover their negated black bodies and psyches in "white masks."[17] With the production of white masks, the epidermal dialectic undergoes a peculiar reversal. These masks increase the need for precisely the kind of white recognition that is not forthcoming from the master self. This need is not for confirmation of one's blackness, but for the confirmation of one's humanity as a self-conscious and autonomous existence. The tragic possibilities contained in this response and how deeply concealed they can be were major concerns of Fanon. It was the extremity of some of these responses that prompted Fanon's statement: "The Negro is comparison."[18] Compared to tower and veil, the production of white masks is clearly a much more contradictory and self-negating response to black racialization.

Lewis Gordon further extends this tradition of Africana phenomenology by examining the role of Sartrean bad faith in the production of both black and white racialized identities. His focus is on the set of intentional acts by which black humanity, self-consciousness, and autonomy get negated by the master's dead eye in spite of all the evidence to the contrary. For Gordon, this negation is made possible by the acts of bad faith through which we are all capable of lying to ourselves and believing the lie. Here they help to constitute the blindness of that eye through which master sees the African. Behind the bad faith negations of the master self, Gordon suggests that there can be found attempts at evading unresolved self-formative difficulties in regard to human freedom as a dialectic between being and nothingness. Among blacks, Gordon shows, the production of white masks or what he calls "black anti-blackness" can take place only because they are being done in bad faith.[19]

In sum, Africana phenomenology has taken up the task of theorizing black racialization as a distinct outcome of the epidermal dialectic between the African and the Western master self. Phenomenologically speaking, it is this racial duplication within the second moment of the black subaltern self that stands between it and its earlier African understandings of itself as Akan, Yoruba, or Hausa. Given these intersubjective outcomes of blackness and whiteness, our last remaining task is an examination of their current relevance and the racial order responsible for their ongoing reproduction.

BLACK SUBALTERITY: BACK IN THE SHADOWS OF WHITE NATIONALISM

The above conceptions of the white master self and its black subother have not gone unchallenged since the time of Hegel. Indeed, for Africana philosophers to have seriously undertaken the task of investigating black subjectivity, they had to begin by departing from the Hegelian claim that the African self was not established on the plane of self-consciousness but somewhere below it. Rejection of this claim was part of a larger insight that these two racialized identities were nightmarish Western fantasies that had somehow become part of the awakened reality of daily life. Thus Du Bois recognized the master self for the imaginary self-projection that it was: "We whose shame, humiliation and deep insult his aggrandizement so often involved, were never deceived. We looked at him clearly, with world-old eyes, and saw simply a human thing, weak and pitiable and cruel, even as we are and were."[20] However, false as this supremacist mask was, it had, like a hurricane, accumulated a great deal of power which it used to demand confirmation of its reality from others.

Concurrent with these Africana critiques were a series of European analyses and criticisms of the master self. From Marx and Kierkegaard through Nietzsche, Weber, and Freud, to Sartre, Lacan, Derrida, and Irigaray, the autonomy and sovereignty of the master self has been carefully examined or challenged. As noted earlier, Gordon's critique of the master self joined forces with Sartre's. However, although these critiques have wounded the master self, they have not transformed or overthrown it. They have rocked its intentional foundations, forcing it to see itself, and hence others, in less distorted ways. These critiques, by exposing its dead seeing eye, its self-inflations, and its bad faith, have reduced its capacity to manufacture desired social distances between itself and others, to make their humanity disappear—in short, to murder the humanity of others. Thus the African American is no longer three-fifths of a person. He/she is now a person whose self-consciousness it is no longer necessary to deny, but who is still not the equal of the master self.

In spite of such changes produced by these critiques, the white supremacist core of the Western master self has remained largely intact. Hence the need for confirmation of self continues to assert itself in the form of conflicts with others in which the latter are defeated. Then and only then in its intersubjective moment can it know itself as the sovereign, earth-owning freedom that it imagines itself to be. This supremacist need still drives the Western master self and can now be most strongly felt on its American frontier. In this American incarnation, the goal appears to be to eclipse the glories of its European predecessors and to prove itself the most supreme among the supreme. However, this American drive has not gone unchallenged. In the immediate post–World War II period, it had to contend with the rise of the Soviet Union to the status of a major global power. Not long after, there were the challenges from the African-American civil rights movement and from the movements for national liberation in the colonies of the West. Among the latter, the most devastating for the master self was the defeat in Vietnam. Adding yet another set of challenges was the rise of Japan and other Pacific Rim countries to the status of major economic powers that were capable of challenging the West in markets where it had long been dominant.

Challenged on these fronts, the Western master self felt its grip on itself slipping as the resurgent humanity of racialized and colonized subothers began signaling equality rather than the confirmation of its desired white supremacy. This loss of its earlier grip on itself initially forced the master self to go on the defensive. As the challenges peaked, this now embattled self was forced to make concessions and to try to conceal more effectively its delegitimized supremacist needs. The most significant outcome of this period in the United States was the change from the Euro-American racial order to the multicultural one. This shift brought the first formal removal of whiteness as a criterion for ritual entry into the American mainstream. It also established the policy of affirmative action as a new contract between white and black America. It was within the framework of this new policy that the abortive attempt would be made to create acceptable American ethnics out of Africans and other nonwhites.

From the phenomenological standpoint, without some profound transformation in the intentional structures of the master self, this defensive posture and its reforms could not be maintained for very long. Sooner or later the persisting need for confirmation of its supremacist self-image would reassert itself. If not accommodated, the earlier sense of crisis, of losing its grip on itself would only return with greater intensity. Indeed, the deepening of this sense of crisis is precisely what happened as policies of affirmative action began to change the racial landscape of America. The small but significant improvements in the sociopolitical positions of African Americans and other nonwhites precipitated what came to be known as the crisis of white identity.

This crisis moved in two directions. First was the response of many liberal whites, who were immobilized by guilt as they came to fuller realizations of the history and supremacist meaning of their racialized identities. Second was the response of many conservative whites who asserted that whites were now victims of racial discrimination by the policies of affirmative action, and so began to fashion a new white nationalism as a counter-response to affirmative action.[21] Rejecting the liberal multicultural order, they declared America a color-blind society, one in which race no longer mattered. In such a society, policies of affirmative action made whites the primary victims of racial discrimination. Whites, and particularly white males, as victims became the rallying cry of this new white nationalism that framed this particular resurgence of the supremacy needs of the American master self. In the words of Russell Eisenman: "Whites are victims of a quota system called affirmative action which causes them (especially white males) to be discriminated against, to work (as I have in the past) for an incompetent supervisor."[22] It was the second rather than the first of these two responses that would be crucial for the current posture of the American master self.

Exacerbation of these domestic difficulties by the Asian economic challenge marked a new phase in the history of the Western master self. After the shattering impact of the defeat in Vietnam, the project of the new nationalism got an important boost from the invasion of Grenada. On the economic front, neoliberal globalization became the framework for containing the Japanese challenge and at the same time ending affirmative action on the grounds that it was a fetter on capital, which now had to be more mobile than ever before. The master self had thrown off its defensive posture and was now back on its Hegelian tracks, grasping at the confirmation of its supremacy through defeating or imposing its existence on others. The collapse of the Soviet Union reinforced this resurgence of confidence. The major obstacle to its ownership of the earth had imploded. In the now postsocialist world, there is no force to really challenge its claims to the globe. The first major manifestations of this newly unfettered and color-blind master self in the postsocialist world have been amply displayed in its invasion of Iraq. It is in the expanding shadow of this resurgent self, its white nationalism, its neoliberalism, and its imperialism that we now live.

CONCLUSION

Whither will this new imperial phase of the Western master self steer the course of world history? At this point we cannot be sure. However, for blacks in both the United States and the Caribbean it has brought reversals to their multicultural and postcolonial orders that have produced significant losses of power. In the United States, behind the façade of color blindness, white power continues to rise at astronomical rates. Unfortunately, this growing asymmetry has already forced both Afro-Caribbeans and African Americans to readopt compensatory responses to black racialization that had long been in decline. In contrast to the veils and towers of black self-assertion during the civil rights and multicultural eras, we are now confronted with disturbing increases in the production of Fanonian white masks. Cases in point are the return of bleaching creams to the shelves of black drugstores; the progressive whitening of the appearance of black hair, as Afros and other black styles have declined with the growing number of blacks who have gone blonde; the return of the mulatto or light-skinned person as the standard of beauty to magazines like *Ebony*, and also now to music videos; poor black women in Jamaica injecting themselves with chicken hormones in the hope of lightening the color of their skin; and finally the growth of black conservative thought. The latter takes as its point of departure the defense of whites as the victimized group of the current color-blind racial order. Thus Shelby Steele's anger is reserved mostly for blacks, whom he sees as continuing this practice of victimization through a combination of manipulating the guilt of white liberals and the making of outdated defenses of affirmative action.[23] John McWhorter goes so far as to define "the new double consciousness" as the mechanism of deceptive self-presentation by which blacks play this game of discriminating against whites.[24]

Given these disturbing outcomes of the color-blind racial order, Africana phenomenologists have no choice but to take up once again the question of the need to dominate, to own the earth that feeds the supremacist image of the Western master self. In other words, we must renew the tradition of critique directed at this imperial self with the hope that our politics of recognition will be joined by a mass-based politics of economic and political redistribution. In particular, we can begin by turning our critical gaze on the changes in the intentional foundations of the dead seeing eye and the bad faith of this now supposedly color-blind master self.

NOTES

1. W.E.B. Du Bois, *Darkwater* (New York: Dover Publications, 1999), p.18.
2. G.W.F. Hegel, *The Phenomenology of Mind* (New York: Harper & Row, 1967), p.231.
3. Ibid.
4. Ibid., p. 229.
5. Ibid.
6. Wilson Harris, *The Guyana Quartet* (London: Faber & Faber, 1985), p. 19.
7. Alexander Kojeve, *Introduction to the Reading of Hegel* (New York: Basic Books, 1969), p. 7.
8. Frantz Fanon, *Black Skin, White Masks*, trans. Charles Lam Markmann (New York: Grove Press, 1967); Ato Sekyi-Otu, *Fanon's Dialectic of Experience* (Cambridge, MA: Harvard University Press, 1996); Lewis Gordon, *Bad Faith and Antiblack Racism* (Atlantic Highlands, NJ: Humanities Press, 1995); Lou Turner, "On the Difference between the Hegelian and Fanonian Dialectic of Lordship and Bondage," in *Fanon: A Critical Reader*, ed. L. Gordon, T. Denean Sharpley-Whiting, Renee White (Oxford: Blackwell Publishers, 1996), pp. 134–51; Nelson Maldonado-Torres, *Thinking from the Limits of Being* (forthcoming).
9. G.W.F. Hegel, *The Philosophy of History* (New York: Dover Publications, 1956), pp. 94–98.
10. Conversation with the author.
11. Maldonado-Torres, *Thinking from the Limits of Being*.
12. Fanon, *Black Skin, White Masks*, p. 220.
13. W.E.B. Du Bois, *The Souls of Black Folk* (New York: Fawcett Publications, 1969), pp. 16–17.
14. Ibid., p. 16.
15. Du Bois, *Darkwater*, p. 17.
16. Frantz Fanon, *The Wretched of the Earth* (New York: Grove Press, 1968), p. 312.
17. Fanon, *Black Skin, White Masks*, pp. 109–40.
18. Ibid., p. 211.
19. Gordon, *Bad Faith and Antiblack Racism*, pp. 104–16.
20. Du Bois, *Darkwater*, p. 20.
21. Carol Swain, *The New White Nationalism in America* (New York: Cambridge University Press, 2002).
22. Russell Eisenman, "Taking Pride in Being White," *Chronicle of Higher Education* 134 (October 1995): 10.
23. Shelby Steele, "The Age of White Guilt," *Harper's*, November 2002, pp. 33–42.
24. John McWhorter, *Authentically Black* (New York: Gotham Books, 2003), pp. 1–35.

10

ON THE NATURE OF WHITENESS
AND THE ONTOLOGY OF RACE
Toward a Dialectical Materialist Analysis

John H. McClendon III

THE CURRENT PHILOSOPHICAL DISCUSSIONS (in many instances what are more precisely debates) over whiteness signal not only the importance of whiteness as a philosophical problem but, more important, the ever-pressing reality of race. The ontological force of race is shaping the character of social institutions, relations, and practices in this country. Hence, such philosophical discussions about the nature of whiteness cannot be removed from broader debates about race. The nature of whiteness is inexorably and dialectically connected to the ontology of race. For example, whether one deems race to be of real substance or assumes that it is in some manner a kind of fiction, thus lacking onto-logical status, ultimately influences how one philosophically appre-hends and theorizes whiteness.

Therefore, in this chapter, I initially address the general problem of race to establish the broader context for elaborations on whiteness. Whiteness, in my estimation, is a particular instantiation of the more general idea of race. Logically, notions about whiteness must derive from general conceptions about race. The import of this presumption coincides with my philosophical perspective and method.

My philosophical standpoint is that of dialectical materialism. Di-alectical materialism, the philosophy of Marxism-Leninism, holds that there is a material reality that is independent of our social consciousness and also that material reality is the basis for consciousness. Although material reality, from the vantage point of dialectical materialism, is independent of consciousness, it is nonetheless open to our cognition; knowledge is a form of social consciousness that provides an objectively approximate cognition of material reality.[1] Herein there is no place for agnosticism and skepticism. Furthermore, race has an ontological status, and I demonstrate, in the course of this chapter, that whiteness possesses an ontological status as well. However, the essential problem at hand revolves around my critique of the prevailing notion that the ontological status of white supremacy can be subsumed within theoretical formulations about whiteness. I argue for a conceptual demarcation separating whiteness from white supremacy. This demarcation allows a critique of the concrete specificities adjoined to white supremacy and practically suggests possibilities for its eradication. In turn, the alternative view, which posits the need for the elimination of whiteness as such, the putative race traitor theory, is called into question.

RACE: FACT OR FICTION

Some philosophers, responding to the inadequacies of so-called "scientific" racism and its attempts to biologically ground the notion of race, declare that race is merely an ontological illusion.[2] Let us call arguments conveying such an ontological conviction about race, *the arguments from illusion*. In light of scientific advances that effectively undermined earlier pseudo-scientific formulations on race, proponents of the arguments from illusion assume that the very notion of race itself constitutes a pseudo-scientific notion. Subsequently, they conclude that race lacks any and all ontological legitimacy.[3] The arguments from illusion, I contend, turn on a particular confusion about the nature of science, its various modes of investigation, and how these modes of investigation are connected to understanding the nature of reality. This confusion about the disposition of scientific inquiry into material reality I term the *paradox of ontological conflation*.

Here the paradox of ontological conflation derives from a type of category mistake about how we are to determine what constitutes the scientific process for establishing how various social entities—social categories like race—assume their relevant ontological rank. The paradox of ontological conflation consists in the fact that the domain of the social sciences is conflated with what is more appropriately rendered in the employment of natural sciences. The paradox of ontological illusion comes with the presupposition that all ontological descriptions and accounts are confined to and exhausted in the natural sciences.[4]

Paradoxically, the arguments from illusion are founded on the same philosophy of science on which the pseudo-scientists anchor their views about race. Both groups share in the reduction of all sciences to natural science. For the former group, since the categories, methods and theories associated with natural science prove untenable in any account of race, they conclude that race is without scientific foundation. While the latter group believes that natural science can adequately explain race because, in their estimation, race is preeminently a biological category.[5]

Yet another paradox arises with the arguments from illusion. This is because the reality of race continually emerges and has enormous social effects. Somehow we are still faced with the nagging fact that "Race Matters."[6] And if "Race Matters," then we are obliged to ask, how do we account for its presence? Does not the social presence of race indicate its reality? Moreover, we discover that race as an idea finds supporters not only with the advocates of pseudo-science, but also among their most strident opponents. The arguments from illusion therefore are directed not only at pseudo-scientists, but also at their opponents since the very idea of race is under contention and not merely the means on which it is grounded. In this light, I contend that it is not fortuitous that Anthony Appiah, a proponent of the arguments from illusion, becomes ensnared in efforts to call into question Dr. W.E.B. Du Bois's ideas about race.[7]

The argument from illusion is often expressed as a conditional proposition: "If the reality of race cannot be scientifically proven—if there is no proof of its existence in *nature*—then race cannot in all *reality* exist." What follows from this proposition is the conclusion that "to the extent that we discover proponents of the idea of race, what transpires is the continuation of an illusion." More broadly, the arguments from illusion are established on the basis of ontological conflation. This is because such arguments restrict the scientific concept of race to what are pseudo-conceptions of science. Here we witness the conflation of pseudo-scientific theories of race with the actual scientific formulations. The scientific investigation of race is thrown out like the proverbial baby with the bathwater.[8]

Can we in view of the pseudo-scientific character of biological determinism, for instance, claim that the scientific analysis of race is exhausted? What if we think of race in reference to it being a social category? We thereby uncover that its ontological basis is not the product of nature and instead is linked to social reality. What about other forms of socially derived phenomena, commonly studied by the social sciences? Being in nature does not limit the boundaries of reality. Social reality, though distinct from natural reality, is nevertheless real. Race derives its ontological status from social reality.[9]

Clearly, with the arguments from illusion, it becomes apparent that the absence of natural scientific foundation, foundations which natural science erroneously attaches to race, on this account, is equated with how race lacks ontological status. When the arguments from illusion are taken to its logical conclusion, they portend to engulf all social entities tout court; all social categories are bereft of any ontological status.

But if ontological status is restricted only to the objects under the purview of natural science then it follows that social science is excluded from the realm of science. In effect, given this kind of reductionism, any and all sciences (outside of the realm of natural sciences) become a virtual impossibility. In fact, what we have is the reformulation of no less than a positivist philosophy of science, whereby natural science is the sole basis for grounding all entities on firm ontological foundations.[10]

Therefore, the argument from illusion overlooks the irreducible character of social reality vis-à-vis natural reality. Moreover, it constrains the possibility for the emergence of social science. Social reality is the object of inquiry for social science. Race as social reality cannot be overridden by the fact that it is not scientifically grounded in nature or natural reality. The displacement of race from natural reality results from the confirmation via social science of its ontological status vis-à-vis social reality. This irreducibility claim ought not be taken as an assertion that natural and social reality are unconnected; I am not adopting a form of dualism. Rather, it is a specification of a determinate difference within a broader framework of interconnected relationships. Natural and social realities are intrinsically linked via the fact that human beings are natural beings who realize natural needs and wants in a social way.[11]

Thus social relations and social practice via social production transform nature as well as human nature whose substance is social relations. The irreducibility of natural and social reality allows for the emergence of social categories, which in a material sense are both objective and real. The argument from illusion thus overlooks this historic transformation, the ontological affirmation of race as a social category. Therein resides how the arguments from illusion and the pseudo-scientific ideas about race share common ground in their neglect of the historical and social reality of race.[12]

The idea of race and the practice of racism are historical/social categories that emerge with the advent of capitalist slave trade and slavery.

The enslavement of Africans and the exclusive designation to and destination in their capacity as chattel required an ideological justification. The historic facts of the United States tell us a most glaring story about the genesis of the racial categories black and white. Although all black people were not slaves, the fact remains that *all slaves were black*. The idea of whiteness and the practice of white supremacy were crucial and central to how slavery became exclusively the province of Africans and their descendants.[13]

Before the downfall of indentured servitude, we discover that a great number of white people were relegated to the status of indentured servants. Yet the very demise of this system of labor exploitation can be directly explained by the institutionalization of slavery on the basis of race. Only a racialized social order could sustain Africans and their progeny in their permanent place at the bottom rung of a social hierarchy. This social hierarchy, which was founded on bourgeois class divisions, nevertheless branded workers in black skin as none other than slaves. In order to attain increasing rates of profit, capitalists ruthlessly exploited cheap slave labor and rationalized and justified this exploitation by means of racialized social categories.

Unlike other prior forms of slavery, capitalist slavery relentlessly and savagely denied the humanity of slaves. Chief Justice Roger B. Taney's declaration for the U.S. Supreme Court in the Dred Scott decision—which stated that a black person had no rights that a white man was bound to respect—made utterly transparent that blackness and whiteness was rooted in the fabric of the bourgeois legal order. The notions of whiteness and blackness were arranged on firm material foundations and gained juridical justification via the United States Constitution. The whole legal, moral, and ideological superstructure of capitalism in the United States rested on the configuration of bourgeois property relations, and the vast majority of black people were relegated to the position of chattel, property without basic human and civil rights.

RACE AS SOCIAL AND HISTORICAL CATEGORY

The institutionalization of slavery on the basis of race necessitated not only a system of labor but also a system that could account for who was white and who was black. It is at this juncture that whiteness developed into a living category. Whiteness grew out the material imperative to solve the problem of situating and locating people in a racialized social order. In turn, this racialized social arrangement furthered the exploitation of black labor.

Of course, after slavery the deployment of racial categories continued. Since the legal justification for slavery was swept aside with the Thirteenth Amendment, new means were found to subordinate black people to white power. Jim Crow, whose genesis and maturation all happened in the so-called "free" states of the antebellum period, maintained harsh lines of racial separation attendant with segregation. In fact, under segregation in the South, the rate of cotton production, so crucial to the institution of slavery, grew to higher levels in the postbellum period. In the last quarter of the nineteenth century, the United States was the leading exporter of cotton on the world capitalist market, and black labor was the chief source of production. The intense forms of exploitation of black labor, both in the antebellum and postbellum periods, justified on the basis of race, meant that racial categories had to be developed to specifically locate one's position within the social order. The utilization of phenotypic description was the principal means to this end.

Phenotypic description functions as the primary means for locating groups of people within the context of racially derived social relations. Social relations of capitalist exploitation serve as both the grounds for and purpose of racialized relations. The aim of social location is the major purpose of this system of racialized identity, and bourgeois social relations are its material foundation.

Phenotypic descriptions are instrumental, which, of necessity, means that they are secondary in the order of logical rank. Whiteness is a social category that designates how one may enter into what are ostensibly racialized social relations, institutions, and practices. The most immediate way of acknowledging differences on racial terms is to institute phenotypic descriptions. A certain phenomenology of appearances eases the complex problem of deciding who belongs where within the social order.

However, phenotypic description falters when miscegenation arises and eliminates clear lines of demarcation based on how racial types appear. All who appear to be white are not necessarily so. Yet, since they appear to be white, it follows that they do not appear to be black. It is precisely this fault line on which the arguments from illusion direct their attacks. Given that race is a social category that facilitates social location, phenotypic description is only one part of the equation.

Phenotypic descriptions are then supplemented by genotypic classification to overcome the blurred lines of racial morphology. The categories of octoroon, quadroon, mulatto and other such classificatory measures are applied to overcome the problems associated with strict phenotypic description. Genotypic classification or what is more popularly expressed as "the one-drop rule" is ultimately an attempt to shore up the fragile instrument of phenotypic description.

The case of Homer Plessy graphically amplifies this point. Despite his phenotype, Plessy's minimal amount of African ancestry (genotype) was a sufficient condition for socially locating him among black people. The *essence* of Plessy's blackness, if you will, derived from his designated social position and not from his physical appearance. Race is a social place, within an objective set of social relations, of which phenotypic description acts as a means to social location. Race, in this instance, is dialectically apprehended as a concrete expression of the contradiction between appearance and essence, via its embedded locus in material relations, institutions, and practices.

Race as a social category is ontologically valid and true, if and when our starting point is material relations of production. The material reality of race as a social category does not require an appeal to nature, natural science, or biology. Just as value, a political economics category, is not rooted in any state of nature but instead in a given set of social relations of production.[14] Yet race and value both possess definitive forms of ontological rank due to their groundings in materially determinate sets of social relations. These materially determinate sets of social relations thus anchoring race and value mean that they are not mere constructions and more appropriately are objective reflections of material reality. Marx comments:

> [A]s a value, the commodity is an equivalent; as an equivalent, all its *natural properties* are extinguished; it no longer takes up a separate special, qualitative relationship towards the other commodities. . . . Its property of being a value not only can but must achieve an existence different from its *natural* one. . . . [O]nly if the commodity achieves a double existence, not only a natural but also a purely economic existence, in which the latter is a mere symbol, a cipher for a [*social*] relations of production, a mere symbol for its own value. As a value, every commodity is equally divisible; in its *natural existence* it is not the case.[15]

If phenotypic descriptions are the sole means of determining race, then the idea of race as a social category is lost. If one relies only on phenotypic descriptions then we encounter the serious mistake of taking appearance for essence. This allows discussions on race to proceed in an antiscientific fashion. When we are concerned with whiteness as a category of race we cannot fall prey to thinking that whiteness is a matter solely contained in physical appearances. Karl Marx's comments on appearance and essence are most appropriate here. Marx in *Capital* makes the point transparent: "All science would be superfluous if the outward appearance and the essence of things directly coincided."[16]

The *essence* of race (as category) is *social* in character. Though, pheno-typic descriptions have a very important role, it is a subordinate role because its functions *instrumentally* and consequently cannot serve as an *ultimate* aim or purpose. More specifically, phenotypic descriptions are the necessary *form* of the social *content* constituting race as a social category.

Following from my comments with respect to value, the value form of the commodity as exchange value is a *necessary* form, which ulti-mately *appears* as the money form of value. This appearance is not merely an ideological illusion but is a *real* aspect of the commodity. Relevant to our discussion of phenotypic description as appearances and the adjoining social content of race, we find the same dialectical relation between appearance and essence is expressed in the corre-sponding dialectic of form and content. Thus phenotypic descriptions as appearances, on this account, hold an ontological status: they are real and not mere phantasms. As forms, phenotypic descriptions are the necessary expression or *manifest* form of race as social content. With this in mind, we can now proceed to an exploration on the nature of whiteness.

ON THE NATURE OF WHITENESS AND THE PROBLEM OF WHITE SUPREMACY

The salient presupposition of so-called whiteness studies, along with its ancillary theory about the function and role of race traitors, is that *whiteness* instead of *white supremacy* is the primary focus in our analy-sis of race. I submit that one of the dangerous implications in locating the concept of whiteness at the center of analysis is the inclination to ascribe attributes that are more appropriate to white supremacy than to whiteness. In more practical terms, whiteness becomes the crucial problem, and white supremacy is enveloped in various definitions and descriptions of whiteness.[17]

I think it is imperative to draw a distinction between white supremacy and whiteness. Whiteness and white supremacy, as philosophical concep-tions of material reality, present us with distinctive ontological and axio-logical issues. The grounds for the philosophical critique of whiteness, of course, are not detached from that of white supremacy. However, there is a fundamental *differentia specifica* demarcating the two. I take it that whiteness derives from the more general category—race—just as black-ness results from such a general category. What we mean by race entails offering concrete specifications about whiteness (and blackness) as a so-cial category. A description and definition of a white person does not of necessity entail a description and definition of a white supremacist. White supremacy, from the standpoint of dialectical materialist (philosophical) analysis, entails an evaluation of particular practices and values connected to how certain white people relate to racialized social conditions within a complex of power relations and within determinate historical conditions. We cannot appropriately and correctly talk of whiteness in abstraction of historical and social conditions.

Debates about the racial makeup of the ancient Egyptians (Kemet) among certain scholars and intellectuals are an ostensible case of an ahistorical approach to race and discourse about whiteness versus blackness. These debates are consumed in phenotypic descriptions of the ancient Egyptians.[18] Therein we observe that race is transformed from its locus as a social category, which includes not only phenotypic description but also social location within a particular set of social relations. The relationship of phenotypic description and genotypic classification is embedded in definitive social relations, which is the material substance behind the concept of race, particularly when viewed in reference to social categories such as white and black.

If we presume that whiteness forms the heart of the problem, rather than white supremacy, then there is a decided tendency to become less cognizant of the requisite values that are distinctively attached to white supremacy and which can be demarcated from those we have adjoined to whiteness. Moreover, the accent of whiteness and its ancillary valuation proves to be problematic especially if we intend to make the transition toward the critical examination of white supremacy, wherein white supremacy is studied both in terms of its materialist foundations and its dialectical development. To amplify this claim, let us develop a hypothetical proposition to explicate the process of centering whiteness, where in our analysis the differentiation between whiteness and white supremacy and their attributes are lost due to subsuming the latter under the former.

Our hypothetical proposition is a generalization for the purpose of generating a heuristic devise rather than a comprehensive summation that offers a substantive elaboration on the whiteness/race traitor thesis. Accordingly, we have the following claims.

The concept of whiteness comprises an ensemble of harmful, oppressive, and exploitive social practices, wherein the phrase "social practices" denotes most general forms of action—political, economic, psychological, aesthetic, religious, ideological, and so on. It follows that whiteness cannot be confined to any particular area of social relations and institutions, especially when viewed in light of its ascribed character—instantiated forms of harmful, oppressive and exploitive social practices.

Consequently, whiteness is *global* rather than *local* in scope and impact. (Here the terms "global" and "local" indicate philosophical rather than geographical denotation.) Specifically the global nature of whiteness means it has institutional as well as individual dimensions, material as well as ideological and psychological aspects. In fact, global whiteness is *primarily* institutional and material. Consequently, any specified beliefs or intentional actions functioning in accordance with such social practices are not necessary conditions for the exercise of whiteness. The aforementioned negative values, harm, oppression, and exploitation embodied in whiteness are *social practices* and thus assume a lived character and an existential dimension.

I think this hypothetical proposition conveys a charitable portrayal of the whiteness/race traitor thesis, or at least that remains my intention. There are six key points to be made in our explication of the whiteness/race traitor thesis.

First, let us begin our explication by noting that values such as harm, oppression, and exploitation all can be subsumed, in a determinative fashion, under the category "whiteness." By determinative fashion I mean that the exercise of whiteness can involve each value separately, any assorted combination thereof, or all of these values simultaneously functioning in modes characterized by a process of overdetermination.

Second, we can assume that these associated negative values of harm, oppression, and exploitation are either *minimally* the effects of whiteness or *maximally* the expression of it. Where they are effects then whiteness is the cause of harmful, oppressive, and exploitative practices. When whites act in a harmful way, oppressive manner, and exploitative fashion toward African Americans, for example, then to account for these practices we should to start with their whiteness as the causal variable and not begin with their harm, oppression, and exploitation taken sui generis. The latter are the effects of a deeper cause (whiteness) and only in uprooting the cause can we effectively deal with the effects.

In the maximal instance, when these values are taken to be expressive forms, then whiteness is one and the same with these expressions, and thus whiteness shares an ontological identity with said values. Whiteness is an ontological category marked by features that are axiological in kind. On the maximalist account, whiteness is harmful, oppressive, and exploitative in a racialized context. Whiteness, in a word, is the problem.

Third, within this range of minimal and maximal possibilities, there resides the overriding principle that whiteness is the source of such values. The location of whiteness either seen in terms of the cause of negative value effects or the essence behind expressions of harm, oppression, and exploitation lends support to a structural analysis of whiteness.

Fourth, in this respect, whiteness is structurally foundational to our host of negative values. Any derivative philosophy of social science aimed at the investigation of the values under consideration within the racialized context, for instance, must be the elaboration of a framework where whiteness is thought of as foundational.

Fifth, given the foundational character of whiteness, the aforementioned values are inexorably contained within whiteness. Whether we presume that these values are minimally the effects of whiteness or maximally expressive of it, nonetheless, they emanate from whiteness. Since whiteness is a social category and requires some form of social analysis, all social categories employed in our analysis that are not part and parcel of whiteness have an external locus to the cause or essence of harm, oppression, and exploitation in racialized circumstances.

Sixth, all investigation and discussion of white supremacy, on this account, is consequently subsumed *within* the category of whiteness. The reprehensible values adjoined with the social practices that are subsequently described in terms of whiteness are manifestly interior and internal in character. Whiteness becomes an insular and autonomous social category and this results in the propensity to discount (if not dismiss) such values as rooted in other social categories and relations because they are exterior or external to whiteness. Now let us move from our explication to a critique of this view on the nature of whiteness.

Here with our hypothetical proposition, the meaning and import of whiteness supervenes on white supremacy in such a way that investigation into and discussion about white supremacy semantically offers us instances of redundancy. Given this blurring of the distinctions between whiteness and white supremacy one can proceed with the presumption that inquiry into the nature of whiteness is a sufficient condition for inquiry into white supremacy. Nevertheless, I began by asserting that we ought to distinguish between whiteness and white supremacy. So we must first address the question, why is white supremacy not subsumed under the category of whiteness?

White supremacy means white power, that is, the power of whites to exercise control over and hence dominate all groups of people that are defined, described, and consequently existentially designated "nonwhite." It follows that "nonwhiteness" is a socially ascribed category that is affixed to the social and more broadly existential position of people deemed to be not white. I contend that white supremacy is quintessentially, although not exclusively, social (material) practices, on the part of white people, wherein putatively nonwhite races (black people) are harmed, oppressed, and exploited because they are not white. Black people, for instance, are cast as inferior because they are not white. The point is that white supremacy (think here of the KKK) indicates oppression and harm. Yet, oppression and harm do not necessarily include exploitation.

Exploitation derives from class positions where power is attached to having or not having wealth. Black and white workers share in being exploited under capitalism, while white supremacy allows for the superexploitation of black working people. On the one hand, we know that not all black people are exploited and oppressed, and, on the other hand, that some black people are exploiters and oppressors. Race analysis cannot be disjoined from the class character of capitalism. Race is not equivalent or even reducible to class as a social category. However, race analysis separated from a critique of capitalism and its material conditions can only achieve at best superficial descriptions and at worst a distorted conception of reality.[19]

Thus, we can argue with warrant that given the class nature of capitalism, the power exercised by white supremacy over black people need not be limited to whites in that capacity. Unlike slavery, when all the slaves were black, there are a sizable number of exploited and oppressed white people who do not have the power that some black people have today. Can we in all honesty say that Colin Powell is not an oppressor and that he does not serve the interests of the ruling class? Or that Powell's power to make decisions about war against Iraq did not send scores of poor white and black people to be made into cannon fodder? Or that the wealth of Robert Johnson or John Johnson or Oprah Winfrey put them in a position where white poor people maintain some advantage or benefit over them due to their whiteness?[20]

Given the above examples, would we really want to call all white people, by virtue of their whiteness, white supremacists? Even if we argue that some whites unconsciously reap the benefits of being white, does this sufficiently indicate they are white supremacists? From a class analysis of whiteness, we can argue that whiteness is not always a benefit for all whites. Whiteness, on numerous occasions, has been used as a smokescreen to render the fight against class exploitation vulnerable to ruling-class hegemony. The objective class interests of the working class are often sacrificed because whiteness is perceived in terms of white supremacy.[21] The conflation of whiteness with white supremacy is the bane of the white proletarian struggle in the United

States in particular. White workers have many times fallen prey to the ruling ideology of white supremacy and often at their own peril as workers who have more in common, in regard to material interests, with black working people than their white counterparts in the ruling class.

Here we can say that whiteness has a certain invisible quality. Many oppressed and exploited whites do not see how whiteness is situated in power relations and neglect their own powerlessness because they derive comfort (psychological respite) in being white. Yet since a great number of poor whites have no real material power in bourgeois society they seek to find the cause of their own misery via perceived threats to their racialized existence. Hence they become not only deluded by whiteness but also other forms of bourgeois ideology such as patriotism and xenophobia. Whiteness cannot be abstracted from the ensemble of social relations where power and wealth are the material foundations for exploitation and oppression. The dialectics of ideological domination, the ruling ideas are those of the ruling class, is a complexity that cannot be reduced to any monolithic description of whiteness as an instrument that all whites hold over all black people.[22]

What if we consider the thesis that white people in general gain benefits from whiteness and thus the accrual of benefits is in some measure equivalent with white supremacy? The presumption is that there is a certain invisible power to whiteness whereby whites gain and black people lose out. Let us take the white person who is never stopped by the police. The idea that some privilege is affixed to such circumstances is generally unknown. Is this because she/he participates in the invisibility of being white? Furthermore, is such a person, by virtue of being white and never stopped, really a white supremacist? What about a white child who will, by virtue of being white, typically receive better health care and better education than a black child of comparable age—would we call such a person a white supremacist? Or what about a white teenage girl who thinks that she is more beautiful than any black girl but does not fully understand that she is the victim of commercial adds, white-controlled cinema, commercial beauty products, and so on?[23]

In short, she has only come to think this way because she has bought into the "normativity" of whiteness. Because she thinks this, can we say she is a white supremacist? My sense is that in each case we would want to say, no. What is problematic is that in a racist society the categories white and black as social categories reflect concrete racialized material and cultural conditions. The transformation of such conditions inevitably requires the transformation of the categories, that is, to the extent that they perpetuate racial subordination. What we mean by black and white takes on a qualitative change. Rather than calls for race traitors, I think we need to focus on reconstituting the social relations, institutions, and practices that give rise to white supremacy. Whiteness in abstraction from concrete relations is not a particular seat of power. It is attached to power only in certain prescribed instances, as outlined above, and then it is dialectically transposed into white supremacy.[24]

The manifestation of white supremacy is not the province of all whites and it can be, and has been, detrimental to powerless whites who, because of their class position, fail to actualize their material interests. In the same instance, blackness is not in itself negative or virtuous.[25] Simply being black does not necessarily point to what in real terms is an anti–white supremacist posture or an allegiance to the mass struggles of black people. Celebrating Condoleezza Rice or Colin Powell during black History Month, does not make them very different from George Bush or Donald Rumsfeld—that is, if our objective is a materialist assessment of history. Moreover, some black intellectuals can and do offer their services to white supremacy and ruling-class ideology.[26] Can we seriously claim that because of their blackness, Condoleezza Rice, Colin Powell, or Thomas Sowell are at a disadvantage with respect to the privileges afforded to white people? Are these highly acclaimed black figures in some manner virtuous because they are black? Whiteness and blackness are value-free notions when considered apart from concrete social relations, institutions, and practices.

Whiteness, and, for that matter, blackness, are not problems in themselves. However, white supremacy is pivotal. My argument is not that race is reducible to class relations; rather, it is grounded in the material conditions of capitalism. The material roots of white supremacy must be attacked. This means both the scientific critique of, and the practical struggle against, white supremacy. This, therefore, becomes our paramount issue.

NOTES

1. Theodore Oizerman, *Problems of the History of Philosophy* (Moscow: Progress Publishers, 1973); V. I. Lenin, *Philosophical Notebooks*, Vol. 38 of *Collected Works* (Moscow: Progress Publishers, 1972).

2. See Kwame Anthony Appiah, *In My Father's House* (New York: Oxford University Press, 1992), and "The Uncompleted Argument: Du Bois and the Illusion of Race," in *African Philosophy: Selected Readings* ed. A. Mosely (Englewood Cliffs, NJ: Prentice Hall, 1995); and Naomi Zack, *Race and Mixed Race* (Philadelphia: Temple University Press, 1993).

3. Victor Anderson, *Beyond Ontological Blackness* (New York: Continuum Publishing Company, 1993).

4. Kwame Anthony Appiah and Amy Gutman, *Color Consciousness* (Princeton, NJ: Princeton University Press, 1996).

5. William H. Tucker, *The Science and Politics of Racial Research* (Urbana: University of Illinois Press, 1994).

6. Cornel West, *Race Matters* (Boston: Beacon Press, 1993).

7. See W.E.B. Du Bois, *Dusk of Dawn: An Essay toward an Autobiography of a Race Concept* (New York: Schocken Books, 1968); Appiah, "Uncompleted Argument"; and Lucius T. Outlaw, *On Race and Philosophy* (New York: Routledge, 1996).

8. Appiah, "Uncompleted Argument"; and Appiah and Gutman, *Color Consciousness.*

9. David Theo Goldberg, *Racial Subjects: Writing on Race in America* (New York: Routledge, 1997).

10. Patrick Murray, *Marx's Theory of Scientific Knowledge* (Atlantic Highlands, NJ: Humanities Press, 1990).

11. Karl Marx and Friedrich Engels, *The German Ideology*, ed. C. J. Arthur (New York: International Publishers, 1972).

12. Appiah, "Uncompleted Argument"; Paul S. Ehrlich and Shirley Feldman, *The Race Bomb* (New York: Quadrangle/The New York Times Book Co., 1977).

13. W.E.B. Du Bois, *Black Folk, Then and Now; An Essay in the History and Sociology of the Negro Race* (New York: Henry Holt & Co., 1939); Clarence J. Munford, *Production Relations, Class, and Black Liberation: A Marxist Perspective in Afro-American Studies* (Amsterdam: B. R. Gruner, 1978).

14. Karl Marx, *Grundrisse* (Baltimore: Penguin Books, 1973).

15. Ibid., p.141.

16. Karl Marx, *Capital, Vol. 3* (New York: International Publishers, 1967), p. 817.

17. Noel Ignatiev and John Garvey, eds., *Race Traitor* (New York: Routledge, 1996); Terrence Epperson, "Whiteness in Early Virginia," *Race Traitor* 7 (1997): 9–20.

18. Chancellor Williams, *The Destruction of Black Civilization* (Chicago: Third World Press, 1976); St. Clair Drake, *Black Folk Here and There: An Essay in History and Anthropology* (Los Angeles: CAAS Publications, 1987).

19. John H. McClendon, "Black and White contra Left and Right? The Dialectics of Ideological Critique in African American Studies," *APA Newsletter on Philosophy and the Black Experience* 2, no. 1 (2002).

20. Ellis Cose, *The Rage of a Privileged Class* (New York: Harper/Perennial, 1995).

21. William M. Tuttle Jr., "Labor Conflict and Racial Violence," *Labor History* 10, no. 3 (1969): 408–32.

22. Oliver C. Cox, "Modern Democracy," in *Race, Class, and the World System*, ed. H. Hunter and Sameer Abraham (New York: Monthly Review Press, 1987).

23. Patricia J. Williams, "The Ethnic Scaring of American Whiteness," in *The House That Race Built*, ed. W. Lubiano (New York: Pantheon Books, 1997).

24. Ibid.

25. Victor Anderson, *Beyond Ontological Blackness*, (New York: The Cortinuum Publishing Company, 1993).

26. Thomas Sowell, *Race and Culture* (New York: Basic Books, 1994).

11

SILENCE AND SYMPATHY

Dewey's Whiteness

Paul C. Taylor

JOHN DEWEY INTRODUCES AN EDITION of Claude McKay's *Selected Poems* by saying, more or less, that there is nothing he can say.[1] He begins with a lament about how commentary and praise seem "impertinent" and "idle," and he ends, a few paragraphs later, by confessing that the poet's depiction of life under white supremacy leaves white men able to express only "humiliated sympathy." My first encounter—my first several, actually—with this text left me thinking of it as an expression of a familiar aspect of whiteness, as we have been led to understand it by the critical race theorists who explore such things. And this led me to think of it as a straightforwardly problematic moment in Dewey's corpus, deeply in need of illumination and correction. But now I wonder whether the lines of illumination might run in the opposite direction as well.

I wonder whether Dewey's silence might have something to contribute to current discussions of whiteness; and I wonder this mainly because I have never quite known what to make of these discussions. As one critic has recently put it, the "core concept"—whiteness—fairly "defies singular definition," in ways that I will say more about below.[2] And the arguments sometimes unfold without specifying the level of abstraction at which they are meant to apply. (I am not happy with that last sentence, but I will leave it as a sign of the problem: I cannot even identify as precisely as I would like the mode of puzzlement I have sometimes fallen into.) Perhaps Dewey's introduction to McKay's book was a response to something that is also at work in whiteness studies, something that also demands silence. You will not be surprised to learn that it will take me some time, and many words, to decide.

I should begin by saying more about what I take to be the main lessons of the critical whiteness literature. The first lesson is that we have to distinguish recent antiracist work on whiteness from the likes of Thomas Dixon's *The Clansman* or Stoddard's *The Passing of the Great Race*. This is why I keep referring to the *critical* study of whiteness. It is also why I have to tell you that what follows will focus exclusively on this critical work, even though I will usually just say "whiteness" for ease of exposition.

The second lesson is that the academic enshrinement of "whiteness studies," or whatever we call it, has at least a couple of dangers that we should consider. One is that we will think of this mode of inquiry as something new, without regard for the people, particularly nonwhite writers and artists, who have been critiquing whiteness for some time. I recognize the contributions of figures like Baldwin and Du Bois; but my particular target is the work that contemporary writers, mostly academics, have done to develop the insights of these earlier accounts. The second danger is that this new field of inquiry will compete for resources and attention with the fields, programs, and departments of, for example, African-American studies and Chicano studies. Considering this danger would require far exceeding the scope of this essay. All I can say here is that the writers I will consider do not propose that we establish departments of white studies, and they explicitly try to fold their efforts into the kind of counter-racist, often archaeological approach to knowledge production that dovetails with and supports the work of, for example, African- American studies.

The third lesson of the whiteness literature has to do with what whiteness is. This is a lesson I have found hard to learn, mainly because the literature I have encountered has in some ways been more suggestive than clear. Where one might expect to find definitions, one often finds a metaphor or list of similes—whiteness-as-property, whiteness-as-terror, whiteness-as-invisibility, and so on. The similes do point us to useful phenomena, and the definitional murkiness is often intentional, meant to indicate that whiteness is variable and contextual, demanding different treatments in different contexts. But still, we ought to be able to say just *what it is* that requires this treatment. So I will try to provide a summary answer to this question by translating some key points of the literature into radical constructionist terms.[3] (I will particularly have in mind Ruth Frankenberg's gloss of these points.)[4]

"White," like all the components of racial discourse, refers to a social position on a properly racialized landscape, where by "social location" we mean a probabilistically and counterfactually specifiable social condition or mode of treatment. Du Bois said in 1940 that a black person is one who has to ride Jim Crow in Georgia. We can take this, mutatis mutandis, as an adequate formula even today: a black person is one who *would have to* ride Jim Crow (or enact the psychosocial drama of passing) *if he or she were* in 1940s Georgia. By extension, a white person is someone who would have to ride in the "whites only" car. The whiteness of such a person consists not in their phenotypic traits, but in the social meaning that Western society assigns to people with the correct bodies and "bloodlines."

In a society still structured by racial dominance, it is easy enough to update Du Bois's test. Belonging to a race means, one might say, being the subject of certain probabilistic inferences by virtue of one's appearance and ancestry, inferences that principally concern one's life chances—net worth, job prospects, access to health care, and so on. These inferences will be complicated and defeasible, as they will take into account the processes by which race, class, gender, region, sexual orientation, age, and all the other principles of social differentiation mutually and simultaneously determine each other, thereby giving a unique shape to the experiences of each individual. But committing to a racial vocabulary or frame of analysis means committing to the proposition that we can specify the difference that race—the condition of being someone who would have to take up a certain place in the Jim Crow car, or the internment camp, or wherever—will make in the unfolding of experience. Or: yes, it is true that white people are distributed across economic classes; but once we specify the class, it is still the case that white people overwhelmingly tend to have, for example, greater stores of financial assets than their similarly situated black counterparts—in every class.[5]

On one level, then, whiteness consists of occupying a social location of structural privilege in the right kind of racialized society—or, if we insist on the interpenetration of social determinants, of occupying one of a set of social locations. But on another level, whiteness involves, as Frankenberg says, an epistemic position: we might follow Marilyn Frye in saying that this means seeing the world *whitely*. Seeing whitely involves a set of context-dependent and variable commitments, which of course individual white people—defined either by phenotype or by social location—need not accept. But part of the social location is an increased likelihood of seeing whitely: this is the lesson of the opinion polls that routinely show white and black people drawing different conclusions on controversial issues.

Seeing whitely tends to involve a commitment to the centrality of white people and their perspectives. Here we return to the idea that whiteness is normative, which allows us to generate some of the other characteristic ideas about whiteness. Critical analysts follow Cheryl Harris in linking whiteness with property in part to argue that whitely perception takes its race-based entitlements as a baseline. Racial privilege becomes a natural right, and establishes the starting point for deliberations about distributive justice. The result, of course, is that proposals to distribute social goods in ways that deviate from the old, asymmetric, racist distributions strike whitely perceivers as *unjust.*

Similarly, we link whiteness with invisibility to highlight the norm-setters' privilege of leaving their perspectives and practices unexcavated and unmarked, and of ignoring the perspectival nature of their perspectives. The way they see the world just is the way the world is, and the way they get around in the world just is the right way to get around. This is, in part, why the nonwhites to whom whiteness was quite visible had to invent programs like Asian American studies—to make up for the implicit white bias of mainstream academic disciplines. (The mainstream discipline was not "white history"; it was, simply, "history.") It is also why some of us still take the European immigrant experience as the paradigm for the American experience—which is to say, in this spirit, the U.S. experience; it is why we can still ask why freed slaves and nonwhite immigrants somehow failed to prosper in the way the new arrivals did. And it is why we refer to some foods and not others with markers like "ethnic" and "cultural." (A flyer I once saw advertised a party at which "cultural foods" were to be served. What food is not cultural? Hamburgers? French—er, *freedom*—fries?)

The ideology of whiteliness, then, gives us a second level of meaning behind contemporary invocations of "whiteness." It also points to a third level. We might think of individual white ideologies as the point at which individuals encounter, appropriate, and revise broader systems of meaning. Seeing whitely means participating in something much larger than oneself; it means tapping into a system of ideas and images that provides a kind of commonsense background for much of Western culture. We can consider this discourse of whiteness in relative isolation from its individual vehicles, participants, or bearers. Here we are concerned with the systematic ordering of social meanings and the patterned structuring of social roles and relations. Here we can speak of the way whiteness shapes labor politics, or of the way it reproduces itself in film narratives, and so on.

So whiteness is a property of individuals—a social location of structural privilege; it is a generic sensibility, perspective, or mind-set, and sometimes one that remains resolutely unaware of its distinctiveness; and it is a discourse, or a system of meanings that is dialectically co-constitutive with individual sensibilities. Whiteness, understood in each of these senses, has the features and limitations of any other occupant of the racialized social world. It is contextual in the sense that it takes on meaning relative to its specific contexts. It is variable and contested in the sense that its meaning shifts, usually in the process of political struggle. It is efficacious in the sense that things happen on account of it. And it is relational in the sense that it gets articulated, and often conflated, with other principles of social differentiation.

As I have said, Dewey's silence evoked for me one particular aspect of this framework, call it a theory of whiteness. This is the idea of whiteness denying itself, or remaining invisible to itself. The fact of silence and the metaphor of invisibility invoke different sensory registers, of course, but the basic mechanism, of failed or flawed perception, is the same. Embracing silence means denying oneself a voice; and this means rejecting the validity of one's personal stake in some subject, and the importance of finding words for one's perspective. This is why we so often speak of political empowerment as a matter of acquiring, finding, and using one's *voice*. Political participation means expressing oneself, expressing one's *self*; and this is a process not so much of delivering oneself of a fully formed set of propositions, but of discovering, shaping, and cultivating the bundle of interests, beliefs, desires, and so on that constitutes the self. "Expression" is the name Dewey gives to this process of excavation, invention, and externalization;[6] and "voice" is the name we give, often enough, to the public face of this capacity for expression.

Declining to speak on a matter that manifestly concerns me is a way of denying my own voice; but I can do this without denying to myself my connection to the subject. Perhaps I just do not care to talk to *you* about it. But claiming that there is *nothing I can say* on a matter that manifestly concerns me, if I claim this sincerely, is way of denying my connection, and, at the same time, of refusing to examine myself closely enough to uncover and find words for the connection.

The parallels between whiteness and this idea of voice,[7] or the act of silencing this voice, are not far to seek. Participating in whiteness-as-invisibility means denying that one has a perspective on or stake in the racial terrain. It means rejecting, or ignoring, the burden of identifying—of conceptualizing, of seeing which words apply to—one's place in a system of social forces and relations. If this is right, then Dewey's embrace of silence is a way of declining to identify his own perspective, his personal perspective, on racial injustice. He never took up the burden of *explain-*

ing, to himself and others, his connection to white supremacy. And that is a paradigmatically whitely thing to do. (Even more disappointing in the case of Dewey, it is also a typically philosophical thing to do. A kind of self-denial has long been a mainstay of the philosophic method, as it is often conceived. Descartes's "I think" was really, as Kant and others saw, just some thinking going on—the "I" had not been specified and did not, could not, do any work. More recently, conceptual analysis, what is left of it, asks us to consider what some "we" means when we say this or that, but typically declines to say who or what or where this we is. But Dewey, like Nietzsche and William James, was always critical of this. He always insisted on context, on tracing philosophic assumptions to their motivating conditions. In some moods, he even took this excavation or archaeology as philosophy's principal mission. It is all the more troubling, then, that he would refuse to orient himself vis-à-vis the specifically racial mode of structuring dominance in U.S. society.)

Reading Dewey's silence as a refusal, and as a matter of the social epistemology or moral psychology of race, goes a long way toward explaining some puzzling lacunae in his career. For example, and as Cornel West has pointed out, the otherwise plausible claim that Dewey was the most outstanding public intellectual in the twentieth-century United States has to grapple with his refusal to endorse or even mention the Dyer Bill, which would have made lynching a federal crime. A search of Dewey's collected works and correspondence, the sort of search that modern databases make possible, finds no mention of the bill, and only a few occurrences of "lynch" and its cognate terms—none related to African-American people, or to the South's "strange fruit." Every reference (that does not involve a person *named* "Lynch") is metaphorical, invoking the general idea of "lynch law"—as if in a Hollywood western—to complain, for example, about the improperly precipitate way in which public opinion can take shape and make itself manifest. As Shannon Sullivan has pointed out, even in an address before the NAACP, Dewey managed to say little more than that racial stratification was a function of more general economic and political forces—a reductionist posture that he would have abhorred in a Marxist.[8]

To be fair, it is worth noting that the NAACP was itself ambivalent for a time about the Dyer Bill, to the extent that at least one historian blames the bill's death in part on the indifference of its advocates.[9] But worries about that particular bill, usually about its constitutionality, did not prevent the organization from strenuously and frequently denouncing the terrorist institution of race-based lynching. Dewey could not bring himself to do even that much (in print, at least).

Also to be fair, Dewey was a founding member of the NAACP, and regularly spoke out against racism in all its forms. As early as 1909—in an address to the conference that would lead to the founding of the NAACP—he endorsed the view that there was no scientific support for biological racialism or for scientific racism.[10] And he frequently spoke out against all forms of racist exclusion, including the mistreatment of the European immigrants whom we now think of as "ethnic" but who still constituted explicitly racialized populations at the time. Consider, for example, his 1916 address to the National Education Association, in which he praises teachers for trying to create an inclusive American identity, blending the best of all races and national origin groups.[11] So it is not as if Dewey said *nothing* about racism. Not only did he speak out, he acted. So maybe he says *there is nothing I can say* not out of a reluctance or inability to confront his own whiteness, understood as his location on a white supremacist social terrain, but out of a sense of the futility of further talk. Perhaps we have here not so much the refusal to find a voice but the determination to privilege antiracist action over concerned hand-wringing.

Unfortunately for this more sympathetic reading, further talk, or clearer talk, would have been far from futile. More precisely: Dewey could have said a great deal more on some subjects, like the Dyer Bill. And he could have said a great deal to clarify or retract what he said on other subjects, as the 1916 address makes clear. As just noted, he recommends in this address that educators insist on and cultivate America's "complex and compound" identity, to create an "internationalist nationalism" of tolerance and possibility. Just after this, though, he raises a second point that bears on "the constitution of a genuine American nationalism." He says: "We have been occupied during the greater part of our history in subduing nature, not one another or other peoples." Apparently unaware that Native Americans, say, or the recently conquered Hawaiians, or (somewhat later in the year) Dominicans under U.S. military occupation would surely have taken issue with this claim, he presses on. "[W]e have had more room, more opportunity" than other nations, he says. "The spaciousness of a continent not previously monopolized by man has . . . diverted activity from the struggle against fellow-man into the struggle against nature."[12] Maybe there is something to this, if the aim is to contrast U.S. history with the birth and history of nationalism in Europe, with its incessant wars and boundary disputes between similarly organized state formations ("similarly organized" in the sense that they were more similar to each other than any were to precolonial American states). If the War of the Austrian Succession is what counts as the struggle against one's fellow men, then maybe this makes sense. Of course, the history of Europe must leave out such events as England's invasion and colonization of Ireland in order for this reading to work. And Native Americans must fail to qualify as fellow men, at least for the purpose of evaluating political violence. And all this would mean that the white experience, in this case the experience of political violence, has once more come to stand in for all experience.

Here we see Dewey even more clearly acting out a script that critical whiteness studies has made familiar. According to this script, and as we have seen, whiteness qua normativity and invisibility involves a kind of false consciousness, what Charles Mills calls an epistemology of ignorance.[13] In fact, Mills makes this one of the provisions of the racial contract that he puts at the heart of Western political society. This contract, like the contract at the core of John Rawls's *Theory of Justice*, is not a document that people sign, but a device for perspicuously rendering certain aspects of our common life. It represents an ongoing set of conventions, often but not necessarily encoded in actual documents or historical agreements (think of the laws establishing the inability of nonwhites to serve as witnesses in legal proceedings). The relevant bits of the contract go something like this: *We, the full persons, call us "white people," agree to accept partial and distorted interpretations of reality concerning the social world, especially where it concerns our relations to, and the condition and nature of, those creatures we agree to constitute as subpersons—call these "niggers," "kikes," "wops," "kaffirs," "pakis," "blackfellas," and so on.* Typically this means seeing black people as muggers or rapists or "welfare queens"; seeing Asians as agents of an inassimilable yellow peril, here to take over; seeing Mexicans as permanent aliens, also inassimilable, and here to take our jobs; and seeing Native Americans as a kind of historical relic or, perhaps, as part of nature, and in any case unrelated to the life of our modern nation. It also tends to involve underestimating the depth of whatever economic and social ills plague these people and ignoring the systemic causes of these ills in favor of causes, or "causes," emanating somehow from the victims.

This myopia is constitutive of a brand of whiteness, and Dewey had a fairly mild case of it. He did not blame the victims, but he was insensitive to the distinctive challenges that they faced, and to how the mechanisms for producing those challenges shaped his own path in the world. He could not see his own whiteness, and the things he did see, he saw whitely. By providing the resources to point this out, the critical study of whiteness has made a useful contribution to the history of philosophy, to Dewey studies, and to the other fields—education theory,

American studies, and so on—that still claim an interest in Dewey. But does this point have anything other than historical interest for students of whiteness? Does the story of Dewey's silence provide any useful lessons for critical approaches to whiteness?

If Dewey's silence has any contribution to make to critical white studies today, it probably will not be a theoretical contribution. We can account for Dewey's case quite well by straightforwardly applying some familiar ideas from the whiteness literature, without coining new metaphors or reconfiguring the conceptual terrain. And proceeding in this way does not seem to leave any remainder, any aspect of his case, at least in the way that I have presented it, that demands further theorization. Of course, the way I have presented it may have something to do with this, which is one reason I say that the lesson of the McKay introduction *probably* will not involve theory. In the fashion of many philosophers, I have taken a scattershot approach to history, focusing on bits of isolated texts without locating them all that carefully along the arc of his career as a writer, activist, and thinker. Let me say that this is my way of respecting the academic division of labor and leaving something for the historians of ideas and literary critics among us to do. Still, my sense is that this is a good beginning, and it indicates where the drift of that work will take us.

I am guessing that future work will not need any novel theoretical resources to account for Dewey's silence in part because I am not sure there is any more theoretical work to do. This is not the sort of thing I can prove, of course. I cannot show that a discourse has become saturated, that a way of going on has exhausted its possibilities, not least because I am not Hegel. But I can report my suspicion, and I can point you to some moments in the whiteness literature that inspire that suspicion in me. I am thinking of a pair of essays in an interesting anthology called *The Making and Unmaking of Whiteness.*

We have already encountered one of the essays, a piece by Ruth Frankenberg. I used this essay a bit earlier as a point of departure for a conceptual geography of whiteness; but there is more to the essay than summary discussion. There is some original analysis, the point of which we can glean from the essay's title: "The Mirage of an Unmarked Whiteness."

Frankenberg's claim is that whiteness is not nearly as invisible, as often, as it has been made out to be—that it goes unmarked much less often than we are led to believe. This is worth noting, but the point is not exactly new; worse, it is not even clear that anyone holds the view that she is rejecting. Of course white people have, under various circumstances, gone to great trouble to declare their whiteness and specify its meaning. There are old examples, from the Jim Crow South and earlier, and newer examples, from, say, Ronald Reagan's mobilization of the resentments of unreconstructed southerners, and others. No one who argued for whiteness-as-invisibility really denied this. They were just concerned with explaining the things that the idea of invisibility does illuminate—like the peculiarity of Dewey's refusal, if I have read it properly. As I understand the invisibility move, the point was always that whiteness *has made itself* invisible in various ways, especially since we started identifying color blindness as the principal moral of the twentieth-century civil rights movement. But saying this does not bar one from also noting that specifically white identities have openly taken on new forms during the same period, and not just among the resurgent white supremacist movement.

The danger that Frankenberg really warns against, quite without meaning to, is the danger of vagueness and imprecision, of making a quite limited claim about sociohistorical phenomena in language that suggests something much more ambitious. This is a danger that the whiteness literature continually flirts with, but one that makes it easier to achieve what strikes me as the main accomplishment of Frankenberg's essay. She has essentially made some elbow room for herself, with a space-clearing gesture that allows her to mark out her own location on an increasingly crowded discursive terrain. I do not mean this cynically; I am not claiming that her aim all along was self-aggrandizement. My point is that she was doing something that seemed to need doing, but that it seemed this way only because of the state of the literature, *and* that we can see this from considering the real import of the moves she ends up making.

I am led to a similar conclusion by Howard Winant's essay in the same collection.[14] His piece is intelligent, as his work always is; and it includes a well-deserved complaint about the "sophistry" of Walter Benn Michaels. But two other moves are central. First, he uses the racial formation theory that he and Michael Omi developed some years ago to uncover three contemporary white racial projects. (A racial project in his sense is an interpretation of "race" and a proposal for racializing some distribution of social goods.) Then he offers a brief criticism of the last racial project, the "new abolitionism" that calls for the repudiation of white identity and privilege. The worry about abolitionism is, well, its abolitionism. David Roediger, the main spokesperson for the view, heralds the "withering away" of whiteness, as antiracist whites disaffiliate and choose not to be white.[15] Winant worries that this is a utopian gesture, oversimplifying the degree to which whiteness is "embedded in a highly articulated social structure and system of significations." Accordingly, the call for abolition reduces either to an apolitical "act of will," detached from the social contexts in which whiteness takes on its particular meanings, or to a call for the elimination of the race concept—"an outcome as undesirable as it is impossible." Instead of abolition, Winant urges on us the strategy of "rethinking . . . ideas about white identity and reorienting the practices consequent upon these ideas."[16] (Unhappily, he chooses the overworked term "deconstruction" to name this alternative to abolition.)

I share Winant's sense that racial eliminativism is problematic, though this is not the place to argue for the point. I agree that the proper response to whiteness involves the "reorientation" of social practice. And I agree that Roediger's call for whites to repudiate whiteness and "enter politics as non-whites" is puzzling, especially against the backdrop of his claims about whiteness being "infinitely more false" than other racial positions.[17] But there is room for puzzlement here only because Roediger has presented his position too vaguely, or imprecisely. If we take seriously his demand that we focus on "exposing, demystifying, and demeaning the particular ideology of whiteness, rather than on calling into question the concept of race generally," then he *has* to mean by abolition more or less what Winant means by "deconstruction."[18] Once again, there is a moment, or more, of conceptual slipperiness in a canonical position in the whiteness literature, and once again an intelligent critic engages the position at just that point, interpreting it in a way that makes room for another intervention.

There are three points here. First, there is a great deal of agreement behind the disputes in the critical study of whiteness—call this the consensus against unreconstructed whiteness. Second, the fuzziness of the central claims sometimes obscures this consensus. And third, intellectual work has certain imperatives—such as *if someone invites you to a conference, come up with something to say*, which is to say, *find a point of entry for your own view, one way or another*—and these imperatives can militate against the charitable readings that might uncover the consensus and build on it. We saw that Frankenberg capitalized on the uncertain scope of claims about invisibility to make her stand. Now we see Winant focusing on the conceptual elusiveness of Roediger's abolitionism to recommend his eminently sensible view. But I take it that Roediger uses "whiteness" to signify a particular *way* of engaging with Winant's social structures and systems of meaning; and that he uses "non-white" to signify the condition of having rejected those modes of engagement. He need not be claiming that the newly nonwhite person can simply opt out of systems of privilege; he is claiming that ceasing to see oneself as white is the first step toward disrupting those systems, toward Winant's rethinking and reorientation. True to the New Left roots that Winant notes on his behalf, Roediger is making an essentially epistemic point. He is offering a therapeutic, consciousness-raising device for shocking oneself out of a complacent acceptance of the white person's place in the scheme of things—hence his talk of whiteness as an ideology.

I am suggesting that Winant and Roediger are talking past each other, and past the common ground they share. This idea brings me back, finally, to my sense that the theory of whiteness has done its work. *The basic moves have been made*, and agreed upon, though our different disciplinary vocabularies and backgrounds—and, I have suggested, the pressures of intellectual work—obscure this fact. All that is left now is to see how and where the basic points apply, by asking, for example, just where and when whiteness remains unmarked. This is essentially an empirical inquiry, and it is the sort of empirical enquiry that theorists of whiteness are perfectly willing to undertake. In fact, writers like Roediger most often use the "whiteness-as" framework mainly to guide more detailed empirical work. Whether the framework serves well in this capacity is a controversial question that I cannot take up here.[19] I am more interested in the basic move—a move to the empirical and the concrete, informed by theoretical categories but refusing to remain at the level of sheer abstraction. The frequency with which people make this move, along with the frequency with which apparently theoretical disputes turn out, as I have suggested, to be problems of vagueness and misunderstanding, suggest to me that the real work of whiteness studies lies in cashing out, in concrete terms, the social realities that the epistemic reorientation—consciousness-raising—of the language is supposed to uncover.

I have suggested that whiteness studies sets up a framework for examining racial conditions after the decline of de jure white supremacy. This is its principal virtue and function, despite the confusion introduced by overly ambitious locutions and escalating metaphors (one writer in the *Making and Unmaking* volume argues, plausibly, for whiteness-as-water/ice—sometimes fluid, sometimes solid). The point now should be to find concrete strategies for confronting the practices and institutions of white supremacy, and to test these guiding metaphors against the demands of empirical investigation.

This appeal to the concrete, to revisionary practice and empirical "cashing out," at last leads me back to the lessons of Dewey's silence. In particular, it forces on me two more possible reasons for his refusal, or inability, to engage more fully with what he referred to as McKay's well-motivated "hatred." First, perhaps Dewey thought further talk was futile because he believed that he had substantial common ground with people like McKay. They shared the basic aim of improving the condition of America's oppressed peoples, and, he thought, he had a satisfactory account of that oppression (based mostly on the economic reductionism of his NAACP address, which McKay at one point in his career would have accepted). Of course, he was wrong about some of this; he needed instruction regarding the nature of white supremacist oppression and, hence, about the depth of the antiracist struggle. But if he had been right, there might have been little to say. There would have been a great deal to say about tactics and methods; about how we might, to put it in Deweyan terms, uproot the old habits of thought and replace them with ones more suitable for a real democracy. But there would have been little to say *to* McKay other than *Yes, you are right to feel that way*, or *I understand, as best I can*. This, I have been suggesting, is what scholars of whiteness can learn from Dewey. They agree on a great deal regarding the nature of the problem. Surely the thing to do now is not to keep reinterpreting a world structured in white supremacist dominance, but to change it.

A second alternative reason for Dewey's silence, and a second lesson we might apply to the whiteness literature, points once more to the analogy between whiteness studies and the older, post–civil rights programs in (nonwhite, I guess we should now say) ethnic and racial studies. Perhaps Dewey limited himself to "humiliated sympathy" because he knew that McKay's poetry represented the struggle of a certain kind of American perspective to find its own voice. Perhaps he thought that it was not his place to say too much, as that would mean intruding on McKay's attempt to find words for his experience as a black man. Silence, on this reading, is the complement to *the other's voice*; it signals one's willingness to receive the other's struggle to find words both for his or her experiences and for the self that those experiences have conspired with the act of expression to create. Silence, I am suggesting, is part of listening for a voice.

How does this idea of silence-as-listening implicate the connection between whiteness studies and ethnic studies? Ethnic and racial studies programs grew from two basic imperatives: to correct for the whitely bias of the mainstream disciplines, and to respond to the demands from nonwhite students and communities for intellectual work that spoke to their experiences and circumstances. There are analogous objectives behind the recent emergence of whiteness studies. It aims to correct for whiteliness in the perception of whiteness, and it responds to a particular set of white experiences—that of being continually reminded of how whiteness worked before the civil rights reforms, and that of having formerly legitimate expectations continually frustrated in the post–civil rights era (this is often the field's subject, not its motivation). Perhaps whiteness studies is, in a way, an internal discussion, a way of finding a voice, of coming to terms with the question, as Linda Alcoff has put it, of what white people should do now, after the collapse of classical racialism and de jure white supremacy.[20] If so, Dewey's example would suggest that while white people work out what to do—and how to talk about what to do, which I have suggested is what they are most often arguing about—nonwhite people should prepare themselves to listen, in sympathetic silence.

As I say: perhaps. I am more inclined to say that silence is no more effective here than in Dewey's original case—and for good, Deweyan reasons. As Roediger points out, nonwhite peoples have long traditions of examining and criticizing whiteness; there is no reason to turn our backs on all that now. Also, as Winant points out, and as Alcoff makes clear, whiteness has always been hybrid or, as Dewey says, compound and complex. In light of these facts, I can complicate the picture I just presented of receiving the other's voice in silence. Democracy is a mode of conjoint life that we can profitably liken to a conversation. In conversation our ideas gather words to themselves thanks to the aid and the tutelage of others—think of Plato, and Socratic "midwifery." We do not find our voices especially well in silence; we do better with the assistance of collaborators, joint inquirers, and fellow citizens. In keeping with this transactional condition on human flourishing, we can hardly leave whiteness studies to develop, or not, on its own.

NOTES

1. John Dewey, "Introduction to *Selected Poems of Claude McKay*," in *The Later Works of John Dewey, Vol. 17, 1925–53*, ed. Jo Ann Boydston (Carbondale: Southern Illinois University Press, 1990), pp. 58–62.
2. Eric Arnesen, "A Paler Shade of White," *New Republic*, June 24, 2002.
3. For radical constructionism, see Paul C. Taylor, *Race* (Cambridge, UK: Polity Press, 2003).
4. Ruth Frankenberg, "The Mirage of an Unmarked Whiteness," in *The Making and Unmaking of Whiteness*, ed. Birgit Brander Rasmussen, Eric Klineberg, Irene J. Nexica, and Matt Wray (Durham, NC: Duke University Press, 2001), pp. 72–96.
5. Melvin Thomas and Thomas Shapiro, *Black Wealth/White Wealth* (New York: Routledge, 1997).
6. John Dewey, *Art as Experience* (1934; New York: Capricorn-Putnam, 1958).
7. I am encouraged to think of voice in this way by Stanley Cavell, and by a commentator who says on his behalf that to speak of voice is to take up "the possibility of . . . summoning the resources of the self and its situation in order to *mean* some passage

of words as a passage of a particular mind." From Timothy Gould, *Hearing Things: Voice and Method in the Writing of Stanley Cavell* (Chicago: University of Chicago Press, 1998), p. 109.

8. John Dewey, "Address to the National Association for the Advancement of Colored People," *The Later Works of John Dewey, Vol. 6, 1931–32*, ed. Jo Ann Boydston (Carbondale: Southern Illinois University Press, 1985), pp. 224–31. See Shannon Sullivan, "Racialized Habits: Dewey on Race and the Roma," in *Pragmatism and Values*, ed. John Ryder and Emil Visnorski (Amsterdam: Rodopi Press, forthcoming).

9. Robert Zangrando, *The NAACP Crusade against Lynching, 1909–1950* (Philadelphia, PA Temple University Press, 1980).

10. John Dewey, "Address to National Negro Conference," *The Middle Works of John Dewey, Vol. 4: 1907–09*, ed. Jo Ann Boydston (Carbondale: Southern Illinois University Press, 1977), pp. 156–58.

11. John Dewey, "Nationalizing Education," *The Middle Works of John Dewey, Vol. 10, 1916–17*, ed. Jo Ann Boydston (Carbondale: Southern Illinois University Press, 1980), pp. 202–10.

12. Ibid., p. 207.

13. Charles Mills, *The Racial Contract* (Ithaca, NY: Cornell University Press, 1997).

14. Howard Winant, "White Racial Projects," in *The Making and Unmaking of Whiteness*, ed. Birgit Brander Rasmussen, Eric Klineberg, Irene J. Nexica, and Matt Wray (Durham, NC: Duke University Press, 2001), pp. 97–112.

15. David Roediger, *Towards the Abolition of Whiteness* (New York: Verso, 1994), p. 12.

16. Winant, "White Racial Projects," p. 107.

17. Roediger, *Abolition of Whiteness*, pp. 15, 12.

18. Ibid., p. 12.

19. See Arnesen, "Paler Shade of White."

20. Linda Alcoff, "What Should White People Do?" *Hypatia* 13, no. 3 (summer 1998): pp. 6, 21.

12

WHITENESS AND FEMINISM
Déjà Vu Discourses, What's Next?

Blanche Radford Curry

INTRODUCTION

THIS CHAPTER CRITICALLY EXAMINES, and offers viable alternative philosophical and experiential discourse concerning, the traditionally accepted and familiar feminist discourses offered by many "white" women/feminists.[1] Within the confines of this chapter, I will address the problem of whiteness in feminism in a very specific manner: acknowledgment of the "known" and populist version of feminism; the presentation of womanist discourse from the framework of "otherness"; and, the introduction of a *third* womanist/feminist voice grounded in the discourse of transformation.

As I contemplated examining the problem of whiteness in feminism, I was presented with multiple déjà vu discourses in both theory and praxis from white women/feminists and African-American women/womanists. By definition, déjà vu discourses are communicative structures characterized by repetition, stasis and marginalization. The continuation of these déjà vu discourses suggests a legitimation of such discourses, when, in reality, this continuation is not legitimate. This form of déjà vu introduces martinalization as a problematic consequential subtext of these discourses. I examined the ideologies of these multiple déjà vu discourses from a philosophical and historical perspective in two essays: "Racism and Sexism: Twenty-First-Century Challenges for Feminists" and "Transforming Feminist Theory and Practice: Beyond the Politics of Commonalities and Differences to an Inclusive Multicultural Feminist Framework."[2] The same discourses about theory and praxis that white women/feminists expressed during the birth of the twenty-first century, the 1960s, and the 1800s are prevalent today. Likewise, the responding discourses by African-American women/womanists are also the same today as they were in the past. The philosophical and historical analysis I provide addresses standpoints by white feminists about the "whiteness" that binds them in a shared racial identity and racism. It is a racial binding that is often denied by white feminists, but African-American womanist critic bell hooks reminds us that to deny that it exists is comparable to sexist men denying their sexism.[3] The familiar discourses of racism I presented in 1995 and 1998 were déjà vu discourses before 1995 and after 1998.

What's Next? What remains is a *third* womanist/feminist futuristic voice that goes beyond the déjà vu discourses in theory and praxis from both white women/feminists and African-American women/womanists to an alternate discourse grounded in transformation. This alternate discourse from a *third* womanist/feminist voice considers three positions underlining the ideologies of déjà vu discourses that have persisted to date. These positions are as follows: (1) white women/feminists who are uninformed about "race matters" and other multiple, legitimate differences; (2) white women/feminists who are educated but choose to ignore legitimate alternative discourses; (3) educated white women/feminists who have begun to understand "Other" discourses as valid and African-American women/ womanists who are actively reevaluating their own discourses. I contend these positions are linked to two problems: the message has gone unheard; and, second, when it has been heard, too often it has been misappropriated and subverted. The *third* womanist/feminist voice grounded in the discourse of transformation offers a framework that acknowledges points of intersection when the familiarity of the white woman's discourse crosses over into that of the African-American woman's world—the link truly being gender. Yet, the framework also recognizes overwhelming points that keep women of both races mired within their own destinies. For despite the similarities between the discourses, there are unique and significant differences.

The beginning of this journey to *What's Next?* involves, first, an understanding of the construction of "whiteness." Second, there must be an acknowledgment of the history of feminism, namely white women's feminism. Third, there must be an acknowledgment of the framework of *Otherness* by African-American womanists. Finally, we must consider a framework that positions women as potential agents for engaging transformative behavior.

CONCEPTUALIZING AND CONTEXTUALIZING WHITENESS

Historical and philosophical analyses of whiteness help explain the inequities of our society, the unconstitutional acts of our government, and people's immoral behavior—all of which prevent the realization of a more just world. "Whiteness," according to Ruth Frankenberg, is a social construction, and it may be defined as a set of:

> locations, discourses, and material relations. . . . [These] locations are historically, socially, politically, and culturally produced and moreover are intrinsically linked to unfolding relations of domination. Naming 'whiteness' displaces it from the unmarked, unnamed status that is itself an effect of its dominance.[4]

Frankenberg's analysis of whiteness is supported by others such as George Yancy, who holds that whiteness claims an epistemological and ontological position of absolute authority and superiority. Yancy argues that whiteness represents the universal standard of authority, truth, and absolute power, placing itself at the center, while marginalizing Others, resulting in white privilege and multiple atrocities of racism, elitism, powerlessness, and invisibility for Others:

> Whiteness creates a binary relationship of self-Other, subject-object, dominator-dominated, center-margin, universal-particular, etc. Whiteness arranges these binary terms hierarchically, where the former term is normatively superior to the latter. As the presumed sovereign voice, treating itself as hypernormative and unmarked, whiteness conceals its status as raciated, located and positioned.[5]

Accordingly, whiteness is a position of privilege that assumes the role of a sovereign voice along with the narcissistic and psychological power of whiteness.[6] Often the concept of privilege is a given, with the speaker operating as subject and assigning the role of object to the listener without asking the latter's permission. In the following pages, this assumed position of privilege is often indicative of white women/ feminists' discourse as they attempt to dialogue with Others of their gender.

"Whiteness" also represents race, though whites seldom refer to themselves in racial terms. Part of the reasoning for this social oddity lies within the concept of race itself. Race, like whiteness, can be characterized as a social construction from the minds of America's forefathers. For Frankenberg, "it is a [privileged]'standpoint,' a place from which white people look at themselves, at others, and at society."[7] Because whiteness and race have moved from the mind-set of the inventors, moving from theory to praxis, they have become social

realities. In the words of Frankenberg, race and whiteness "refer to a set of cultural practices that are usually unmarked and unnamed."[8] This definition of race as a social construction reveals for Frankenberg links between race, whiteness, and their relation to power and the processes of struggle, as well as the evolution of cultural definition.[9]

Whiteness and *race* are "real." Like gender, they help shape an individual's sense of self, experiences, and life chances, and they have lasting, real, tangible, and complex effects. Race privilege is manifested through social organization in ways that result in residential, social, and educational segregation.[10] Moreton-Robinson notes that when white women are not racialized, "race privilege remains uninterrogated as a source of oppression and inequality."[11] The links between *feminism* and *race* must be interrogated before true transformative dialogue between white women/feminists and African-American women/womanists can occur.

FEMINISM AND RACISM

Upon close examination of whiteness, race and white women, one can clearly see a linkage among histories, social processes and *racism*. To consider racism by white women/feminists in this chapter is very déjà vu for me. In my 1995 analysis of feminism and racism, I provided historical evidence from the 1800s through the early 1900s of racism by white women, white feminists. When Sojourner Truth rose to speak at the Second National Women's Suffrage Convention in Akron, Ohio, in 1852, white feminists screamed, "Don't let her speak!" Sojourner Truth's retorted, with her famous "Ain't I a Woman?" speech. In reference to the same incident, Yancy notes: "Truth's question raises the dialectics of recognition. Her questions critiqued the white ideological framework that would deny her true womanhood because of her Blackness. Her questioning, in short, is not one of self-doubt, but functions as a demand placed upon white women to critique their own standpoint."[12] Ironically, while there was overwhelming racism by white women suffragists and fear of being embarrassed by Sojourner Truth, I contend that it was the content of her speech and the vigor with which she delivered it that gave historical significance to the convention.[13]

Another account of white women/feminists' shared racial identity and racism can be found in Belle Kearney's 1903 statement representing the National American Women's Suffrage Association's response to the Fifteenth Amendment granting African-American men the right to vote. She stated, "Just as surely as the North will be forced to turn to the South for the nation's salvation, just so surely will the South be compelled to look to its Anglo-Saxon women as the medium through which to retain the supremacy of the white race over the African."[14] This statement emphatically expresses white women's value of their whiteness.

Implicit in Kearney's statement was a refusal to consider African-American women as belonging to a larger group of women within society; her emphasis on race precluded the possibility of considering African-American women as a group separate and distinct from African American men. Indeed, during this time, white women's suffrage groups were concerned with social equality only for white women, not all women; these white women had abandoned their alliances with African Americans over the passage of the Fifteenth Amendment in 1870. It was these white women's designation of their "whiteness" as essential that led them to form the National American Women's Suffrage Association (NAWSA) or the General Federation of Women's Clubs in 1890 and at the same time prompted African-American women to form the National Association of Colored Women (NACW). Of significance is the inclusive position of NACW versus the exclusive position of NAWSA. The motto for NACW was "Lifting as We Climb," and its mission statement declared that the organization "is led and directed by women for the good of women and men, for the benefit of *all* humanity."[15]

The same allegiance to whiteness by white suffragists was demonstrated by white women abolitionists. bell hooks contends that while white women abolitionists in the 1830s fought against slavery, racism was not an issue for them; they valued the power of their white privilege too much to support ending the racial hierarchy.[16] Similar histories of racism by white women/feminists are documented by other African-American women/womanists such as Rosalyn Terborg-Penn, Pauline Terrelong Stone, and Angela Davis. Terborg-Penn states that racism is an essentialistic stance for white women.[17] Similarly, Stone reminds us:

> Racism is so ingrained in American culture, and so entrenched among white women, . . . many Black women have tended to see all whites regardless of sex, as sharing the same objective interest and clearly the behavior of many white women vis-à-vis Blacks has helped to validate this reaction.[18]

Davis asserts that our focus of concern in the 1990s is the same as the concerns that black women faced in the three distinct waves of the women's movement—the 1840s, the 1960s, and the 1980s—namely, the invisibility of black women in theory and praxis.[19]

Frankenberg notes:

> [R]acism was and is something that shapes white women's lives, rather than something that people of color have to live and deal with in a way

that bears no relationship or relevance to the lives of white people. . . .
[W]e tend to view it as an issue that people of color face and have to
struggle with, but not as an issue that generally involves or implicates
us. . . . Racism can, in short, be conceived as something
external to us rather than as a system that shapes our daily experiences
and sense of self.[20]

She argues further that because white women have a standpoint forged
on dominance and race privilege, they have no recognition of the
effects of racism on their lives or on the shaping of our society.[21]

I can recall my own encounters with racism from white women/
feminists as if they had occurred yesterday. Once, Angela Davis delivered a provocative speech at the institution where I was teaching, and a
philosophy professor there made plans to have Davis, other guest
speakers, and faculty at his home. Aside from Angela Davis, I was the
only African American among the group. The host professor commented that there was not enough space to accommodate me. One of
the white feminists challenged him on not having enough space for
one more person and vigorously expressed her disbelief and disgust,
stating that if there was not enough space for me, then she would not
join them. She related that she had recently obtained tenure, and with
nothing to lose, she was committed to standing up to this kind of
racism. But another white feminist said that she was going to join the
group because she needed to converse/network with a couple of important [white male] philosophers. Later at this same conference, I
tried to raise a question regarding her presentation, but was not recognized by her. I attempted to follow up with her after her presentation,
only to be ignored again.

There is definitely an interrelatedness among the concepts and reality of whiteness, race, and racism for white women/feminists. In their
analyses of these linkages, as well as analyses by others, it is evident
that *race difference* between African-American women and white
women has been substantially underappreciated and therein lies part
of the déjà vu discourses.

THEORIZING RACE DIFFERENCE

There is no denying that *race* is an indicator of *difference*. Often race,
one of the first indicators for determining a person's identity, is the
initial illustrator of difference. Janet Elsea asserts:

The way we process information about each other when meeting one another for the first time focuses on what we can see: Our differences. We

see: Color of skin, gender, age, appearance, facial expressions, eye contact, movement, personal space and touch. Social scientists disagree on the precise sequence of this processing, but agree otherwise.[22]

Similar to the analyses of white women/feminists from perspectives of déjà vu, analyses of race *difference* by African American women/womanists in terms of placing exclusive emphasis upon racial difference also resonate déjà vu. In my analysis of differences for African-American women, I discussed the dilemmas of racism and sexism for African American women.[23] Historically, many African-American women have denied sexism or made it secondary to racism, claiming racism destroys African-American men, women, and children and prevents the formation of economically and socially stable communities.[24] It has been evidenced that the position of African-American women has changed since the late 1960s. And like white women's false claims that sexism is more fundamental and oppressive than racism, so too have African-American women's claims regarding the prominence of racism in their lives has proven to be false as well.[25]

Several African-American feminists have pointed out connections between racism and sexism. Deborah K. King explains racism and sexism as phenomena of a "both/or" orientation in which African American women simultaneously belong and do not belong to a group.[26] African-American women are at the tail end for Shirley Chisholm.[27] Their problems are not addressed by the black movement or the women's movement. bell hooks points out that in the discourse about African-American people, sexism militates against acknowledging the interests of African-American women, and in the discourse about women, racism militates against recognizing African-American women's interests.[28]

Racism and sexism represent different forms of oppression for African-American women. We share the psychological structures of racism with African-American men, while we share sexism with other women. Patricia Hill Collins reminds us that there are ways in which African-American women are not part of either of these groups.[29] Moreover, beyond race and sex, many other differences must be contended with: class, culture, gender, religion, age, and ethnicity. Our differences have varying points of intersection, depending on the given circumstances. On some days, it may be our race and religion that are at issue, while on others it is our class and gender.

There remains a huge gap between African-American women's and white women's day-to-day lives. The freedom from domesticity and the road to professional growth remain significantly different for

African-American and white women. Indeed, Elsa Brown maintains that white women's lives are largely the result of the lives African-American women live, because they are the caregivers and housekeepers for white women.[30] Similarly, there are far fewer professional opportunities for us than there are for white women. Contrary to the notion that being both African American and female strengthens one's position, the reality is that too often the two militate against each other.

While white feminists readily recognize the domination of sexism, they tend not to see the domination of racism or the interconnections between sexism and racism that African-American feminists must negotiate. African-American womanists and white feminists have different experiences of domination, subjugation, devaluation, and dismissal. Being a mother and a homemaker, Davis explains, does not have the same meaning for African-American women who experience racism that it does for white women who do not experience racism.[31] Similarly, for white feminists to compare white women's oppression under sexism to African-American women's position in slavery, or to construct analogies between the women's movement and the civil rights movement are unacceptable forms of appropriation of African-American women's experiences. Elizabeth V. Spelman explains that there are some experiences that one can have and that others cannot.[32] Unacceptable appropriation of another's experience disrespects the other person's situation and overlooks the differences in options available to people.

To be sure, some white women/feminists have heard and adhered to the message from African-American women/womanists. Frankenberg points out that in the 1980s white feminists could no longer ignore[33] the critique of their racism by women of color. "When confronted, white feminists had a limited repertoire of responses: confusion over accusations of racism; guilt over racism; anger over repeated criticism; dismissal; stasis."[34] For Frankenberg, racism was and remains all too relevant to the course of every white woman's life. It is not something that is defined by externals; rather, it is indigenous to the fabric of American culture.

Moreton-Robinson points out that during the mid-1980s there was a transition in the thinking and writing by white feminists about what constitutes difference. And in the 1990s, analyses of women of color, lesbians, and black feminists revealed theoretical limitations to the traditional gender/sex difference and the need for feminism "to develop critical theories which are inclusive of differences and reflexive."[35] She concludes from her critique of several leading white feminists' theories of a more inclusive position on difference that each one is inadequate.

While problematic theoretically, I contend that each of them presents a principle which becomes meaningful when reconstructed in the *third* womanist/feminist voice of transformation that I offer in this chapter. It is not their principle that is problematic. Rather, much work is needed in the theoretical discourse explaining the given principles and elaboration on transforming them into praxis. The principles themselves represent a substantial core of fundamental norms to be acknowledged and embellished in order to begin the journey of the *third* womanist/feminist voice of transformation.

In this regard, much might be gained from a number of theories critiqued by Moreton-Robinson: Iris Young's idea of a "democratic pluralism based on multiple differences which are not fixed"; Sandra Harding's idea of white women learning from the insights of marginalized women; Marilyn Frye's idea of recognizing the necessity for differences; Shane Phelan's idea of recognizing our multiple identities and locations in power, recognizing differences and our shared communities, and valuing both relationality and individuality; Elaine Jeffreys' idea that differences should not be ordered hierarchically or my own similar idea that we avoid an Olympics of oppression; and Anna Yeatman's idea of multiple and interlocking oppressions.[36] All of the aforementioned feminist theories have some degree of validity. One need not accept binary opposition in locating answers. This kind of conceptualization is the focus of feminist pedagogical paradigms.

There are several important white feminists, publically acknowledged, who have heard and adhered to the message from African American women/womanists. For example, Catherine Stimpson examines the comparison of white women's situation to that of blacks, pointing out the habit of white people not only to define the black experience and make it their own, but to do so in a way that leaves their own views unexamined: "The analogy evades, in the rhetorical haze, the harsh fact of white women's racism."[37] Margaret Simons concludes from her analysis of several works by white feminists that little attention is given to racism and the oppression of minority women.[38] And she noted that when white feminists produce works that do not render minority women invisible, other white feminists seldom accept their insights.

Simons explains that too frequently white feminists provide analogies that undermine significant dissimilarities among themselves and African-American feminists. It is the frequent habit of white feminists to deemphasize women's differences in order to emphasize the shared experiences of sexism. Adrienne Rich writes that many white feminists view the world through a tunnel vision that claims white women's experiences as the absolute center of the world.[39] She has termed this tendency *white solipsism*: "[T]o think, image and speak as if whiteness described the world . . . a tunnel-vision which simply does not see nonwhite experience or existences as precious or significant"[40] Elizabeth V. Spelman writes that white feminists posture their experiences as essentialistic and the universal model for all women's experiences.[41] Marilyn Frye sees this as white women's practice of "whiteliness" that is an ingrained way of being in the world.[42]

Some white feminists have offered personal accounts of having *heard* the message that African-American women/womanists try to convey. Ruth Frankenberg's valuable work on the social construction of whiteness and the impact of race in shaping white women's lives marked a turning point for her. She notes that her work, and analyses such as the Combahee River Collective, points to the structural subordination of women of color and explains to well-meaning white feminists that they are part of the problem of racism resulting in

> an inventory of meanings of racism, of racist behaviors began, de facto, to accumulate in [her] consciousness. . . . I learned by proximity what it means to navigate through a largely hostile terrain, to deal with institutions that do not operate by one's own logic nor in one's interests, and to need those institutions to function in one's favor if one is to survive, let alone to achieve. I realized for almost the first time in my life the gulf of experience and meaning between individuals differentially positioned in relation to systems of domination, and the profundity of cultural difference.[43]

Lucius Outlaw interprets another white feminist's personal experience of having *heard* the message. While discussing the history of Philosophy Born of Struggle, the African American Philosophical Association, at the Fourth Annual Alain Locke Conference, Outlaw shared the scenario of Sandra Harding's attendance at the early Philosophy Born of Struggle conferences. He contends that it was her interaction with members of the association that enabled Harding to effectively theorize and engage in standpoint theory.[44] Indeed, my own encounters with Harding and familiarity with her work lead me to the same conclusion of her engaging in the journey of the *third* womanist/feminist voice of transformative discourse. There are similarly personal accounts of other white feminists such as Margaret A. Simons, Linda Bell, and others to be encountered.

TRANSFORMING DÉJÀ VU THEORY AND PRAXIS

Transforming white women/feminists' and African-American women/ womanists' multiple déjà vu discourses of theory and praxis involves examining the limited discourses presented by them. Let us begin with *those white women/feminists who have heard and adhered to the message from African-American women/womanists.* How did they accept their own discourses, while recognizing those of African-American women/ womanists? How did these white women/feminists resist racism and other multiple injustices of whiteness—elitism, powerlessness, and invisibility? How are they different from those white women/feminists who have not heard the message, and thereby have not adhered to it or those who have heard and refused to adhere?

The beginning of this journey to *What's Next?* a *third* womanist/ feminist voice is grounded in a framework of transformative discourse. Frankenburg's study of white women's whiteness and "race matters" discusses those whose limited contacts/interactions with African-American women have prevented them from recognizing and understanding the impact of their white privilege and their perpetuation of those social problems. Such women can change, she says, once they are educated.[45] Once *educated*, their naivete dissipates, and they become inclusive, self-liberated, and more globally conscious, beginning the journey to become agents of resistance to the reproduction of racism and other social constructs of white privilege.

In contrast, there are others who remain unchanged. For Anthony Appiah, these women lack cognizant capacity.[46] The element of choice is not available for these white women. The condition of these women is recognized and accepted by the *third* womanist/feminist voice of transformation, and their incapacity for dialogue does not significantly hinder the proposed transformative framework of discourse. Nevertheless, the experiences of historical movements—African-American slavery, the Holocaust, and women's suffrage—which are replete with individuals who have lacked cognizant capacity prove that social ills can be eradicated through transformative discourse.

There are other white women/feminists who recognize and understand the reality of whiteness and "race matters," but choose to be subversive, discriminatory, and provincial and are driven by binary constraints of Western hierarchy that are contrary to a shared sense of power. They maintain a historical/hierarchical sense of power that many of their white male counterparts have assumed. They cloak in the name of better womanhood, while appropriating the mind-set of the white male hierarchy and choosing not to transcend their exclusive domains that prohibit dialogue with others, especially women of color, who are actively engaged in the womanist/feminist struggle. For them, education is a valid transformative tool, but they choose to be disingenuous and deny it.

What can we say about the white women/feminists, the *educated*, who have *heard the message and adhered to it*? They express an authenticity of consciousness, commitment, and courage to "do the right thing." They have, according to Martín Alcoff,[47] an awakened white consciousness and willingness to make significant sacrifices to journey beyond white privilege. They are grounded in feminist ontology, the importance of standpoint theory, and the purpose of feminist pedagogy. Moreton-Robinson reminds us that feminist ontology argues that women theorize from their own standpoints.[48] Personal experience is viewed as an essential component of the learning and teaching process for feminist pedagogy. The consideration of personal reference for feminist pedagogy is to suggest different notions of how to view knowledge and how to teach it.

Akin to understanding that there are distinct ways of knowing is the idea of true collaborative exchange. The goal of this framework of "feminist process" is a democratization of the collaborators to the end of realizing a more egalitarian society that improves the quality of life for all people. If there is not a true transformation of a personal epistemological claim into a radical form of praxis, then no real progress will be made; the situation becomes one more instance of déjà vu in which there is empty theory and no praxis.

Frankenberg relates the same position regarding feminist pedagogy. She explains: "Theorizing 'from experience' rested on several key epistemological claims, staples of feminist 'common sense.' The first of these was a critique of 'objectivity' or 'distance' as the best stances from which to generate knowledge. For feminists argued there is a link between where one stands in society and what one perceives." This epistemological stance also claimed that the oppressed person's clarity of vision is more comprehensive, providing insight into the minds of the oppressor/privileged and a more extensive knowledge of the entire society.[49] Still further, for Frankenberg, it is the work mostly by African-American feminists that transformed feminists' analyses, pointing out white-centeredness and false universalizing claims by many white feminists. She states that "the racial specificity of white women's lives limit feminist analysis and strategy in relation to issues such as the family and reproductive rights and intersection in women's lives of gender, sexuality, race and class as well as visions and concepts of multiracial coalition work."[50]

Lucius Outlaw reminds us that *race* is here to stay.[51] He explains that race as a social construction is a reality and the way that Western society, and in particular, America, has dealt with *race has been the problem*. With that understanding, I will approach the problem differently—accepting *race* in a positive way. In *A Promise and a Way of Life: White Antiracist Activism*,[52] Becky Thompson also agrees. Like Outlaw, she believes that part of a viable solution is not the ignoring of race but the recognition of race, as an integral part of one's personal epistemology.

Similarly, Alain Locke, from the standpoint of a metaphorical feminism, in the provocative and informative text, *The Philosophy of Alain Locke: Harlem Renaissance and Beyond* also uses the paradigms of values and education as vehicles for transformation of our mind-set about *race*.[53] Although he presents several levels of approach, most pertinent is his continual reference to reedification of value systems and education as primary texts for societal renewal. And it is from recognition of this foundational knowledge that we can shape another method of constructing a pedagogy essential for reconstruction of institutions, such as education, culture, and societal history.

In short, this means not taking a position of color blindness because there is a false consciousness in such a stance. Race is real. If race is eradicated, then I cannot fully tell my story, because the recipient would see my version only as it replicates hers. The listener would still be telling her story, not mine. In the spirit of the "cooperating imagination," a concept associated traditionally with Keatsian poetry[54] but equally relevant to philosophy, personal epistemology will not overshadow the larger humanistic message that transcends gender, race, and class. Historically, a deconstruction of humanism has meant a removal, consciously and /or subconsciously, of references to non-whiteness and a positioning of "whiteness" as the essential trope of that which is "human." (This kind of thought involves hierarchy, binary opposition, and exclusion.) This designation of race, which is a social construct, as a sign of universal humanism is inappropriate. What I propose by way of the *third* womanist/feminist voice is a new interpretation of the term in which race and other legitimate differences are defined as part of a comprehensive humanity, which recognizes commonalities and simultaneously acknowledges our differences.

Liberating discourse must involve a comprehensive rendering of the truth. Each raconteur must be allowed to tell her story and construct her world along lines other than those of binary opposition. Society will then reflect an inclusiveness of all people, leading to a truer picture of reality in which blackness, whiteness, womanism, feminism, and our other multiple selves, generated by gender, sex, class, religion, and so on, will maintain their respective identities, while not over-shadowing the larger world to which they contribute.

In order for society to be transformed under the auspices of reformed white women/feminists' discourse, it is necessary to acknowledge the sign of *race* as a positive force that embellishes rather than diminishes the feminist/womanist's experience. The histories of the social construction of race have perpetuated negative and inferior discourses about race difference. *More theorizing* is needed which emphasizes the value of *difference* rather than maintaining the devaluing of difference and/or the deemphasis of difference in favor of universality and essentialism where the latter result is racism. Audre Lorde maintained, "It is not [the] differences between us that are separating us. It is rather our refusal to recognize those differences."[55] We can consider each other's standpoints without devaluing our own or another's. Elsa Barkley Brown asserts: "[A]ll people can learn to center in another experience, validate it, and judge it by its own standards without need of comparison or need to adopt that framework as their own. Thus, one has no need to 'decenter' anyone in order to center someone else; one has only to constantly, appropriately, 'pivot the center.'"[56] There is space for everyone. Valuing differences requires us to interact with one another, understanding one another's traditions, values, race, gender, culture, class, shared ideas, and the like. While we recognize our shared ideas, we must appropriately acknowledge and learn from our differences.[57]

More praxis, interaction, and *contact* between white feminists and African-American women/womanists are needed. Margaret A. Simons notes: "[E]fforts on a theoretical level are not sufficient. We must extend our efforts to a personal and practical level as well. . . . As feminists, we must. . . . confront racism . . . , as well as sexism, on both a personal and theoretical level."[58] Patricia Hill Collins argues that our choices to confront racism and sexism are related to our ethics of personal accountability. She asserts: "[P]eople are expected to be accountable for their knowledge claims. . . . [It is] essential for individuals to have personal positions on issues and assume full responsibility for arguing their validity. . . . [It involves] utilizing emotion, ethics, and reason as interconnected, essential components in assessing knowledge claims."[59] Moreton-Robinson explains that white feminists' social lives are restricted to being with women of their own race. They experience limited sociality with *other women*, thereby perpetuating their "disparity in experience, knowledge and meaning between women who are 'Other' and white feminists in relation to systems of domination and the depth of differences." Their unexamined white race privilege prevents them from examining their sociality or their knowledge.[60] White feminists would do well to recall and to reengage their discourses and personal experiences of whiteness and feminism. In doing so, "white feminist academics" may begin to transcend the historical invisibility of whiteness. In particular, Moreton-Robinson's "white feminist academics" could engage in the journey of the *third* womanist/feminist voice of transformative discourse. Moreton-Robinson's scenario of "white feminist academics" could be turned upside down in the words of Sojourner Truth. She explains:

> "Race" as "Other" and "racism" are important politics of white feminist academics as an intellectual engagement. However, their anti-racist practice is reduced to teaching within a limited paradigm, which has little impact on their standpoints both outside, and within the university context. They all used skin colour and physical features as a marker of difference in thinking and talking on race and cultural difference. [Only nonwhites] were the categories of "Others" that were spoken about by feminists in their discussions on race and pedagogy. [T]hey did not interrogate whiteness in their teaching on "race." By not naming and interrogating whiteness in their pedagogy "race" remained extrinsic and extraneous for feminist and their students. Its relevance as a "difference" was reserved for those positioned as "Other." Whiteness was centered but invisible in their pedagogy.[61]

The conclusion of Moreton-Robinson's scenario is that white feminists' discourse and their mere theoretical engagement with white race privilege is inadequate for them to know about their privilege, to deal with it by writing about it and thereby moving beyond it. By choice, white race privilege remains invisible in the work of white feminists along with the influences of patriarchal whiteness on their work in the academy. Accordingly, "[c]ultural differences are erased within the academy because the cultural values and beliefs of racialised 'Others' are subordinated to those of the institution." These white feminists fail to recognize how their thinking, knowing, and writing mirror those of their white male counterparts. To transform this scenario, Moreton-Robinson suggests the need to reconfigure "theory to deal with how to give up power to inform strategies to liberate us all from the oppressive and painful actualities of this very troubling and risky business."[62] This is the idea of shared power that empowers everyone versus hierarchical power, which is limiting.

CONCLUSION

Inherent within the concept of déjà vu is historical precedence. I am reminded of numerous principles for engaging in a new consciousness. In literature, Alice Walker has the conviction that genuine writing cannot be separated from the way we live our lives.[63] In sociology, Paulo Freire explains that transformation begins first with thinking; second, speaking; third, writing; and fourth, giving meaning to our actions, thereby engaging in transformation.[64] Within the same discipline, Patricia Hill Collins explains the need to honestly engage in accountability of our actions.[65] And, finally, I strongly concur with the following philosophers: Martín Alcoff, who offers "new traditions" for eradicating white privilege;[66] George Yancy, who incorporates the importance of the "*philosophical i*";[67] Sandra Harding, who promotes "reinventing ourselves as Other";[68] Linda Bell, who acknowledges white privilege, and has heard and adhered to the message;[69] and the unknown white feminist voice (1996) who commented during a conversation at an American Philosophical Association conference that she had used "Racism and Sexism: Twenty-First-Century Challenges for Feminists," in her undergraduate course at Chicago Circle and found it to be very valuable.

What's Next? I see the vision of my own "new horizons." While it is important to recognize the theoretic mantra of philosophical discourse, if true transformation is to occur there must be specific norms that transgress boundaries imposed by race, gender, and class. When referencing feminist discourse, I spoke about the voices of white women/feminists, African-American women/womanists and the *third* womanist/feminist, the most liberating position of all. This author calls for an authenticity of consciousness, commitment, and courage from white women/feminists and African-American women/womanists to journey with the *third* womanists/feminists for meaningful transformation.

This *third* voice has accessed the true energy that provides the foundation of all life. It is a force, whose essential foundation is literally part of the mysterious fountain of being. It is a place that is invisible but something that is accessible to those with the proper mind-set. Only those fortunate individuals do so; they acknowledge the societal constructions of race, class, gender, and so on, which constitute personal identity, but also realize and transcend these entities which have been historically configured as necessary, essential, unabridgeable barriers and differences. They reconfigure them as important sites of identity formation in a truly liberating new world consciousness which finds a place for fluid differences within the framework of fluid similarities.

The *third* womanist/feminist voice, which is comprehensive in insight and possesses a moral ethos to do the right thing, will be able to effect the goal of a better world order for everyone.

By virtue of history, the African-American womanist of the "third voice" womanist/feminist is in a uniquely comprehensive, knowledgeable position to lead in the transformation of déjà vu theory and praxis. Even though, historically, there has been much debate about their ability to do so, they are the ones whose courage founded in multiple foundations must take the lead in transforming themselves and by extension others. In the words of D. E. Smith, "[T]he situated knower is always also a participant in the social she is discovering. Her inquiry is developed as a form of that participation. Her experience is always active as a way of knowing whether or not she makes it an explicit resource."[70]

Not only have they been forced by all aspects of society to know their "story," but also in order for them to carve out an existence, they had to know the "history" of white males and the "herstory" of white females. It is not an issue of the avenues that produced such knowledge, it is simply a matter of fact that if the African-American women/womanists were to be successful, often they had to sublimate their own texts to those of others. Their voices were not silenced for long; the "cooperative" spirit of their imagination allowed them to operate on several levels and live a life of multiple selves. While aware of the "rightness" of their own history, they had not only to validate it in the eyes of white men with norms predicated on a hierarchy of values but to teach white women/feminists who, while espousing another ideology that deplored binary opposition, in reality were mouthing a discourse similar to their white male counterparts.

In this chapter, several distinct variables have been outlined as they pertain to the déjà vu discourses of white women/feminists; African-American women/womanists; and the third voice of the womanist/feminist. It has been established that the cycle of déjà vu discourse can be broken only through the transformative ideology posited by the women of the *third* voice, who are new African-American womanists and new white feminists. Within that final group, the societal constructions of race, gender, and class are recognized but transcended because the discourse must operate out of a life principle that is grounded in the humanity that foregrounds all personal identities.

In order to effectively transition from déjà vu discourse of the white women/feminists and African-American women/womanist to the post–déjà vu discourse and praxis of the futuristic *third* womanist/feminist voice, these women must effectively coordinate transcendence and transformation. Not only must there be a recognition of the socially constructed variables of gender, race, and class, there must be an acknowledgment of the manner in which they operate in terms of the societal correlatives relatives of time, space, and humanity. In essence, a more comprehensive humanity involves the following process:

- All races of women must engage in individual re-evaluation of personal discourses as well as collective discourse revealed in history and society at large.
- After acknowledging problematic areas, they must seek reeducation through informal and formal interaction with different races, classes, genders, while recognizing multiple legitimate differences.
- In reeducation, personal identity is redefined within but not limited to the space of its own integrity. We are individuals, but we share a common humanity.

Accordingly, the *third* futuristic womanist/feminist voice ushers in the age of not only a post–déjà vu feminism but a new world humanism. No longer is one's personal identity absorbed, denied, marginalized, or decentered; rather it is appropriately acknowledged within the new, comprehensive humanity that enhances the quality of life for all people.

NOTES

1. I am indebted to Beverly D. Miller, George Yancy, Earnest Curry, and Howard McGary for their helpful comments on earlier drafts of this chapter.
2. See my articles "Racism and Sexism: Twenty-First-Century Challenges for Feminists," in *Overcoming Racism and Sexism*, ed. L. A. Bell and D. Blumefield (Lanham, MD: Rowman & Littlefield, 1995); and "Transforming Feminist Theory and Practice: Beyond the Politics of Commonalities and Differences to an Inclusive Multicultural Feminist Framework," in *Women's Studies in Transition: The Pursuit of Interdisciplinarity*, ed. Kate Conway-Turner, Susanne Cherrin, Jessica Schiffman, and Kathleen Doherty Turkel (Newark: University of Delaware Press, 1998).
3. bell hooks, *Feminist Theory: From Margin to Center* (Boston, MA: South End Press, 1984), p. 55.
4. Ruth Frankenberg, *White Women, Race Matters: The Social Construction of Whiteness* (Minneapolis: University of Minnesota Press, 1993), p. 6.
5. George Yancy, "Feminism and the Subtext of Whiteness: Black Women's Experiences as a Site of Identity Formation and Contestation of Whiteness," *Western Journal of Black Studies* 24, no. 3 (Fall: 2000): 1–2.
6. Ibid., p. 6.
7. Frankenberg, *White Women, Race Matters*, p. 1.
8. Ibid.
9. Ibid., p. 11.
10. Ibid.
11. Aileen Moreton-Robinson "Troubling Business: Difference and Whiteness within Feminism," *Australian Feminist Studies* 15, no. 33 (2000): 344–45.
12. Yancy, "Feminism and Subtext," pp. 10–11. For a different reading of the context of Sojourner Truth's speech, see K. A. Appiah and H. L. Gates eds, *Africana: The*

Encyclopedia of the African and African American Experience. New York: Basic Civitas Books, 1999; J. C. Smith and J. M. Palmisano, eds, *Reference Library of Black America*. Farmington Hills, MI: Gale Group, Inc., Distributed by African American Publications, Proteus Enterprises, 2000; and Jeffrey C. Stewart's *1001 Things Everyone Should Know about African American History*. New York: Doubleday, 1996.

13. Radford Curry, "Racism and Sexism."

14. Belle Kearney, quoted in Aileen Kraditor, *The Ideas of the Woman Suffrage Movement 1880–1920* (New York: Columbia University Press, 1965), p. 202.

15. Radford Curry, "Racism and Sexism."

16. bell hooks, *Ain't I a Woman: Black Women and Feminism* (Boston: South End Press, 1981).

17. Rosalyn Terborg-Penn, "Discrimination against Afro-American Women in the Women's Movement, 1830–1920," in *The Afro-American Woman: Struggles and Images*, ed. Rosalyn Terborg-Penn and Sharon. Harley (New York: Kennikat Press, 1987).

18. P. T. Stone, "Feminist Consciousness and Black Women," in *Women: A Feminist Perspective*, ed. J. Freeman (Mountain View, CA: Mayfield, 1979), p. 583.

19. Angela Davis, *Women, Culture and Politics* (New York: Random House), 1989.

20. Frankenberg, *White Women, Race Matters*, p. 6.

21. Ibid., p. 9.

22. Janet G. Elsea, *The Four Minute Sell* (New York: Simon & Schuster, 1984), pp. 9–11.

23. Radford Curry, "Racism and Sexism."

24. Elizeabeth Hood, " Black Women, White Women: Separate Paths to Liberation," *Black Scholar* (April 1978); pp. 48–55.

25. See Elizabeth V. Spelman, "Changing the Subject: Studies in the Appropriation of Pain." Paper presented at the "Symposium on Racism and Sexism: Differences and Connections," Georgia State University, Atlanta, Ga, 1991; Toni Morrison, "Friday on the Potomac," introduction to *"Race-ing Justice, En-gendering Power: Essays on Anita Hill, Clarence Thomas, and the Construction of Social Reality*, ed. Toni Morrison (New York: Pantheon Books, 1992); and Paula Giddings, "The Last Taboo," in *Race-ing Justice, En-gendering Power: Essays on Anita Hill, Clarence Thomas, and the Construction of Social Reality*, ed. Toni Morrison (New York: Pantheon Books, 1992) pp. 441–463.

26. Deborah K. King, "Multiple Jeopardy, Multiple Consciousness: The Context of a Black Feminist Ideology," *Signs* 14, no. 1 (1998), pp. 42–72.

27. Shirley Chisholm, *Unbought and Unbossed* (New York: Avon, 1970).

28. bell hooks, *Ain't I a Woman*.

29. Patricia Hill Collins, *Black Feminist Thought* (New York: Routledge, 1989).

30. Elsa Barkley Brown, "African-American Women's Quilting: A Framework for Conceptualizing and Teaching African-American Women's History," in *Black Women in America: Social Science Perspective*, ed. M. R. Malson et al. (Chicago: University of Chicago Press, 1990), pp. 9–10.

31. Angela Davis, 1981. *Women, Race, and Class* (New York: Random House, 1981).

32. Spelman, 1991.

33. Radford Curry, "Racism and Sexism."

34. Frankenberg, *White Women, Race Matters*, p. z.

35. Moreton-Robinson, "Troubling Business," p. 343.

36. Ibid., pp. 344–47.

37. Catherine Stimpson, "Thy Neighbor's Wife, Thy Neighbor's Servants: Women's Liberation and Black Civil Rights," in *Woman in Sexist Society: Studies in Power and Powerlessness*, ed. V. Cornick and B. K. Moran (New York: New American Library, Signet Books, 1971), p. 650.

38. Margaret Simons, "Racism and Feminism: A Schism in the Sisterhood," *Feminist Studies* 5, no. 2 (1979).

39. Adrienne Rich, *On Lies, Secrets, and Silence* (New York: Norton, 1979).

40. Ibid., p. 229.

41. Elizabeth B. *Inessential Woman: Problems of Exclusion in Feminist Thought* (Boston: Beacon Press, 1998).

42. Marilyn Frye, *The Politics of Reality: Essays in Feminist Theory* (Trumanburg, NY: Crossing Press, 1983) and *Willful Virgin: Essays in Feminism* (Freedom, CA: Crossing Press, 1992).

43. Frankenberg, *White Women, Race Matters*, p. 4.

44. Lucius T. Outlaw, comments at the Fourth Annual Alain Locke Conference, Howard University, Wahington, D.C., April 4–5, 2003.

45. Frankenberg, *White Women, Race Matters*.

46. Kwame Anthony Appiah, *In My Father's House* (New York: Oxford University Press, 1992).

47. Linda Martín Alcoff, "What Should White People do?" *Hypatia* 3, no. 3 (summer 1998), p. 6.

48. Moreton-Robinson, "Troubling Business," p. 343.

49. Frankenberg, *White Women, Race Matters*, p. 8.

50. Ibid.

51. Lucius T. Outlaw, *On Race and Philosophy* (New York: Routledge, 1996).

52. Becky Thompson, *A Promise and a Way of Life: White Antiracist Activism* (Minneapolis: University of Minnesota Press, 2001).

53. Leonard Harris, *The Philosophy of Alain Locke: Harlem Renaissance and Beyond.* (Philadephia: Temple University Press, 1983).

54. W. J. Bate, *John Keats* (Cambridge, MA: Harvard University Press, 1963).

55. Audre Lorde, *Sister Outsider* (New York: Crossing Press, 1984), p. 115.

56. Barkley Brown, "African-American Women's Quilting," p. 10.

57. Judith Mary Green and Blanche Radford Curry, "Recognizing Each Other amidst Diversity: Beyond Essentialism in Collaborative Multi-Cultural Feminist Theory," *Sage: A Scholarly Journal on Black Women* 8, no. 1. (1991): pp. 39–40.

58. Simons, "Racism and Feminism," pp. 397–99.

59. Hill Collins, *Black Feminist Thought*, pp. 768–69.

60. Moreton-Robinson, "Troubling Business," p. 350.

61. Ibid., pp. 349–50.

62. Ibid., pp. 350–51.

63. Alice Walker, *In Search of Our Mothers' Gardens: Womanist Prose* (New York: Harcourt Brace & Company, 1983).

64. Paulo Freire, *Pedagogy of the Oppressed* (New York: Seabury Press, 1973).

65. Hill Collins, *Black Feminist Thought*.

66. Martín Alcoff, "What Should White People Do?"

67. George Yancy, *The Philosophical i: Personal Reflections on Life in Philosophy* (Lanham, MD: Rowman & Littlefield, 2002).

68. Sandra Harding, "Reinventing Ourselves as Other," in *American Feminist Thought at Century's End: A Reader* (Cambridge, Mass.: Blackwell Publishers, 1991): pp. 140–164.

69. Linda Bell, "The Allure and Hold of Privilege," in *Overcoming Racism and Sexism,* ed. L. A. Bell and David Blumefield (Lanham, MD: Rowman & Littlefield, 1995): pp. 37–44.

70. Dorothy E. Smith, *Writing the Social: Critique, Theory, and Investigations* (Toronto, Buffalo: University of Toranto Press, 1999), p. 6.

13

THE ACADEMIC ADDICT

Mainlining (& Kicking) White Supremacy (WS)

Joy James

I HAVE BEEN MAINLINING WHITE SUPREMACY (WS) for so long that I have lost clarity and spirit.[1] I do not remember what it means to be without addiction, that is, how to be truly alive. I could blame this on the university, the degrees, publishing, narcissism, and careerism (my own, and that of my colleagues and students), as well as player-haters (being high eases the pain of being played or playing, hated or hating). Yet, I was hooked long before I went to graduate school and long before I got the green light for tenure track, tenure, and promotion.

I likely started off in my preacademic years in incremental dosages, sniffing rather than shooting. But the supply was so plentiful and pervasive. It was (is) neither cheap nor scarce, but *free* and mandatory, ostensibly so in order to inoculate against some greater ill. (As with the anthrax vaccine required of troops who serve in global warfare, the government supplies clean needles. Those who refuse injections are stigmatized and/or arrested.)

To clearly view WS addiction as disease is akin to researching and teaching about government complicity in cocaine trafficking and the sex trade. Clarity raises difficult questions that are often shunned—questions about the underground drug and sex economy as a structural feature of "market" capitalism, about the nature of institutional WS addictions, and about the power of influential or wealthy WS addicts in shaping democratic and intellectual cultures.

Conventional truism: Addicts are known to exaggerate (a euphemism for "lie"). Yet, which addicts: government leaders, corporate CEOs, police and military chiefs, academic administrators, professors, or students? For decades, those taking WS (to speak of intergenerational addiction, one must include those born of parents who were users) have built personal, national, and imperial wealth on WS. The false dichotomies between classroom purveyor and street pusher, suburban recreational user and urban junkie, bank launderer and immigrant mule suggest that words have become weapons in a rhetorical war on WS. Regardless of Senator Trent Lott's apology, this nation is incredibly strung out.

Another truism: The trouble with addicts is that they are so troubled—full of self-loathing, half of the time unintelligible, the other half, prophetic. This is where the role of academics and scholars-intellectuals (their functions are not synonymous) is so crucial. Yet it's difficult to distinguish between gibberish and prophecy, academic and intellectual. Partly because of the overlap between the entities and functions, partly because in a culture of denial most people are closet users and with such a high dependency on WS, few resources have gone into finding reliable healing programs.

In an addicted culture, or a culture of addicts, academic addicts likely distinguish themselves in their search for getting clean or becoming increasingly lost by words, usually those found in their articles or on their reading lists. Syllabi and bibliographies are paraphernalia. Addiction makes you convoluted, hiding in words, pumping something into a vein or artery for an infusion of self-worth. Sometimes words bring clarity, like talking in tongues.

How to describe the felt need to perform, to be on stage, to fake sobriety, to mask shooting up on synthetic substances such as "master race" narratives or discourses only to long for a conscience? First, talk nonsense. Then (re)gain enough consciousness to speak in the "double consciousness" of the antiracist addict, critiquing the master narratives for occlusion of "race" and collusion with racism. Next realize that your very deconstruction of the masters' narrative(s) reveals addiction. The addict's trap. To embrace or reject WS, pick up or put down the needle—all require a concentration of energy, nerve, and mind on "whiteness."

It would be "highly offensive," I am told, to seriously suggest some correlation between academics and addicts. Perhaps those offended disdain the status of the common addict, who in this culture is usually constructed as impoverished and black. One could hardly wish to embrace bodies so policed, imprisoned, and despised given the punitive aspects associated with certain strains of addiction in a stratified culture.

White addicts are assumed to be able to handle their addictions with dignity and civility while black addicts are presumed to be emboldened by theirs into a savagery only recently relinquished. Hence, black addicts are policed and sentenced differently from white addicts. The black addicts tend to be restrained in the academic carceral at higher rates with more repressive measures than those used against their white counterparts. Those not completely high know that Michel Foucault exaggerated in *Discipline and Punish*. Torture had not "disappeared" from the landscape; it had "disappeared" into black or racially marked bodies. (The addict housed in the academic carceral has some relation to the addict warehoused in the state's penal sites, but it would be surreal in this missive to enter into a serious discussion of Attica, Guantanamo, or your local prison or INS detention center; such important information is readily available in reports from human rights organizations such as Amnesty International.)

If you do "white time," you are more likely to be sentenced to rehab through seminars on diversity. If you do "black time," you are more likely to be caged, to be pimped by guards and guardians of the containment center, and to be profiled when driving, or walking, or voting, or teaching. It is commonly argued, another truism, that those so held deserve to be imprisoned. How then do the racially "different" (read *deviant*) survive addiction?

The faith-based initiative currently promoted by the secular government suggests religious revival as an essential component of survival and rehabilitation. Signing up for rehab (I have class privilege) led me to an interview on black women's religious responses to 9/11, conducted in early 2002 for the now-defunct women's publication *Sojourners*. I turned the interview into a referendum on white supremacy and militarism in a duly unelected government. The interview was never published, perhaps because of my refusal to take personal responsibility and my habit of blaming the government and corporate-military elites for excessive dysfunctionalism, violence, and a WS pandemic. As part of a program to kick WS, I have reworked the interviewer's questions and my responses into my own five-step program.

1. Find examples of religion/spirituality in history and your own family or personal experience to help you stay strong [and sober].

The historical wells that black people drew from are the sources of contemporary strength and courage. Spirituality existed and exists outside of and beyond religions, which are often set by rules that attempt to contain and articulate a deeper consciousness in peace and grace. Blacks drew and draw from the love and compassion that we have for each other, and for ourselves, the love that leads to a determination that we survive, despite being lied to, stolen, and stolen from. We were caged, and mobilized for or made passive in the face of destructive practices and policies. The peace we found or fought for, that we find or fight for, is embodied in a respect for life, for others' lives and the spirit that surrounds us. Strength is reflected in struggle. The ocean, mountains, winter sunlight offer space for calm and insight.

2. Identify particular women whose lives inspire you in times of crisis [and offer instructions for sobriety].

In my academic writings, I remember the ancestors. It is opportunistic to call them only in prefaces, and, immature to run to them only in crises (like calling out "Jesus!" only in desperation). I am still evolving. So I remember more often antilynching crusader Ida B. Wells and civil rights mentor Ella Baker. Of the living, my mothers include the twins who raised and reraised me (an incomplete work), and, my god-mother, a priestess of Yemoya.

3. [Question if] religion and spirituality have helped you to cope with the September 11 tragedy [and its tragic aftermath, U.S. warfare and occupation].

In religion I have heard the chant often: "'With God on our side', we can kill [without remorse]." The multicultural collage of state terrorists and insurgent terrorists all claim to be men (and women) of faith. Such religious people have managed to destroy and kill at a shocking and awesome rate.

The aftermath of September 11 includes the killing of more people. Why should I "cope" with that? Religion can incite war or bring comfort that helps survivors, but it does not necessarily bring resistance to war and killing. There was so much American indifference to those dying before September 11 in Africa, in the Middle East (including hundreds of thousands of Iraqi children affected by U.S. sanctions), in Latin America, in Europe, in Asia from poverty, disease, wars, torture, and prison.

Fortunately, there have always been those (not all claim a religion) who love humanity and who condemn not only the tragedy of September 11, 2001, but also the killings before and after. Our ability to love despite the horror—to not give in to mindless patriotism, police state powers, or exhortations to shop in order to feel better (and boost the economy)—allows us to seek peace and justice. It also allows grief to unfold, not as a numbing weight but as a girder, in our bodies.

Spirit guides resistance in ways that are very old and familiar. So, very much in the tradition, I allow myself to reject authoritarian figures, to hear in presidential speeches about "crusades," "evildoers," and the "absolute good" embodied by the United States another religious fanatic, another instrument of death.

So spirit(s) comes full circle, with its instructions: We have the same duties and obligations that our foremothers and fathers had— to survive and to go beyond survival to freedom. Not as individuals or (affluent) families stockpiling Cipro[2] and purchasing country homes but as international communities who, with their international bodies, arrest the spread of terror and warfare, repression and incarceration, and daily violence and poverty.

4. Adjust your vision of peace for the world and the alterations to it by current events.

My vision(s) centers on people in right relation with themselves, nature, creation, and life itself. Peace for the world ideally is the absence of physical want and coercion or force. Things are so imbalanced: income disparities, dictatorships, dysfunctional democracies, pacified populaces. Read Octavia Butler, 1 Corinthians 13.

Life is not different now; nor is death. It is the same (although some are more attentive or anesthetized to suffering and struggle). Resistance to repression that indigenous, black, and poor peoples have historically known mandates a moratorium on warfare, on its industries, on corporate profiteering, on its racist opportunism, on its hatred of or indifference to families and communities, its violence against women and children. Peace would be a rejection of paternal leadership, of police state and prison expansion, of greed. Peace would mean the inclusion of life-affirming nonelites into the decision-making processes of the governments and corporations and military and police centers that adjudicate lives. Democracy, of course, requires the same. So to struggle for a true democracy is to be in struggle for peace. To be in struggle for peace is to work to alter or abolish repressive institutions and governments and addictions.

5. Say something to our children to help them.

Tell them how we love; how we've failed at it; how we've managed to triumph in loving; how our lives are committed to them and their learning compassion, demanding justice, and freedom. Freedom from violence, hunger, fear, ignorance: Those are our true legacies for children. All of the ideals that make living and dying dignified and filled with grace and beauty, ideals not to be hoarded but to be spread, with spirit, globally.

NOTES

1. I offer no definition of "white supremacy" here. As a recovering black WS addict, I know that WS is part fantasy, part nightmare, an artificially or chemically induced altered state, one that promotes an exaggerated sense of self shaped by the presence (or absence) of mythical value. The reader may refer to the considerable literature in print (and performance) on the contradictions of black WS addiction.

2. Cipro is a prescription drug used to counter bacterial infection. Following 9/11 it was promoted by some as a potential "antidote" to biological warfare.

INDEX